Praying in the Dark

Praying in the Dark

Spirituality, Nonviolence, and the Emerging World

DANIEL O. SNYDER

CASCADE *Books* • Eugene, Oregon

PRAYING IN THE DARK
Spirituality, Nonviolence, and the Emerging World

Cascade Books
An Imprint of Wipf and Stock Publishers
199 W. 8th Ave., Suite 3
Eugene, OR 97401

www.wipfandstock.com

PAPERBACK ISBN: 978-1-6667-3191-0
HARDCOVER ISBN: 978-1-6667-2496-7
EBOOK ISBN: 978-1-6667-2497-4

Cataloguing-in-Publication data:

Names: Snyder, Daniel O., author.

Title: Praying in the dark : spirituality, nonviolence, and the emerging world / Daniel O. Snyder.

Description: Eugene, OR: Cascade Books, 2022 | Includes bibliographical references.

Identifiers: ISBN 978-1-6667-3191-0 (paperback) | ISBN 978-1-6667-2496-7 (hardcover) | ISBN 978-1-6667-2497-4 (ebook)

Subjects: LCSH: Spirituality—Society of Friends. | Nonviolence. | Social change.

Classification: BX7738 S60 2022 (paperback) | BX7738 (ebook)

VERSION NUMBER 093022

See, I am doing a new thing!
Now it springs up; do you not perceive it?
I am making a way in the wilderness
and streams in the wasteland.

—Isaiah 43:19

Contents

Acknowledgments

THIS BOOK WAS BORN shortly after 9/11. The faculty and students at Pendle Hill, a Quaker Center devoted to worship, study, and spiritually grounded activism, struggled deeply with discerning a faithful response to those events. I am grateful for the many students who participated in my classes and shared their reflections, papers, and personal stories. They were essential conversation partners. Steve Baumgartner, Pendle Hill's director at the time, was an early encourager. Steve was excited about what I was trying to do and developed a program we called "Pendle Hill on the Road" that supported my offering these classes as weekend workshops to be shared with Quaker meetings around the country. The challenge to go deep in a short time concentrated my focus. Without Steve's vision, the ideas in this book might never have fully taken shape.

Mel and Beth Keiser, retired professors from Guilford College, answered a call to develop "The Common Light Meetingplace," a Quaker initiative in spirituality and activism. Their invitation to bring my workshops to North Carolina opened a door to a rich spiritual friendship. Their reading of my work and their deeply insightful commentary has greatly enriched my writing and understanding of our shared tradition. Beth's years as Charles A. Dana Professor of English, and Mel's years of teaching religious studies and Quakerism, have made them invaluable conversation partners. Both of them seasoned this writing with their wisdom.

Of the many soul friends that I have found along the way, two have been especially helpful. Mahan Siler and Guy Sayles, both retired pastors and committed contemplative activists, came together with me in a writer's group. We seasoned our writing and friendship with many rich conversations about matters of faith and this book is the better for their sharp eyes and wise feedback.

Mahan and I have also been a part of a Lectio group that has been meeting for more than a decade. Also in the group are Liz Canham, Marvin

Schrock, and James Hyde, who have all been strong encouragers along the way. Ann Bohan joined us some years later and Bill Ratliff became a part of this group after his retirement from teaching pastoral care and counseling at Earlham School of Religion. They both brought much wisdom to our gatherings and gave us the gift of allowing us to accompany them into their passing.

I have kept up with some of my classmates from Pacifica Graduate Institute over the years, and one of them, Judith Lamp, very generously read many of my chapters. My other readers were almost all theologically trained, so Judith, steeped in depth psychology, and outside the theological world, brought a fresh perspective and immensely helpful critique and commentary.

My brothers and sister have been lifelong conversation partners on matters of psychology and spirituality. Our conversations over many decades have always challenged and inspired my reflections. My sister, Demaris Wehr, a Jungian psychotherapist, teacher, writer, and fellow explorer in the world of peacemaking, has always shared my curiosity about matters of the spirit. Some of the best books on my bookshelf are gifts from her. My brother Tim, passionate about his work with youth at risk, is an adventurer who loves to sail on both the inward and outward seas. We have shared many adventures on the inward seas, although on the outward ones I tend to turn green and hug the rails, so out of an abundance of compassion he has stopped inviting me. Tim's son, Mike, one of my many amazing nephews and nieces, is a gifted writer, adventurer, documentary filmmaker, and husband and father extraordinaire. Mike took time from his busy life to read my manuscript and ask sharp questions that helped me out of my own generation into language and concepts that speak to his. My brother, T. G., who prefers his initials to his full name, is a psychiatrist who has spent much of his career in the world of ACTT (Assertive Community Treatment Teams), a public mental health initiative designed to provide in-community treatment for those who suffer severe mental illness. T. G. brings his compassion and medical training to his patients, in their homes, in shelters, and sometimes under the bridges. My brothers and sister and I have regular conversations, support each other in prayer, and are each other's best encouragers. They generously agreed that I may share stories about our family. Naturally, our perspectives may differ, as is always the case with families. We all fell from the same tree, but not onto the same ground.

Parker Palmer has earned immense gratitude from his readers over the years, and his gift of friendship and enthusiasm for this book has been invaluable. Parker was there at the beginning of my awakening to spiritual hunger, when I was a student at Pendle Hill in the seventies. Now, all these years later, he continues to offer himself as encourager, elder, teacher, and friend. I'm grateful that we have been fishing together in the same pond all these years. Elaine Prevallet, SL, was also Pendle Hill faculty at the time. My first spiritual director, she was a profound nurturer of the soul. She and Parker encouraged me to trust the leadings that opened my life in surprising ways.

The monks at St. Benedict's Monastery in Snowmass, Colorado welcomed me into their community for a year of vocational discernment, and carried me in their prayers. Fr. Michael Abdo and Fr. Joseph Boyle were especially warm and encouraging. Brothers Thomas, George, Charles, Raphael, John, Bernie, and Frs. Tom and William each looked for and found opportunities to bring me their love, good humor, and kindness.

I had wonderful teachers and classmates at Earlham School of Religion, Boston University School of Theology, and Pacifica Graduate Institute who invited me into profound learning conversations. Woody Sheetz-Willard, a classmate at Boston University, became a soul friend with whom I have stayed in close contact for nearly forty years. Woody also read my manuscript and gave very helpful feedback. David Tatgenhorst, soul brother for almost fifty years, ever since our days together in the Philadelphia Life Center and Movement for a New Society, has been a constant encourager. Gareth Higgins and Brian Ammons, more recent soul friends, have also brought much love, encouragement, and laughter into my life.

Many others, too numerous to mention, have loved, forgiven, challenged, and blessed me over the years. Among all these fellow pilgrims, I include my clients. For reasons of confidentiality, they cannot be named, but their immense courage and faithfulness has been a constant source of inspiration and hope. They share their lives, their struggles, hopes, and awakenings with breathtaking honesty. They have blessed me beyond measure with their invitations to walk alongside.

Finally, there is one whose love and nurture has been unwavering: Anne Marx, a soul friend of the rarest kind, has been an encourager from the first gathering of ideas for this book over twenty years ago. She always calls me deeper into the work. She gave me an inside view of what it was like growing up under Communist rule in East Germany, helped me as I struggled to understand the East German revolution and eventual reunification with the West, and put up with my frequently mangled German. Anne refused to join the *Jungendweihe* (the Communist Youth organization) when in school, and then later carried candles at the Magdeburg peace prayers. She listens with heart, asks big questions, and persistently loves me into my better self.

Introduction

WHO IN THEIR RIGHT mind thinks it's a good idea to wake up at 3:45 AM to go pray? That was my first thought when one of the brothers came around with his wake-up bell the first morning after my arrival at the monastery deep in the Colorado Rockies. I was a young Quaker, had recently discovered and been inspired by the writings of Thomas Merton, and was hungry for an inward depth to match the outward activist work of previous years. The Trappists welcomed me into their community as an "observer" for a year, during which I would try to discern if I had a call to monastic life.

I soon learned that the hours spent in prayer in the deepest part of the night tend to strip away defenses. The monastery taught me to face the hard truths of my unacknowledged sorrows and regrets, my unexplored doubts, and my uncertainties and fears. In those dark hours I found a bottomless stillness where it was impossible to deny my human fragility, my inevitable death, and my dependency on mysteries beyond my ability to comprehend. I also found the voice of my longing in the psalms and the Gregorian chants we sang in brotherly unison that reverberated off the stone walls. I don't know what I thought was going to happen in this place, but it was not this. Behind those cloister walls, deep into the night, souls are laid bare. Praying in the dark is a free fall into the wilderness of the heart.

I came to love that life and the brother monks who welcomed me and supported me as I tried to find my way, but I eventually discerned that my call is to live on the boundary between the contemplative and active life, and to let each one infuse the other. I left the monastery and have spent the more than four decades since then wandering in the worlds of strategic nonviolence, theology, depth psychology, and spirituality—studying, teaching, practicing, and then digging in for further study. This book is the harvest of a long season of growth and learning. It brings these four disciplines into conversation, against the backdrop of my Quaker heritage and with my own story woven throughout. It is the fruit of one Quaker's lifetime of living on the boundary between contemplation and action.

The path has taken me in many surprising directions, and I have lived into identity labels like beads on a string—activist, monk, teacher, pastoral psychotherapist, spiritual director, writer—and I have learned that my life was never in the beads but always in the thread that runs through them, a thread that always took me deeper into the kinds of questions that now inform this book: How do I love America and live my American life in a way that does not require yet another war, or risk climate collapse, a life that doesn't depend on building empires on the backs of others? Given that I was born into oppressive structures that were already in place before I was born, how do I free myself and others of their legacy? How do I honor and cherish my white life in a way that doesn't suck up all the air so that Black lives can't breathe? How can I live my Christian life in a way that honors its profound spirituality while fiercely opposing its many ideological distortions that cause so much harm, and how can I answer a call that came from somewhere far outside the bounds of the world I was born into? Leaving the familiar for an unknown world is a wilderness journey. I had to learn how to pray in the dark because there was no map, no light showing me the way. Now, I can finally say that there is a wonderful light in that darkness, but it has taken me many years to learn this.

I have made my peace with being a wilderness dweller, and in fact an original title for this book was *A Report from the Wilderness*. But *Praying in the Dark* is better because there is an intentionality in prayer. We experience the wildly unknown and mysterious nature of life, but the mystery also encounters us. We are inevitably a presence within the wilderness just as it is a presence within us. Merely showing up is already to bring a certain attitude and orientation to the encounter. I pray in the dark because prayer is how I want to orient myself in the world. I want to live my spiritual, psychological, and political life from a stance that places me in service to the heart and soul, certainly my own, but also the heart and soul in others, in the world, and in nature. Someone else might engage the mysteries of life from a different orientation and with different questions, but my call has been to dig deep into theology, depth psychology, and the dynamics of nonviolence, and to then to weave these strands together into a spirituality.

I know that my prayerful orientation is not universally shared. Some people have been so wounded by religious words that any mention of prayer already sets off alarm bells. So, just to be clear, I offer the reflections in this book conversationally and not ideologically. I speak and write with conviction and often with passion, but always my aim is to invite dialogue, not to make pronouncements. I am painfully aware of the immense harm that has been done in the name of religion, and the temptation to abandon the field is powerful, but I'm too stubborn for that. I've seen too many good people stiffen and retreat at any mention of matters of faith, no doubt the result of encountering ideologues who use religious words like battering rams. But I am unwilling to retreat, unwilling to surrender to people who drag perfectly good words through the mud. It can be a difficult discernment to know when to fight for words like "God," "Soul," "prayer," and many others, and when to let them go, but for better or worse, I have declared my fidelity to them even though others cheapen them with shallow meanings. My digging deep into theology, psychology, nonviolence, and spirituality has been one way I have staked my claim on these words, and planted my battle flag in the fight to take them back.

Out of this work has come my conviction that these words and the disciplines behind them are themselves conversation partners. Every theology is latently psychological, and every psychology is latently theological, and no spirituality can be lifted free of the whole cloth that includes not only theological and psychological ideas but also a way of living in the world. We need the whole cloth. Forced into isolation, these words and their underlying disciplines tend to harden into fixed ideas and images that we then impose on lived experience. But the imposition of interpretive patterns and ideologies onto experience tends to freeze meaning in place, and our spiritual, political, and psychological lives are far too dynamic and mysterious for that. Trying to capture the mystery in a single idea is like trying to put a cat in a box. We need good ideas. But ideas are like budding fruits that need the sunlight of vigorous conversation in order to ripen.

Our world is currently in the midst of a difficult labor. It must be midwifed by people who have learned new ways of being religious and political with each other. A new world comes with a new consciousness and both are born much like people are, with a lot of labor and a willingness to give oneself wholeheartedly to the journey. A new birth means that one's life will never again be the same. It means a lot of new responsibility, but it also brings a lot of surprise and wonder, and a love that fills the heart with amazement. I lean all of my hope in the direction of a safe and healthy birth. I offer this book in service to that hope.

I have organized it into four parts. Part I explores prayer in three movements, asking first "What Is Spirituality?" Anyone searching the internet or bookstores for resources on spirituality is immediately overwhelmed with possibilities. Finding a clear drink of water in a flood is nearly as difficult as finding one in a desert. This chapter offers an approach to spirituality that begins in the underlying human impulses that drive spiritual practice and that introduces the idea of navigating by Soul.[1] Chapter 2 takes up silence as a central feature of praying in the dark. Silence invites all guests to enter, trailing as much baggage as they care to bring along, allowing by its very hospitality an ever-deepening relinquishment. Eventually we come to the Great Stillness that is beyond distinctions. Chapter 3 offers my own Quaker tradition as one contemporary model for creative, spiritually grounded engagement in the world. The "holy experiment" that came to be the Quaker movement is inspired by a hope, a "what-if" possibility. Gandhi conducted "Experiments in Truth."[2] Like all experimenters, he learned a lot about what doesn't work on the path toward perfecting the way of nonviolence. He has even been compared to Thomas Edison, someone who learned a lot about how *not* to make a light bulb before finally making one. Quakers are also experimenters in Truth, worship, and life. Like both Gandhi and Edison, we often miss the mark, but we are certain that what we are reaching for is possible. Life can be animated and guided, inspired, breath by breath. We can be rightly placed, gifted, and brought into meaningful and effective engagement in the world.

Part II begins in the assumption that we all want a world without war but that we don't agree on whether that's even possible let alone on how to achieve it. This section draws on key insights and contrasts between what scholars have called "the domination system" and "partnership systems." Violence and nonviolence are the strategic visions that arise from each system respectively. Chapter 4 lifts into view the violent "peace" of systems that create the cruel stability of suppressed conflict in the inward and outward dimensions of experience. Oppression, suppression, repression, and depression all share a common dynamic. Nonviolent conflict, the theme of chapter 5, is the partnership system's response to violent "peace." Nonviolent action is a kind of therapy for the culture, and therapy, at its best, is a kind of nonviolence for the soul. What heals the world also heals the psyche. What heals the psyche also heals the world. There are both moral and strategic arguments for nonviolence, but the deepest argument, and the most persuasive in my view, is that nonviolence heals a deeply embedded cultural wound of the collective soul. Violent revolution never reaches the root cause of the disease. Violent revolution fails to unearth the domination

1. In my idiosyncratic usage, "the soul," in lowercase and accompanied with an article, refers to our more common understanding of the central essence of our being. When I omit the article and capitalize "Soul" I am referring to that which is more of a relational space, that is both transpersonal and a dynamic center, within which a transformational encounter may occur. When we move from "the soul" into "Soul," it is like stepping off the riverbank into the river.

2. Gandhi, *Autobiography*.

system's archetypal influence and merely yields another version of violent "peace," only with a different set of actors in the dominant role. Nonviolent peace, the theme of chapter 6, is the fruit of nonviolent conflict. It is structurally different, and more sustainable, than violent "peace." The partnership system liberates both conflict and peace from the domination system's violent distortions and sets them within an ecological frame where both are revealed to be essential features of any lasting, creative, dynamic world. If nonviolent conflict is the "good trouble" that civil rights veteran and congressional representative John Lewis spoke of, then nonviolent peace is the fertile and dynamic possibility that arises in the awakening that follows. Life is revolutionary in its essence, always plowing up the ground, birthing itself over and over.

Part III brings nonviolence to the inner world and imagines spirituality as a fierce and persistent inward activism. Chapter 7 draws on the profound contributions of depth psychology and emerging spiritual practices to show how nonviolence for the soul can rescue prayer from being reduced to mere form, and restore it to its original transformational power. Chapter 8 brings that power to bear on a systemic analysis of privilege and oppression. In both of these chapters there is an insistence that there can be an inward/outward nonviolent revolution that brings all of us to an undivided home. Healing must uncover and treat the soul wound that occurs with the internalization of domination hierarchies. Because I cannot presume to write for voices that are not my own, this chapter is primarily about the spiritual journey for those of us who are born to systemic privileges, taking the ongoing fits and starts of my own life as an example. Chapter 9 offers a theological reflection on these themes as a complement to the earlier chapters' more psychological and political views. Here I offer a nonviolent theodicy, that is, a theological reflection on the question of how to understand the goodness of God in relation to evil. The theological and spiritual dilemmas created by the sheer brutality of evil in our lives are immense, and many faith journeys have shipwrecked on those unforgiving shoals. A conversational weaving of depth psychology, theology, and politics, as each one is viewed through the lens of nonviolence, invites a shift in the archetypal frame that holds this question.

Part IV turns the focus back to the outward dimension and suggests that all of life can be sacramental, or outward prayer. Chapter 10 considers Jesus as a model. Discarding frames that picture him exclusively as zealot, prophet, or sacrificial lamb, and following New Testament scholar Walter Wink, I engage Jesus as an image and model of the whole human being.[3]

3. Wink, *Human Being*.

I have never been able to ignore Jesus, despite the horrendous abuses that his followers have perpetrated in his name. Jesus is the very embodiment of wilderness, resisting every attempt to domesticate him. He defies the expectations of those who claim him as their own because they think they know him, as well as for those who have rejected him because they think they know him. To follow Jesus is to be led into a wilderness where all bets are off, all assumptions are questioned, where the blind see, the lame walk, and the poor hear good news. Jesus not only teaches but also heals, and says pointedly, outrageously, "Go and do likewise." Chapter 11 takes this call seriously and casts a long look at the seemingly impossible possibility of Jesus' invitation to heal. Finally, in chapter 12, I place Truth within a relational metaphor, the wildly creative and authentic world of jazz. Living in the conversations, holding tension, allowing paradox, discovering new harmonies, these are the disciplines that finally free us from the terrible prisons of individualism, relativism, nihilism, narcissism, and ideological self-righteousness. There is an extraordinary beauty in finally letting go into the shared creativity of finding Truth in the music. As in great jazz, there is an awakening that can only happen out beyond the boundaries of the predictable.

I conclude with an epilogue that borrows a line from Lincoln's first inaugural address, where he calls the nation to answer to our better angels. Now for us, as it was for Jesus, the angels of the wilderness appear alongside the wild beasts. This country we call home has given quarter to the wild beasts of genocide and slavery, and it has also been a land of unprecedented generosity and opportunity. Extraordinary freedom and brutal oppression have lived and continue to live side by side in this wounded and beautiful land. There is a promise implicit in our founding documents, only partially realized and largely denied to many, but still there and waiting for full realization. Deep democracy awaits our willingness to create a genuine partnership society. Perhaps if we learn to risk the wilderness journey, we can finally face and heal the great traumas and injustices that are so thoroughly embedded in our national legacy. It is a transformational journey, frightening because the wilderness holds all of our shadows. But if we are willing, and take even a few beginning steps in search of a world that works for all of us, we will find our better angels waiting for us there.

Many fine books offer explorations of the inward/outward life, and like mine, they speak from within the perspectives of a particular human life, lived in a particular culture and context. I write personally, sharing many of the shaping events in my life and in some of my dreams because I believe that Truth cannot simply be proclaimed but is *per-sonare*, or "sounded-through" persons. We are each hand-carved instruments uniquely shaping the breath of God that blows through us. The more instruments in the orchestra, the fuller the sound. We serve best when we are willing to name for each other the unique ways in which our own instrument has been tuned. Then we are better able to participate in Truth's music because we are offering our ideas relationally, rather than ideologically. As in great jazz each voice invites new tensions, new engagements, and new disagreements that resolve into even greater and more complex harmonies. Perhaps our world will find its way again when we finally learn that the more voices, the richer the music, that no one's life or music is expendable, and that we need a fierce commitment to each other, to creative conflict and conversation, all in service to a beautiful, complex, and dynamic whole. Finding our way toward that wholeness will require exploring the wilder edges of prayer and peacemaking, and that is a journey that I suspect can only be thoroughly enjoyed and courageously engaged when we are sustained by what the great religions call love.

PART I

Prayer

SOMETIMES CLIENTS WHO COME for spiritual direction claim that they don't know how to pray. It's not that hard. "Yes" is a complete prayer. "Hello" will work fine. It doesn't take much—desire, willingness, an open heart. Just keep showing up.

The difficulty is not with prayer itself but with the countless ways we get in our own way. Disturbing questions about belief and disbelief crowd into the prayer space. The ways in which psychological and spiritual formation may have closed the heart and set our teeth on edge will interfere and complicate attempts at prayer. The simple gesture of trust implied in a "Yes" or a "Hello" may be extraordinarily difficult for someone whose trust has been repeatedly violated. Prayer itself is simple, but simplicity may be one of the hardest things we ever try to do.

The three chapters in this first section aim to get behind many of these problems by going all the way back to the beginning with the question "What is spirituality?" Let's start there, with a simple gesture of the heart. Matters of belief and disbelief, of trust and mistrust will be lifelong companions. It makes no sense to wait for them to resolve before beginning to pray. Show up, tell the truth, and listen. That's how I answer the "how to" question. We can pray *to* God *about* our gods, about belief and disbelief; we can pray about trust and mistrust. We can even pray about prayer. Honesty is key.

What we hear, God's first response that meets our "Hello," is silence, the theme of the second chapter. Encountered on its own terms, silence resists a projection of either Presence or Absence, and opens onto vast possibilities, inviting curiosity, playfulness, creativity, and courage. Eventually, there is an inward opening toward depths that the discursive mind cannot reach.

In silence, spirituality becomes a "Holy Experiment," the theme of chapter three and a central impulse of the Quaker movement. Silence is an invitation. It is God's way of introducing us to ourselves, to our becoming, deepening, dynamic, alive, creative, and mysterious selves. Individually and collectively, we are God's holy experiment, a work in progress. Holy experimenting becomes a fertile seedbed for peacemaking.

CHAPTER I

What Is Spirituality?

Be brave and walk through the country of your own wild heart.
Be gentle and know that you know nothing.
Be mindful and remember that every moment can be a prayer.[1]

—MIRABAI STARR

WHETHER SPIRITUALITY BEGINS WITH an altar call at a tent revival or gazing at the stars, it is essentially a conversation between the depths of our own being and the mystery of the universe. What does anyone do with the wonder of simply being alive, breath by breath, or what does anyone do with a loved one's suffering and our own helplessness? This world holds us in an exquisitely torturous embrace where her right hand caresses us with astonishing beauty and her left shatters us with unspeakable sorrow. Spirituality in all its forms is fashioned out of eons of human efforts to be fully present to both wonder and tragedy. Beauty elicits a cry of celebration, and sorrow a cry of agony. How does anyone take the raw human experience of undefended vulnerability and turn it into courage, wisdom, hope, and the capacity to love? We never get closure on these questions but we wouldn't be fully human if we didn't keep asking them.

For some inexplicable reason, around three in the morning seems to be the time when my soul wakes me up so I can have it out with God. That's when I go to the mat for those who have found their way into my heart. They say that a good therapist should maintain some detachment from

1. Starr, "Introduction," 2.

clients—don't take their problems home with you; don't let them get under your skin. If you do, then that's your countertransference. I seem to have a lot of that. Clients get under my skin all the time. I hope I get under theirs. Pastoral counseling is not psychoanalysis. I don't sit behind the couch with my notepad and keep an inscrutable silence. We're in a relationship. I come to care very deeply about them, even love them. I don't tell them that, and I'm very careful about boundaries and confidentiality, but I suspect that some of them have figured it out anyway. My clients get to me, they bother me, inspire me, challenge me, and sometimes worry me. I work it all out with God. Sometimes prayer results in new insight into myself and enables me to resolve real countertransferences that are getting in the way of the therapy. At other times, prayer simply allows me to return to the therapy room with a deeper presence and ability to hold a graceful space for whatever needs to unfold. Either way, I'm not done praying until something happens. Either a light comes on and I see something I had missed or I feel a deep release and assurance. Then I can let them go into a greater love than my own. This is heart work. Fortunately, my soul doesn't wake me up for it every morning at three, but when it does, I just need to open up the conversation and don't much care about how I get there. Sometimes I open the prayer space with *Jah!* (a kind of explosive out-breath), something I heard on a Sinéad O'Connor album. But "God" also works fine. That is simply how I address the Great Mystery.

Whether "God" or "*Jah!*" for me, these sounds are gestures of speech; they are cries from the heart. I need to personify the mystery, put a human face on it. I'm fully aware that I'm doing this, and in my more reflective moods I can see that I'm simply walking into the wilderness through the embodied gesture we call language. But when I'm in the throes of the human condition, either my own or for those I care for, all this is way too much thinking. I like Bernice Johnson Reagon's description of prayer. Reagon is a veteran of the civil rights movement. In an interview with Vincent Harding, recorded in his "Veterans of Hope" series, he asks her about her spiritual formation. She says that she grew up in a tradition where calling on God was simple and straightforward: "You know me; you know my condition. Come on down and see about me. I ain't got time to go into no details in this prayer!"[2] That's how it is for me when my soul wakes me up at three in the morning and wants me to pray in the dark. It's mat time, in the trenches, come to Jesus, however you say it. I don't have time for worrying about whether I'm getting the words right.

2. Reagon, "Bernice Johnson Reagon."

Spirituality will always be as varied as the souls that practice it, and as mysterious as the soul is free. There aren't any definitive maps of the wilderness, but there are some trail markers pointing the way and a few others warning of dead ends and washed-out canyons. I want to offer some that have been important to me. I'm sure there are others. Of all the teachings on spirituality, however, the most important one, I am convinced, is that we must never stray far from the living mystery.

Reimagining Spirituality

The key to lost spirituality and numbing materialism is not merely to intensify our quest for spirituality, but to re-imagine it.[3]

—Thomas Moore

My way of praying works for me and helps me stay fully present with my clients and with the sorrows, tragedies, and traumas that they would otherwise be struggling to carry alone. I imagine that Sinéad O'Connor's spirituality works for her. I can hear its power in her music, and I can see the fruits of Bernice Johnson Reagon's spirituality in her life. They have both gone far into the wilderness and come back bearing gifts. What a loss we all would have suffered if they had unquestioningly fit their lives into some predetermined form and not bothered with doubt, mystery, or the struggle to find their own voice and authentic way of being in the world. Spirituality cannot be and must not be limited to predetermined forms and practices, and certainly not by an insistence on the right words, beliefs, or actions. Spirituality, in whatever form, consists of practices that have the single aim of setting the soul free so that it can come unhindered into the unique expression of its gift, and its own astonishing and happy surprise of becoming! Spirituality holds it all—the psychological quest for wholeness, the political quest for community, and the theological quest for a believable intimacy with *Jah*! These are inseparable quests, each one an essential thread woven into the whole cloth of finding a rightly ordered sense of being fully oneself, one's unique way of being meaningfully engaged in the world, and at home within the infinite mystery of the universe.

A vital spirituality must sound a compelling call to each of these threads of a whole life, a call that awakens desire, commitment, and discipline. Not, however, the kind of discipline that many of us have been taught,

3. Moore, *Care of the Soul*, 232.

in the sense of a rigorous adherence to an ideology or a mere rehearsal of it, but rather discipline in its original meaning, which is "to follow," as in being a "disciple." But what or whom are we to follow? Many have looked to mainstream religious institutions, looking for real food for the soul, and have found little more than an insistence on ideological conformity. I see clients every day who are disaffected from mainstream religion. They tell me they are "spiritual but not religious."

This is the dilemma of modern spirituality. When religious institutions abandon the mystical depths of the great traditions and turn their teachings into ideologies, then souls go hungry. When no one is listening to the call of the wilderness, or pointing toward the sacred mysteries, or passing on the wisdom of thousands of years of spiritual teaching, seekers are left merely to follow whatever spiritual fad catches their interest. If our choices are limited to ideological conformity or an open-ended relativism, then neither path is worth following. We need more than institutions that offer predictable and lifeless answers to questions no one is asking, and more than an individualism that wanders aimlessly with questions that have no sustainable answers. The one traps the soul in rigid forms and the other casts it adrift. We are either fighting over which star to follow or we are lost on an endless and unnavigable sea.

Navigating by Soul[4]

If you don't know the kind of person I am
and I don't know the kind of person you are
a pattern that others made may prevail in the world
and following the wrong god home we may miss our star.[5]

—William Stafford

There are many teachers, books, retreats, practices, congregations, and other gatherings of fellow travelers that are not at all lifeless. They serve well and they have earned the trust of a skeptical and sometimes spiritually wounded

4. "Soul" is a liminal word, meaning that it stands at the threshold between knowing and not-knowing, between language and mystery. We use liminal words like we use prayer words: They are not intended to define something but rather to evoke something. Their purpose is to orient us toward something that is ultimately self-defining. "Soul" suggests that our deepest interiority, as well as the deepest interiority of the universe, is ultimately an ungraspable mystery. We know by participation, not by naming.

5. Stafford, "Ritual," 16.

community. When I look for what makes these communities work, what I find is that they engage all three of these threads of vital spirituality, and they do so by inviting dialogue, welcoming serious questioning, and nurturing authenticity. They are more relational than ideological, and they avoid an "anything goes" type of relativism by being rigorously conversational. They work at learning from a wide diversity of voices, both within and beyond their own contexts and communities, and they include the voices of those who have gone this way before, ancestors who struggled with these same dilemmas and who went deep into the mystery and came back bearing gifts. They find a unity of Spirit within a diversity of voices.

A relational approach to spirituality reaches into the past, anticipates the future, and seeks meaningful connections across diversity in the present. We take seriously the wisdom of ancient religious traditions, their wisdom figures, as well as the teachers we encounter in everyday life. In all of these conversations, however, it is understood that we cannot presume to substitute another's journey for our own. There is an Inward Teacher, according to the Quaker tradition, who must also be consulted, especially when engaged with outward teachings. There is an Inward Guide that does not always yield to outward guidance, and an Inward Light that points to what is essentially an unnamed knower embedded in our nature. But this inward depth and center of our being is so easily drowned out by the busyness and noise of our lives that it takes long periods of silence and listening just to begin to restore a felt sense of its presence.

This is wilderness work. How does a fox know how to be a fox, and how does a mouse know how to be a mouse, if not by following their own natures? We humans must follow our own nature too, but unlike most other creatures, we have the unique capacity to be false to ourselves, to be internally divided and off-kilter. How are we to return to our original wholeness if not by deep listening and paying close attention to the soul's inward depths? Programs, beliefs, and well-defined practices can be useful, but they can also become ritual prayers that domesticate the mystery. A reimagined spirituality must include a deepening awareness of an interior alignment, a whole-body awareness, and an increasing capacity to notice when the plumb line has drifted off center. A restored interior alignment enables us to engage teachings and teachers relationally, the better to bring our own authentic voice into conversation with the authentic voices of others.

For much of my life I thought I would find myself in some outward form. I lived in an activist community, a Quaker community, a Trappist monastery; I went to grad school, served the poor, the mentally ill; I preached, taught, and chased after identity, vocation, and meaning like a foxhound on the hunt. I met many deeply authentic and truly called people in each of those communities, and also some who were more like me, trying to find themselves in a life that didn't really fit their nature. I have immense gratitude for the many teachers and fellow pilgrims I met along the way, not least because seeing the gift in others helped me see that it was not my own. These realizations were never easy; often they meant yet another journey into the wilderness. At this point in my life, however, I simply accept that I am often a restless guest in worlds that others inhabit with ease. Now I'm a therapist, a pastoral counselor, but even in this world I play at the edges of form. As labels go, the German *Seelesorger* (one who cares for souls) is a closer fit than "therapist." I certainly want my clients to get better, but I'm less interested in practices that follow a model of alleviating symptoms as quickly as possible than I am in seeing the symptom as a trailhead into the wilderness. What the ego perceives as a symptom to be cured is often the soul's call to a larger and more authentic life. The stance we take in relation to it is critical to whether we will follow the way of Soul or retreat to the perceived safety and illusory comforts of the familiar.

I have a small ceramic sculpture of a hatchling turtle emerging from its shell that sits on a shelf in my office. I keep it there to remind myself, as well as my clients, that what we're here for is not to seal up the cracks but to break through them. The task is to engage life and its difficulties with curiosity and compassion, the better to midwife the soul into new life. Like hatchling turtles, the soul builds strength in its struggle to crack the shell of a world that has become too small. The hatchling dies whose shell is broken either too soon or not at all. But the shell that is broken in Soul-time opens onto a new world, with new horizons, new dangers, and new possibilities. One can only inhabit such a new and larger world by also inhabiting a new and larger identity. In turning toward the symptom rather than away from it, we make it more teacher than adversary. The "self" that engages the symptom relationally is larger than the "self" that is possessed by it. We learn to suffer it legitimately, in the sense of learning to bear or to carry that which is uniquely ours to carry. Then, perhaps, the burden is lifted, or not, but either way the hatchling soul emerges into a new world, with a larger sense of self, stronger, more resilient, and with new vision for making different life choices or for seeing current ones through new eyes.

Now, with more than seven decades behind me, the forms and identities I've put on are mostly broken, and I'm glad. I've been chasing an authenticity that I thought I would find in some outward form when all along it was the Chaser in the chase. All that searching for identity, vocation, and meaning was more fox than foxhound. Soul was the Seeker in the search, the Believer in the belief, the Doubter in the doubt, the Despairer in the despair, and the Hoper in the hope. Now I occasionally catch a glimpse of that old fox in the mirror and I have to laugh. Then he gives me a wink and runs off again. The dance between form and Soul is a dynamic one. The shell breaks and my hatchling soul emerges into a new world that turns out to be yet another womb. Now, after having broken more than a few shells, I've given up the hope of arriving somewhere. Now I've gotten a sense of the pattern and have learned that it is actually the breaking of shells that invites the play. We hold on until we let go. And when the shells are all broken, we've laid down the quest and the wilderness has become home. We learn to navigate by Soul.

We humans have devised a nearly infinite number of ways to keep the lights on in the dark, to put a comfortable face on mystery, to wrap the simple facts of beauty and suffering, love and loss, life and death in reassuring platitudes. We paint mystery's canvas with images that have no shadows. We build ideological houses and then invent gods who will not crack the foundations. Yet none of these have ever sustained me in my relinquishment of each day's concerns as I surrender to the night's vulnerability and sleep's rehearsal of death. For this I must relinquish the day-world and learn to love surprise more than certainty, to sustain awareness in the midst of both wonder and sorrow, and to live with big questions about good and evil, beauty and tragedy, trust and betrayal, love and loss. A spirituality that lacks wildness and freedom also lacks the creativity that is big enough to host such questions. A spirituality that is overdetermined by ideology is forced to split off all that is uncertain and unpredictable. All the remainders fall into exile where they return as shadow gods, those tricksters who are constantly exposing the cracks in our ideological foundations.

Our collective addiction to rigidly held religious beliefs, political ideologies, the unquestioned moral convictions of both the right and the left, even our favorite psychological treatments, are symptoms of the present world's entrapment in shells meant to be broken. Those beliefs and commitments that can survive the breaking are more mythic than literal; they carry more mystery than certainty. Mythic narratives always involve some version of dying into new life, leaving port for unknown waters, being broken open by some impossible challenge, an unbearable tragedy or burden, and then entering the wilderness through the broken places. In our dreams we are threatened by unknown strangers, or pulled into the underworld. There is always some harrowing journey out of enslavement, only to be led into a wilderness. Mythic narratives can survive breaking over and over; they even invite it. They are seaworthy, reliable vessels for stormy waters, for night journeys, and for navigating by Soul.

Myth, Mystery, Mysticism

Those who do not have power over the story that dominates their lives, power to retell it, rethink it, deconstruct it, joke about it, and change it as times change, truly are powerless, because they cannot think new thoughts.[6]

—Salman Rushdie

A reimagined spirituality that navigates by Soul requires a desire and discipline of noticing the stories we inhabit, that form the backdrop against which we live our lives. A primary function of religion is to offer a new story, one that makes it possible to think new thoughts. Without a contrasting story, we can't really see the one we're in; we take it for reality. Until we gain a perspective from the balcony, we are stuck on stage, playing a role, functionally in a state of possession. It is the story that is recognized *as story,* and not taken as the only possible shape of reality, that can be deconstructed, retold, joked about, and eventually mourned and let go. Spiritual practice begins in the recognition that the essential dynamic of religion is not belief but participation in a story.

Mythic religion is narrative, not doctrine. It is poetry, not science (although today's scientists often have more in common with mystics than the conventionally religious do). Mythic speech is evocative, not definitive; it is more an approach to mystery than a replacement of it. In fact, "myth," "mystery," and "mysticism" all share a common root in the Greek *mu*, which signifies a gesture of silence.[7] The language of authentic spirituality does not insist that you believe something; it invites you to participate in something. However diverse we may be in religious language, we can all be brought to a threshold where words give way to silence, and belief to participation, or as one early Quaker mystic put it, to "the knowledge of things beyond what words can utter."[8]

Immersion in myth is also an exercise in identity formation. The narrative invites a new way of being. In a dream, the self that experiences the story is not the same self that narrates it. Dreams give us a glimpse of alternative "selves" to contrast with the limited if not outright false identity that was handed down by culture, family, and sometimes abuse. The promise

6. Rushdie, "One Thousand Days," 17.
7. Moore, "Developing a Mythic Sensibility," 58.
8. Penington, *Mystery of Life Within*, 92.

of the truly healing religious narrative is that the participating self is the larger self, the self that is more truly aligned with our original nature. Every religion offers a promise that we might be much more than we ever dreamed possible, more deeply loved, more thoroughly forgiven, more radically free, and more surely guided to a welcoming home, where we don't have to give up who we are in order to belong, and we don't have to give up belonging in order to be who we are.

Literalism also has a narrative structure, but it is hidden, denied. Religion is offered as fact, not story. The identity formation invited by literalism is the believing self, one who either accepts or rejects the facts. Literalism locates the self outside of the myth, not only as believer, but also as the moral self, or the righteous self, the one who conforms to the rules. There is always a shadow self in such a construction, a doubting, disobedient, rebellious self, and there is always a narrator, an observer self, a commentator who secretly notices the shadow, worries about it, and adopts various strategies for dealing with it. Literalism's shadows must be disowned, denied, repressed, and when this fails, acted out, and then obsessively confessed. We have more than a few painful cultural examples of literalism's shadows acted out in damaging ways, usually sexual, since sex seems to be one of literalism's obsessions.

The self that is constructed by literalism is a divided self, a performer self split off from its shadow, a self that is anxiously trying to be good enough to be loved, where the "goodness" required is always a moving target. When held within the larger participatory self of mythic religion, these conflicts have the breathing room necessary for healing. There, the self is loved apart from any assessments of relative goodness. Shadows can be acknowledged without any risk to our place in the beloved community. Identity is formed and transformed through the mythic journey; it is a work in progress. Healing comes with shadows and scars, and hard-won humility. Jacob wrestles with his night visitor and comes away with both a wound and a new identity.[9]

The participatory structure of mythic religion is relational. Identity is formed in an encounter with God or religious figures such as Jesus or Mary, or perhaps angelic presences. My own Quaker tradition uses a variety of images, such as the Inward Light, the Divine Presence, the Inward Teacher or Guide. However, we are emphatically non-creedal, which is to say that these words are an invitation to discovery, not merely to belief. The Quaker promise says that when we bring all that we are to the Divine Encounter, our lives are not only nourished, they are transformed, and it is the transformed

9. Gen 32:22–31.

life that becomes leaven in the world. It is a transformation that we long for. However, it is also one that terrifies us. The Light not only illumines, it also searches us and reveals our shadows as well as our gifts, and then it calls us to live our lives out of a radical dependence upon the Living Heartbeat of God.

This too, of course, is mythic. *Divine Light, Inward Teacher, God's Heartbeat*: The paradox of religious language is that every attempt to speak meaningfully of the ineffable carries with it the temptation to hear the words as explanation rather than invitation. Religious words are trailheads that open onto the beauty and terrors of the wilderness. Our efforts to domesticate the wilderness with explanations are defensive. Freud was right to call us out on our fantasy projections, our defensive whistling in the dark.[10] He was wrong, however, to dismiss all religious speech as defensive. Jung went deeper. What Jung intuited and spent most of his life exploring is that religious language is mythic, not literal. Like good poetry, mythic language relies on metaphor, constructing a footbridge across a chasm of mystery.[11]

Literalism ignores mystery and reduces faith to an ideological map, requiring only belief and not a journey. Literalism exiles the shadows of religious speech, as mere belief exiles doubt. Mythic language, on the other hand, offers its narrative as a participatory structure that makes creative living possible in spite of the tensions between belief and doubt, light and shadow. Most religious mythologies invoke Divine Love as a fundamental feature, the better to nurture courage and sustain the risks of transformation. However, truly radical love never strays far from the wilderness. It is more like a wild animal than the comforting but domesticated love that we heard about in Sunday school. The radical and fierce Love of God issues a relentless call to awakening. It first drives the soul into the wilderness, and then sustains it there.[12] Love becomes the bridge that allows for two-way traffic between presence and absence, fullness and emptiness, belief and doubt, light and shadow, life and death, beauty and sorrow. Like Sherpas crossing a Himalayan abyss we put our full weight on the bridge. We bet everything on Love.

10. Freud, *Future of an Illusion*.

11. "Metaphor" comes from "meta" (over or across) and "pherein" (to carry or bear). Good metaphors create new meanings by bridging tensions of difference.

12. In the Synoptic Gospels (Mark 1:12, Matt 4:1, Luke 4:1), the Spirit drives Jesus into the wilderness where he undergoes the trials of Satan and is tended by angels amidst the wild beasts. As a mythic narrative this story precisely depicts the soul's journey. The profound inner work of differentiation must endure harrowing confrontations with archetypal depths, out of which emerges an awakened consciousness.

Show Up, Tell the Truth, and Listen

The greatest hindrance to knowledge is our adjustment to conventional notions, to mental clichés. Wonder or radical amazement, the state of maladjustment to words and notions, is, therefore, a prerequisite for an authentic awareness of that which is.[13]

—Abraham Joshua Heschel

The journey to amazement is itself amazing and unpredictable. However, there are trail markers. Those I've offered so far are, first of all, that spirituality is warranted more by its fruits than by its practices, and that it has the single aim of releasing the soul into its native freedom so that it can come more fully into the world bearing its gifts. Another marker offers the possibility that Soul is dynamic, in motion, undomesticated. Trying to contain its fullness in language is like trying to put a cat in a box. Like great jazz, the form shapes itself to Soul rather than the other way around. "Soul," like "God," defies definition, but I'm fairly sure that it is more of a verb than a noun.

Another trail marker is that spirituality is an ongoing exercise in identity formation and transformation. Identity is never fixed but is a work in progress. A spirituality that merely confirms a fixed identity is more a defensive exercise in ideology than a true wilderness journey. More fox than foxhound, the authentic self will always escape ideological traps. Inevitably, literalism is a washed-out canyon, a spiritual dead end, whereas a spirituality that respects myth and mystery, light and shadow, yields a growing ability to inhabit the wilderness.

Another marker is that a vital, mythic spirituality helps us notice the stories we tell ourselves. Mythic stories always locate the self in some relational stance within a narrative that invites transformation. If Love is both the invitation and the goal, then the soul that falls into its depths finds a new ground and center, and new warmth that thaws out all the frozen relational configurations of the provisional self. All these and more, however useful, are still just trail markers left by those who have traveled this way before. The wilderness itself will forever remain unmapped. We will find our way there by a variety of paths, but however we get there, the deep wilderness of spirituality will always open onto amazement.

13. Heschel, *Essential Writings*, 58.

There is no single answer to the "how-to" question. Spirituality is a journey of the soul, and no two are alike. But here too, there are some trail markers. One of them has to do with a distinction between meditation and prayer. I recognize that these terms are used in a variety of ways and my distinctions may be somewhat arbitrary. Nevertheless, I find it useful to see meditation as those practices that are primarily focused on the activity of the practitioner and may or may not have a mythic story intentionally attached to them. Prayer, on the other hand, is relational and takes place within the context of the myths, histories, teachings, and cultures of religion. Prayer is "a naked intent toward God in the depths of your being."[14] It may include observation of the mind, breath, and body; it may anchor attention by means of a mantra or sacred word, but its primary focus is *encounter,* and it comes alive in a relational story within which I am loved into being, moment by moment. In prayer I am sustained through the break*down* of the world-wombs that have become too small, and the subsequent break-*through* into new worlds with ever-widening horizons.

If a loving relationship is the context within which I can risk awareness of a wider and more inclusive truth about who I am, then the spiritual practice of prayer is how I show up for my part in the conversation. In some relationships, I am more container than contained, and my task is to invite and nurture the emerging self of someone else. In other relationships the roles are shared in a mutuality of invitation and nurture. But in prayer, especially in my Quaker/Christian practice of it, I am in a relationship that is infinitely unbalanced. I am always the smaller, emergent self in relation to the larger, inviting Self of God. There is no mutuality of knowing, or wisdom, or loving, there is only the Infinite Knower and the finite known, the Divine Lover and the beloved. The relational dynamics of prayer are unique in this sense. Unlike in human relationships, there is never a condition in which I am unknown or unloved by God; there is only my daily journey toward allowing God's deeper knowing and deeper loving to bring me to the threshold of transformation.

"Show up, tell the truth, and listen" is the short answer I offer those who ask me how to pray. Then the "holy conversation" of spiritual direction begins as we unpack what each of those terms actually means. These are not complex instructions requiring long stretches in a cave or multiple stages of initiation. Their difficulty is more in the living. They are instructions that serve well for any relationship, whether marriage, parenting, pastoring, or therapy. I suspect that most failures of these and other types of relationship

14. Johnston, ed., *Cloud of Unknowing,* 49. Written in the fourteenth century by an anonymous monk, the text is a guide to prayer in the apophatic stream. A central theme throughout the text is that prayer is naked intent toward God.

can be traced back to some neglect of one or more of the elements. They also work for relationship with oneself, with one's multiple states of mind, with shadows as well as angels. They can also be faked, cheapened, worn as masks rather than fully inhabited. One can be in the room but really absent, offer interpretive habits or unseasoned opinion as truth, and one can hear without truly listening. Prayer is the one encounter where fakery never works. A regular practice of prayer quickly exposes the absurdity of any posturing. Who are you kidding?

Let's take a brief look at each of these. Showing up means commitment to the practice. Over time and with deepening awareness it means presence, a willingness to bring one's attention to *this*, what is, without judgment. Showing up means turning toward life, embodied in this breath, this heartbeat, and not running from either its tragedy or its beauty: Either one will break your heart. Sometimes they team up and do it together. A variety of popular practices emphasize showing up, simply being present without resistance or demand that reality meet my needs or conditions. Showing up means simply noticing the flow of experience and the stories I tell about it. Even just recognizing that I am a narrator of my experience, that I love to tell stories about it, and locate myself somewhere within them as either hero or victim, also reveals that I am embarrassingly attached to some of them. Even in the valleys of despair, I have learned that no matter how vulnerable and powerless I feel, this one thing can never be stripped away—my freedom to be present, to show up, to choose life, one breath at a time. Showing up is perhaps the one thing that is truly mine to bring to the relationship.

Once I've decided to show up, I've risked full exposure, and any attempt to say something that is actually true is immediately faced with an undeniable awareness of how far off-center the plumb line can swing. "Truth" is etymologically related to "trust," "troth," and "tree." Truth is treelike; it is faithful to its nature and invites trust. Deep in the silences of wilderness, truth appears in the flight of the hawk, the quickness of the mouse, and in the way the stream flows. In prayer, telling the truth is first of all an exercise in simply avoiding self-deception. It may begin in naming without excuse or apology the simple truth of our brokenness, and the reality of harm we have caused. It may also be an exercise in accurately naming our demons: *Shame, Embarrassment, Depression, Fear, Addiction,* etc. There is great power in naming. Above all, truth-telling is about noticing alignment, becoming treelike in our fidelity to our own nature. Quakers speak of "centering down," an expression that points to an embodied awareness and a deepening attunement to the subtle shifts of the soul's plumb line. Once I've shown up for prayer, I may need a long and silent period of waiting before the plumb line finally becomes still. Only then can I say something that is actually true. Only then can I speak into the wilderness as a hawk flies, or as the river flows.

Finally present and at rest in truth's stillness, prayer falls deep into listening. But this too turns out to be far more than what we imagined it to be. The selective hearing of everyday life widens its range in prayer and we begin to listen at the edges of perception until the barriers that we set up against truly hearing begin to weaken. Listening becomes more than hearing. Deep listening is a kind of whole-body awareness that begins to notice that we are woven into a fabric of interconnected being. The whole world is alive and the cosmos is singing! Even the stones talk, although I don't recommend that you tell very many people that you hear them! In prayer, listening becomes more like the quivering awareness that is everywhere present in the wilderness. Even if I have to live at the edges of what is considered the normal and sane world; even if I have to endure the skepticism of those who prefer to live closer to the world's conventional wisdom, prayer calls me to a new world of wonder and amazement, where nothing is as I assumed it would be, and where I am invited to become more than I ever thought possible.

Love is an invitation, never a demand. Sometimes I am impatient with listening and I want God to barge in, but that would only reinforce my illusion that God is essentially outside, separate, perhaps above it all. But if I imagine God to be the deepest interiority of everything, then God's presence will always be deeper and more patient than mine. I do not arrive at my most profound interiority, I am not even fully inside myself until "self" disappears into "the unbearable wholeness of being."[15] If prayer is never more than my waiting for something outside of me to finally arrive, then the shell of my everyday world will never break open into wonder. But if prayer is more about God's waiting for me to finally show up, to become true, and to learn to listen as the earth listens, then I am the one who needs to come home. God is already there.

15. Delio, *Unbearable Wholeness of Being.*

CHAPTER 2

Silence

We wake, if we ever wake, to the silence of God.[1]

—Annie Dillard

There are many invitations to silence. Some excellent ones hang in the Brandywine River Museum where Andrew Wyeth's paintings blanket the mind and heart with a snow-covered stillness, where plow, stone, barn, and fencerow all sit together like ancient Quakers in a Pennsylvania meeting. Wyeth uses paint like great poets use words—sparely, saying only enough to awaken memory, hope, or longing. My favorite artists and poets all seem to have learned the art of silence from nature—in a snowfall, or watching a cat by a fire, or while tending a fishing line on a still pond. We are the saffron-robed novices constantly being thwacked into awakening by nature's sheer presence. Those who truly inhabit silence no longer need words, which at best are merely an opening into the inexpressible. But I am not awake so I need guides, and I am grateful for artists.

And for musicians. Samuel Barber invokes silence with an extraordinary musical gesture in his "Adagio for Strings" where the listener is thrown aloft by the orchestra, caught and transported higher on the notes of a few violins, and then finally released into still heights where the air becomes too thin to breathe. I am launched to the highest point that gravity will allow. And then silence. Barber does not break my fall. He allows it; there are no receiving arms, no net, only a vast silence within which to descend like a stone. The "Adagio" gathers itself again into sound only when it is clear that

1. Dillard, *Holy the Firm*, 64.

there is no rescue from such a fall, only a rebirth. There are no saving gods there, wanting praise or worship, only the most essential lesson that silence can teach: our small gods are forever betraying us. We fall into the great stillness, and then we are gathered together again into a new beginning. I am grateful for musicians.

Annie Dillard gets down to the raw business of stripping us of our illusions of a kindly old white-haired god who is there just to keep our lives running smoothly: "Of faith I have nothing, only of truth: that this one God is a brute and traitor, abandoning us to time, to necessity and the engines of matter unhinged . . . Have I once turned my hand in this circus, have I ever called it home?"[2] If she were to just declare herself an atheist and be done with it, I wouldn't blame her, but something in her won't let her off that easy. She shows up—for life, however harshly or beautifully it comes to her, paying exquisite attention. Then in a few words, she says something true. She returns to listening and that gets her back on the hook, riveted, noticing, and writing. I am grateful for poets.

Great artists all seem to know silence. Wyeth knows as much about where not to paint, as where to apply a few strokes of the brush. Barber's "Adagio" would be something altogether different were it not for that one great stillness. Whenever I am able to hear a live performance of Handel's *Messiah*, I wonder how long the conductor will hold that immense and cavernous pause that comes just before the final Amen. I want it to last forever. Even the angels are holding their breath.

Mary Oliver, in a poem entitled "Praying," finds a doorway into silence simply by paying attention to a few weeds in a vacant lot.[3] Would it be the same silence without the weeds? Silence is the absence framed by presence, a blank space on the canvas, the rests between the notes, how the poet's words say more by saying less. I have known three great silences in my life, the silence of a Quaker meeting shaped by the simplicity of the meetinghouse and the ancestral presences of our history, a year of silence with the Trappists, shaped by seven daily offices and the liturgical year, and the silence of the Camino de Santiago, shaped by nature, fellow pilgrims, and a soul friend who did not need a lot of words in order to know and be known. These are different silences, not in substance but in how the paint around them is placed on the canvas. Silence is the stillness shaped by fasting from sound, the pause between breathing out and breathing in. In silence all of our named gods die off, leaving only a sacred stillness where the thousand names fall away.

2. Dillard, *Holy the Firm*, 45.

3. Oliver, "Praying," 37.

Going into the Dark

> But when I lean over the chasm of myself—
> it seems my God is dark and like a web:
> a hundred roots silently drinking.[4]
>
> —Rainer Maria Rilke

I suspect that our certainties, successes, accomplishments, and reputations will never be what interests the angels. They want to know what we do with the misdirection, the wrong turn, our losses and failures, the broken heart, even the depression that ultimately breaks our addiction to light and misplaced hope. I suspect that they know that the soul is bottomless and that we reach its depths by falling rather than by climbing. The soul is like a vast root system that reaches into the earth with ever-finer threads until it finally becomes indistinguishable from the ground that nourishes it. It has taken me decades to learn this, but finding my God in the dark is what finally made sense of a recurring nightmare I had as a child.

I am standing outside my family's house. It is dark outside and I am alone. Inside there are bright lights and a party is going on. I can see that everyone is having a good time, laughing, talking, although I can't hear them. Outside, with night descending, it is utterly still. I bang on the window trying to get their attention, hoping that someone will come and let me in, but no one can hear me or see me. As the realization begins to close in on me that no one is going to come and let me in, I slowly turn away from the window and towards the night. Behind our house was a barn, a garden, then a pasture and a woods, and then deep into the woods a ravine dropping steeply for several hundred yards to the Whitewater River making its slow and muddy way to the Ohio. I turn away from home, from the lights, the party, the familiar. I know that I must go into the night alone, into the woods, and then down into the ravine. I wake up in a panic.

I now know that like most dreams, this one is multilayered, addressing both personal and collective themes. It would be true, but not enough, to say that my childhood dream gives narrative form to my experience of being unseen and unheard within a distressed family that had too much going on to pay much attention to its youngest member. It would also be true, but not enough, to say that the dream anticipated and was preparing me for an impending crisis. There were some serious fault lines in my parents' marriage that were beginning to crack open. Children often carry forbidden knowledge, and I knew without words, in the way of a child's knowing,

4. Rilke, *Book of Hours*, 47.

that the container could not hold. Within a few months of my having these dreams my mother would make a precipitous decision to take her sons and flee to another state. The family container shattered like a dropped vase. My dream recurred perhaps three or four times and then suddenly stopped. In hindsight I can see that the dream was telling me that the impending upheaval in my family would throw me into a crisis of identity that could not be resolved by reconstituting an old order. The dream does not tell me how to get back into the family living room. Rather, by placing my dreamer-self outside the family home, the dream shows me that I will be required to grow into a larger identity with wider horizons. As a child, barely eleven years old, I was much too young for this developmental leap, and consequently experienced the dream as a nightmare. It would be more than a decade before I would be able to answer its deeper call. Now I understand it to be a dream of initiation into a wilderness way of knowing.

The dream states in unmistakable terms that there is more to consciousness than what can be seen from within the walls of a well-lit house. It is mythic in structure: there is a challenge or crisis, a persistent attempt to resolve the crisis in a way that doesn't work, and then a call to undertake an arduous journey that will require resourcefulness and courage. It doesn't promise that I will succeed, only that I must undertake the journey. In fact, I almost did not succeed. The journey into the night has taken me into some very dark periods of depression. But over time I learned how to navigate these dark passages by honoring the call to sink deep into silence and to let all my senses become attuned to the night world, an unmapped wilderness that offers itself as a natural habitat for the soul's rebirth. The dream's call is toward humility, humus, earth; I must go *down*, not *up*, into a ravine, not up a mountain. Eventually I learned to pray in the dark.

Now I can enter the landscape of this childhood dream with more confidence because I've learned that the night is a vast and spacious host for the small lights of our day-world ego-consciousness and all its anxious grasping after knowing and certainty.[5] Silence, like darkness, is a womb from which a deeper wisdom is born. My greatest learning always comes when I turn toward the unconscious, toward people who see the world differently than I do, and toward the mystery of God who is always slipping outside the frames of neatly packaged theologies, an ungraspable God who inhabits regions far beyond ego's comfortable living room. Containers break. But the soul is endlessly fertile in its religious imagination and can rebuild our temples again and again.

5. This phrase evokes the poet John Keats, who advocated what he called "negative capability, that is, when a man is capable of being in uncertainties, mysteries, doubts, without any irritable reaching after fact and reason." Keats, *Letter.*

The Apophatic Way

Therefore I pray God that he may quit me of god,
for [God's] unconditioned being is above god and all distinctions[6]

—Meister Eckhart

Some part of me will always long for the well-lit house with its presumed certainties and securities. But I can't un-dream the dream; it now belongs to my awareness like a parable, a teaching narrative whose lesson is inescapable. Fortunately, the wilderness way is a path that has been traveled by many who have come before. There are wonderful teachers and guides. I can draw strength and courage from them. Those who speak most powerfully to my condition are the apophatic mystics.

Apophasis refers to the spiritual gesture of "un-saying or speaking away."[7] Apophatic spirituality is always working to get behind the language and concepts that can too easily fill in the whole canvas, leaving no space for mystery. It is grounded in the awareness that any name for God is not God; any image of God is not God; any assertion about God is not the full truth. Those who practice an apophatic spirituality know that the light of consciousness casts a shadow, much like a campfire creates a circle of light while also darkening the night around it. Apophatic mystics know that the full mystery of God extends far beyond ego-consciousness and its small circle of light. In Christianity apophatic voices can be heard as far back as pseudo-Dionysius in the sixth century. They are also present in the other Abrahamic traditions, and in the Far East, apophatic sensibilities reach back many thousands of years.

Meister Eckhart, a German preacher and theologian of the early fourteenth century, was a major apophatic figure. He longs for a God of "unconditioned being" who lives in a darkness that stretches infinitely beyond our carefully tended light, and in the deep silence that falls into depths far beyond the reach of words. He was intensely aware of the powerful human temptation to reify our beliefs and images into certainties, and to install them as the reigning deities in our personal, relational, and political worlds. Eckhart prays to be rid of these gods. Not surprisingly, he got in trouble with the church, as apophatic mystics tend to do, because their "un-saying, and speaking away" invariably challenges the church's tendency toward institutional hardening into ideological rigidity. Many Quakers find a welcome

6. Eckhart, *Modern Translation*, 231.

7. Sells, *Mystical Languages*, 2.

spiritual friend in Eckhart's writings even though he preceded the Quaker movement by more than three centuries. Jung was also deeply influenced by him and that influence can be discerned in Jung's understanding of ego's relationship to Soul.

When I weave these voices into a Quaker, Jungian, apophatic conversation, I am pointed toward mysticism, myth, and mystery. In Quaker worship, I turn toward the Great Silence. I lean into that which lies hidden beyond all of our knowing, naming, and imaging, and I am weaned off of words. A simple relinquishment of words, however, is not enough. The Jungian voice in this conversation helps me understand that the fall into silence is always narrated by some background story. Maybe the silence is seen merely as an empty container into which I pour my ruminations. Or, maybe the silence feels dangerous, not empty but harboring threats. Or maybe there is some other barely conscious perspective that becomes the functional narrative shaping the practice. Better to make the operative story conscious, and then to ask if I want to keep it or consider another. I prefer to engage the silence by way of a mythic story that gives narrative structure to the processes of transformation, one that invites practices that bring the small, provisional self into dynamic engagement with the mystery I call God. The Jungian voice in this conversation reminds me that we all inhabit some mythic structure—our only choice is whether or not to make it conscious. Finally, the apophatic voice in the conversation negates the hardening of the mythic structure into an ideology of God. The practice of "un-saying or speaking away" holds the paradoxical affirmation that there is a God beyond our gods. Meister Eckhart expresses this when he prays to be rid of "god." His prayer is an act of negation that itself is predicated upon there being an unconditioned God who hears his prayer. What I learn from this three-way conversation leads me to a radical spirituality that expects and surrenders to God's nonviolent revolution within.

Because there is always a "self" that is constellated with its "god," radical spirituality is not only about the transformation of the God-image; it is also about transformation of identity. *Constellation,* in this sense, means "to stand with." Identity is always formed in relation to some god, understood as the orienting center of one's universe. "Selves" and their gods stand with each other; they rise and fall together; they hold each other in orbit. The "self" whose world is defined by the well-lit living room is not the same as the "self" who stands outside the window and turns toward the night. We are always in some provisional self that either co-operates with or defends against its own evolution into ever-larger frames of consciousness. In the silence, I turn toward the dying of a self that is clinging to a dying god, so as to allow, participate in, and even welcome the dying/rising journey that appears to be the way of Soul. To follow the way of longing for the wholeness of God, is to follow a journey in which all of our small selves and all of their small gods ultimately disappear into the mystical union. Our false selves and their false gods fall away and we are left with the hidden wholeness of being.

Surrender

The heart is a beggar.[8]

—James Carse

The apophatic gesture of "un-saying" requires a willingness to give up all hope in all our gods so as to come into a state of surrendered listening and waiting. This is not as easy as it sounds. There is the grasping self, then there is the non-grasping self that congratulates itself in having attained a state of non-grasping! Eventually, I recognize that I have not really attained anything; I have merely arrived at a trailhead. From there on the journey is in darkness. In the wilderness, all of my hard-won competencies are useless. I am stripped down to my most needy and vulnerable. It is frightening to need that which is beyond my capacity to understand or control. Of course, that doesn't stop me from trying. I am shameless in my attempts to appease, entice, trick, or seduce God into meeting me on my terms. But I've learned over and over that I'm helpless to get God to show up for me. I really have no choice other than to adopt the powerless posture of the beggar.

Once when one of our young mothers took her crying infant out of a meeting for worship, we could still hear his cries in another room, and a familiar Quaker saying sounded plainly in my thought: "That Friend speaks my mind!" Then his cries softened and quieted when I imagine he was offered his mother's breast, and my worship deepened into the Great Stillness as I fell deeper into my own hunger and embraced my own powerlessness. False gods are addictive in part because they offer the illusion of control, and as every recovering addict knows, an acknowledgment of powerlessness is the first step.

Like the infant, the praying heart must yield to a mystery that both nurses and weans the heart. So much helplessness, dependency, and surrender! Giving up control feels dangerous! I feel like a kid playing around an abandoned well. What could be more risky? Where are the grown-ups

8. Carse, *Silence of God*, 4.

warning me away; where is Lassie coming to save me? What if I fell in!? I would surely die! I look to the mystics and they just tell me that dying is the whole point. Some comfort! I quickly retreat to safer ground and then occupy myself with another book on prayer or a new practice. Let me get back to my centering prayer word, or maybe do some Lectio with one of the psalms. Or maybe it would be fruitful to ruminate on what prayer practice would be most suited to my Enneagram type. These and many other approaches to prayer all have their place, and for many they take the prayerful heart to the edge of silence and leave it there. But I use them like sacrificial goats. I keep hoping that I can get it right and appease the right gods and entice the mystery into showing up for me. These practices are doorways into silence and surrender; they are not prayers without risk. But I want to be rescued from the edge of the well, or if I *must* fall, then at least I want to be caught by the Everlasting Arms. But that doesn't seem to be my hymn. Maybe I just don't have the hang of it, or I picked the wrong prayer word, or got my type wrong. Maybe I just keep sacrificing the wrong goat.

Or, maybe nobody really knows how to pray. It is such a mystery. Only ego ever pretends to be an expert in prayer. Silence teaches that we are always and forever rank beginners. I have no judgment in me for those who want to name the mystery or devise plans and programs for spiritual practice. I have done my share of throwing words down the well, even though I know that it is the very nature of silence to resist our attempts to find names for it. There is no single right way, no form that unfailingly serves everyone. For some, the outward form with its sacred words and rituals of devotion is exactly the lifeline that they need, and I have on many occasions found myself on my knees before the eucharistic table. But for others these forms are more of a cruise ship than a lifeline, more of a denial of mystery or even a safeguard against it, than they are a way to stay close to it. Our religious gods can become idols as readily as our secular ones.

Whether the outward form of worship is a Quaker meeting or a high church Mass, it is not the form but the inward stance of the worshipper that matters. Let me take a posture of simplicity, and like the beggar or the infant, embrace my vulnerability and hunger. If I take a defensive posture of ideological certainty, if I build a big ship and cling tightly to it, sooner or later, I find that my ship is the *Titanic* and God is the iceberg. I'd rather have a raft. Better to walk into the night, past the barn and garden, through the pasture, into the woods, and down the ravine. Then like Huck Finn, I'll lash together a few logs and let the river carry me all the way to mystery. Silence is an invitation to surrender, not only our words, but also our gods, all those centers around which the false self orbits. Silence invites an immense trust.

In silence we are set free of our false gods. Anything we release that is true and vital will return with the fullness of God.

In a well-seasoned Quaker meeting a collective surrender can be felt as the silence deepens. It may take a while for this to happen, but after some period of time, usually more than just a few minutes, a meeting settles. There is an almost palpable feeling of collective letting go, as egos begin to relax, leaning into the silence. Sometimes spoken messages are offered that arise from egos that have not fully surrendered, and that is understandable given what is being asked of us. But when a well-seasoned meeting is able to allow its collective courage for surrender to carry it into greater depth, the community falls into an abyss of stillness. We know that something may happen here, but we also know that our greatest contribution is in our willingness not to be its agent, but only its willing instrument. This can be serious labor. Ego loves to be in charge and will make many subtle efforts to retreat from the wilderness. Surrender consists in the difficult practice of doing nothing, simply waiting in expectancy. This is hard work. But the fruits are inspiring, especially when someone is lifted into speech and the hawk flies, the river flows, and we hear something true.

The best metaphor I have for this is that in seeking to offer ourselves as instruments, willing to be placed in service in the meeting and in the world, we try to remember that instruments don't play themselves. A simple wooden flute lies on the shelf until it is picked up and the breath moves through it. Our job is to tend to the emptiness inside, to keep clear of the false selves and false gods that would fill us with their pretensions. Yielding to the process of being hollowed out is not an achievement; it is simply our contribution to the music. It is an act of devotion. Another, more recent dream brought this home to me:

I am a novice under the instruction of an old monk. I watch as he goes in and out of his small hut. He is emptying everything out and taking it to an altar where he gives it up in devotion. I think, "Ah, this is the lesson: I should empty myself out like him." But then I realize that is not really the point, because I see that he continues to go in and out of his hut, even after everything is cleared out. I keep watching and now I see him making a gesture that looks like he is scooping up his emptiness. And then he brings that to the altar too.

I wake up humbled by the dream's confrontation of ego's desire to achieve something, to make emptiness into an accomplishment, something to attain. The dream confronts me with the eagerness of my novice-self to learn a lesson and apply it in service to my spiritual "progress." What the Dreamer really wants me to see in this teaching tale is not just that the old monk is empty, nor even that I might become empty like him, but that he is filled with devotion.

He is not attached to his possessions, but neither is he attached to his emptiness. He surrenders everything for love, including his emptiness.

Prayer of the Heart

Just as the quiet lake originates deep down in hidden springs
no eye has seen, so also does a person's love originate
even more deeply in God's love.[9]

—Søren Kierkegaard

For all the insistence that the apophatic mystics place on "un-saying and speaking away," it is clear that these gestures rise from a great devotion. The preference for silence over too many words, or for darkness over too much light, is the same preference that a lover has for solitude over the presence of false suitors. One who waits for the unnamed Beloved fiercely rejects all idols, those imposter gods who trap the mind in a single image or belief, and who demand a loyalty that is unworthy of the heart. For many, fortunately not all, but for many within the institutions of conventional religion, the mystic path has always fallen under great suspicion and mistrust. It feels dangerous to walk into the night where the path of unknowing feels like toying with disbelief, a rejection of church doctrine that could put one at risk of falling into heresy or worse.

Apophatic silence, however, is a *practice* not a doctrine. Its purpose is to move faith from the mind into the heart. Preoccupations with belief or disbelief are a great distraction, red herrings that have taken many souls deep into territory that has nothing to do with faith. A rejection of our gods is not to be confused with atheism, which insists that no god of any description could possibly exist, and is consequently its own form of ideology. Atheism is always rejecting one image or another, and typically focuses on the easiest of targets, rejecting all possible gods in the name of a single caricature. It is essentially reactive to whatever theistic images are current in the culture. Garrison Keillor once commented that everyone in Lake Wobegone is Lutheran, including the atheists.[10] Nor is praying to be rid of our limited and limiting gods to be confused with agnosticism, which while acknowledging uncertainty, nevertheless continues to support the notion that *gnosis*

9. Kierkegaard, *Works of Love*, 9.

10. "It was a Lutheran town. Everybody was Lutheran. Even the atheists were Lutheran—it was a Lutheran God they didn't believe in." Keillor, "Signs Off."

is the key function, either knowing or not knowing. Theism, atheism, and agnosticism all live in a world in which some theistic image is affirmed, rejected, or held in the mind's uncertainty.

But apophasis is a gesture of the heart, and is not focused on the mind's preoccupations. Believing or not believing is beside the point, and once those preoccupations are no longer an issue, I am released into a more deeply contemplative prayer where I can accept the disappearance of the Beloved into pure absence, darkness, and silence. And, I can accept and delight in the reappearance of the Beloved when I simply begin to feel the absence more as a fullness, and the darkness as light. There seems to be a dance between dark and light, desolation and consolation, the desert and the promised land. My relief is immense in the moments of presence and promise. The world is ok again, all is well, and I relax into confidence, and wonder how I ever could have felt lost. Until I do again.

This is the wilderness way. The weather is constantly changing in my inner world. My inner guests come and go. Feeling lost and wondering if I've wasted my life on a fool's quest are regular visitors, as are the feelings of hope and confidence. When they show up at my door, as they inevitably do, I do my best to be a reasonably gracious host, offering a seat and a cup of tea. Rumi has written a wonderful poem about that in "The Guest House."[11] I prefer to host Hope, Trust, and Love, so I'm always tempted to leave my more difficult guests and go looking for some I like better. But inevitably, Despair, Lost, and Hopeless also claim a place at the table. The guests I don't like turn out to be messengers, though their message is harder to hear. They turn me away from the well-lit house back towards the night. Again and again, I hear the call of the wilderness. I turn away from the familiar, leave home, walk past the barn, through the pasture, into the woods, down the ravine, and fall into a deeper silence. I am returned to my spiritual infancy, to the beginning of everything.

Kierkegaard's image of the quiet lake expresses this well, precisely because he insists that our origins are so deeply interior that they are inaccessible to the eye, and by implication, to thought or understanding. His insight is the same as Rilke's, who says that no matter how deeply he goes within, his God is dark, in the sense of being hidden from the light of consciousness. Kierkegaard suggests that we are created by Love, for love. But it is a fierce and costly Love. Anyone who has ever loved deeply knows that the sheer vulnerability of love breaks our hearts over and over. We can't possibly bear love's sorrows or its joys on our own, so we search for love's origin, its funding source, its replenishment. I have to work daily at sinking down to

11. Rumi, *Essential Rumi,* 109.

the depths where the Divine Spring flows, clearing the detritus and slog that would choke it off and turn my little pond into a stagnant swamp. Am I being too dramatic? I don't think so. I've tried loving *without* the "Divine Assistance" that is always invoked in Quaker wedding vows, and I'm not any good at it. My heart *needs* God regardless of whether I am in a state of belief or doubt, trust or mistrust, dying or rising.

The apophatic mystics see the empty spaces on the canvas; they hear the rests between the notes. They invite me to fall into silence, into a daily dying of my many false selves, to fall with expectancy, and an anticipation of being met by yet further transformation. Every out-breath rehearses the final breath of death and every in-breath remembers the first breath of life. The promise of the hidden spring is more credible knowing that Kierkegaard plumbed the depths of existentialism and despair before he found it. Even the resurrection, the central image of hope for Christians, has no meaning apart from the crucifixion. "I face death every day," says St. Paul.[12] Prayers of the heart eventually teach us the art of dying. And then out of our dying comes new life, new freedom, and an extraordinary joy. The awakened heart is freed to live in radically new and authentic ways.

Silence and the Shout

Joy Unspeakable is not silent,
it moans, hums, and bends to the rhythm of a dancing universe.
It is a fractal of transcendent hope, a hologram of God's heart,
a black hole of unknowing.[13]

—Barbara Holmes

Richard Rohr points out that contemporary literature on contemplative prayer emphasizes silence and solitude and is mostly focused through a Eurocentric lens.[14] He's right, at least as far as this chapter is concerned. Everyone I've quoted, until now, is white and most are male. I don't consider that an indictment of silence *per se* but it does raise an interesting question. Why have I been so deeply drawn to silence, to the Danish Kierkegaard, the Germans Rilke and Eckhart, and the Quakers who originated in seventeenth-century England? I suspect that God calls each of us to the practice

12. 1 Cor 15:31.

13. Holmes, *Joy Unspeakable*, xvii.

14. Rohr, *Art*.

that we most need to become whole, and for me, silence has been the heart of prayer. But for many, the night has already been too long and the soul too long silenced. For some, especially those for whom a tightly woven community has been key to survival, the longing for God is expressed communally, and the mystical union is nurtured and experienced in soaring music, transcendent preaching, and the congregational shout. I have no doubt that we are one family, all drinking from a common well, but the Spirit comes into visibility in diverse ways and Barbara Holmes's work opens the contemplative life to new horizons.

Reading about the contemplative practices of the Black church in her book has given me language for what I have long sensed to be true. Often when I read the work of Black writers, I feel like my nose is pressed against a window onto Black experience. I'm an observer, not a participant. In her probing deep into Black religious traditions and experiences, I know that Holmes is not writing about me. She tells a story of Black survival, spiritual resourcefulness, protest, and practices that drink from a deep well. This is not my ancestral community, but woven throughout I also hear a transcendent human story about universal dynamics of suffering and spirituality. She has created a remarkable tapestry that tells the story of Black spirituality and survival that is at the same time archetypal and points beyond the particularities of race and culture toward the beloved community. She lifts up a spiritual vision in which I can find a place in the community, despite the obvious disparities of privilege. Political realities do not ultimately define spiritual ones, and while there is always the danger of misusing the language of common spiritual ground to obscure historical realities and ongoing systemic oppression, there is nevertheless profound and important truth for all of us in her afterword where she says, "We are on a pilgrimage toward the center of our hearts. It is in this place of prayerful repose that joy unspeakable erupts." I want to be included in that "We"! Then, she adds, "It is a joy that lives as comfortably in the shout as it does in silence."[15] Yes!

We don't do much shouting in Quaker meetings. It is certainly in our spiritual DNA, being the spiritual heirs of some pretty noisy preachers. But the worship practices of modern Quakers have become very quiet and subdued. I suspect that we have allowed our cultural habits to shape our worship rather than the other way around. I can only speak for myself, but I know that when I get all the way back into the woods and down into the river of God, something comes to life in me that I know rises from the same Spirit as the shouting I hear in Black churches. I don't give in to my more ecstatic impulses in Quaker meeting because I don't want to shock them all

15. Holmes, *Joy Unspeakable*, 200.

witless. But I have come to know contemplative shouting as well as contemplative silence, and sometimes I go worship with communities that love to sing and preach and make some noise.

However we get there, if we each follow our own trailhead into the collective depths, we will eventually meet at the river. There is a common stream that carries us all, despite chasms of differences and the many cultural and political realities that define our diversity. The contemplative journey, regardless of social location, always moves in the direction of revolutionary love. It is a fierce Love that funds and empowers our liberation, spiritually, psychologically, and politically. Soul has no race. When I fall into the deepest listening I know how to do, I begin to hear things that my Eurocentric world has vigorously suppressed, things that those in the African diaspora have been talking about for a long time. I begin to hear marginalized voices more clearly, those in the world as well as those in my own psyche. I can begin to feel the world talking to me, and to hear the voices of nature, and if I listen deeply enough, I can feel the secret inflowing of Love in the soul. Deep in the silence, I find my way to the river of God. Yielding to its currents I am carried home to an undivided world, and awakened to a joy that "bends to the rhythm of a dancing universe."

CHAPTER 3

A Holy Experiment

Christ [has] come to teach people himself.[1]

—George Fox

A friend once commented that he really appreciates the Quakers, except when one of them speaks! I wonder if I was the one who uttered a few words when he was there to hear them. We are mostly untrained preachers. What rises has not been prepared in advance. It is rarely well crafted and often incomplete. The water always tastes of the pipes, as one Quaker quip has it. For many the deep stillness of a Quaker meeting is already eloquent and is difficult to improve upon with words.

And yet we speak anyway. Often against an internal resistance, we rise to deliver ourselves of that which wants to be born in and through us, conceived in and by the great mystery that lives in the heart. These deliverances aren't polished; they are the raw and unrehearsed "leadings" of the Spirit. It should be no surprise that the messages that are offered in a Quaker meeting are not always drawn from the deepest part of the well, which is no doubt what my friend noticed. Anyone who submits to a deepening Quaker practice inevitably must learn to distinguish the impulses of ego from the leadings of Spirit. Yet, despite the obvious challenges, we persist in our practice in the hope that if we keep listening and responding faithfully, we might catch a glimpse of the angels out of the corner of an eye. The life of a Quaker meeting is a holy experiment, and as with most really good experiments, we fail often at it. The hope and promise, however, is that we

1. Fox, *Journal*, 104.

can live sacramental lives, outward and visible witnesses to an inward and invisible grace.

We are wilderness explorers, living in the borderlands between silence and speech, between contemplation and action. We embrace no formal creed and follow no formal practice except to gather in silent worship, where we listen for the flowing forth of the Spirit. Our resistance to creeds and liturgy has deep roots in our history. Quakerism was born in mid-seventeenth-century England at a time of intense religious persecution. Religious ideology was imposed by ecclesiastical and political power. Anyone who challenged the official creeds and formal religious practices of the established Church of England could be subjected to imprisonment, beatings, or worse. Now, three hundred and fifty years later, in a context of religious freedom and multicultural diversity, an allergic reaction to creeds is no longer warranted. Ideological rigidity is certainly a problem, but I have many friends who experience sacred ritual and affirmations of faith as trailheads into the wilderness. Sometimes I go worship with them. Together we allow the liturgy to carry us to the edge of mystery.

In all traditions, including Quakerism, there are those who live only on the surface, simply putting on the outward form. There are many, however, who fall into the mystical depths of their tradition and these inevitably find spiritual community even with those who follow very different practices. I find a wonderful model for this in Howard Thurman. He once met with the Indian poet Rabindranath Tagore, about whom he made the comment that Tagore "moved deep into the heart of his own spiritual idiom and came up inside all peoples, all cultures, and all faiths."[2] He is not saying all religions are the same, only that the mystic has eyes to see from the inside. On the same trip, Thurman also met with Gandhi, and at the close of their visit, the Hindu Mahatma wanted to sing Christian hymns.

The Church of England in the seventeenth century, however, was not so welcoming of diversity. It was dominant, abusive, and doctrinaire. It held religious authority with one hand and political power with the other. Rebellion ensued, most notably by the Puritans who wanted to reform the established church and sought to "purify" it of its papist leanings. In the chaos of the English civil wars of that period a variety of dissenting groups sprang up proclaiming new practices and doctrines, including the Ranters, the Diggers, the Levelers, and a personal favorite, the Muggletonians. These all died out, but the Quakers persisted primarily due to the efforts of George Fox, a man possessed of an intense religious hunger. Fox records in his *Journal* that he sought out the teachers and professors of all factions, but he found

2. Thurman, *Head and Heart*, 129.

"none among them all that could speak to my condition."[3] Finally, when he had given up on them all, he heard an inward voice that said, "There is one, even Christ Jesus, that can speak to thy condition."[4] Fortunately, he had the good sense not to create his own new doctrine out of this experience or to set himself up as yet another voice of God to be followed and obeyed, but instead joined with others in forming a movement of people who referred to themselves as "Friends in the Truth," apparently in reference to Jesus' saying to his disciples, "I have called you friends, for everything I learned from my father I have made known to you."[5] Others called them "Quakers," derisively, because of their insistence that we must stand in awe and trembling before the Holy Spirit. Then and now, Friends sometimes find themselves "quaking" when uncovering the mystical stream.

The name stuck, perhaps because it was an accurate description of how these early Friends understood and experienced a dramatic shift to a new ground and center for their lives. Fox reports a number of spiritual visions; he was given to prophetic utterances, and was not at all shy about calling out religious authorities on their hypocrisy, as Jesus called out the Pharisees of his day, and like him, Fox got them all into such a rage that they plotted against him. He was something of a firebrand, and was constantly subjected to beatings and imprisonment, which, like Paul, he saw as an occasion for rejoicing, as his loss would be Christ's gain.[6] Yet Fox was not solely a mystic and prophet; he was also an extraordinary organizer. These unique features of personality were probably necessary for someone laying the foundations of a new religious movement in those early days of upheaval, religious turmoil, and persecution. It was a bloody period characterized by violent struggles for political power with the guardians of religious purity justifying all manner of tortures and executions. Sound familiar?

As the young movement sorted itself out, it also had to confront the unrestrained excesses of some of its converts when the release of all outward institutional norms led to an overreliance on the purely inward with little or no communal discernment of "leadings." Eventually the Quaker movement matured and developed practices that allowed the individual and community to work together, with each acting as a restraint on the excesses of the other. The twentieth-century Quaker scholar, Douglas Steere,

3. Fox, *Journal*, 11.
4. Fox, *Journal*, 11.
5. John 15:15.
6. Phil 1:12–20.

called our meetings for worship "laboratories of the Holy Spirit."[7] We are experimenters in the holy, as well as subjects of the experiment. Individually, and together, we seek to listen carefully for how the Spirit will put us to service in the world.

Prophetic Mysticism

There was a care on my mind to so pass my time as to things outward that nothing might hinder me from the most steady attention to the voice of the True Shepherd.[8]

—John Woolman

Born in the American colonies almost thirty years after Fox's death, when Quakers were no longer being imprisoned, tortured, and hanged, John Woolman was a man of profound spiritual sensitivity, whose life was a model of prophetic mysticism. His *Journal* is written in plainness and simplicity, showing us how he looks past the immediately visible to the eternal. He orients his life by a different compass, and that gives him a new way of discerning his course. He wants to rightly order his life in all its dimensions around the central fact of God's love and guidance. Woolman was aware that there is much in the outward world that presents a persistent temptation to become preoccupied with outward things. His solution was not to reject the world, but to maintain a steady inward attention while living in the midst of the world's clamor and drama. In another passage, he says, "I have felt tender breathing in my soul after God, the fountain of comfort, whose inward help hath supplied at times the want of outward convenience."[9] What a gentle affirmation!

Fox and Woolman seem like two very different characters to me, two personalities, distinct in preferred inclinations and styles, as all personalities are, yet each faithfully responding to the needs and demands of their respective cultural and historical contexts. On the surface, it would appear that Fox had an intensely outward and active life, preaching, teaching, organizing, and willingly taking on suffering for his witness. And it might appear that Woolman had an intensely inward and mystical life, continually in an attitude of surrender and devotion. Yet this reading of their lives would

7. Steere, ed., *Quaker Spirituality*, 15.

8. Woolman, *Journal*, 35.

9. Woolman, *Journal*, 172.

widely miss the mark in both cases. Fox had an extraordinary mystical life and Woolman an inspiring and dedicated life of witness, particularly in his tenderness toward the native people of the land, and in his witness against slavery and the oppression of the poor.

Fox and Woolman are well-known among Quakers, often taken as models for the Quaker faith. There are many more, and with every Quaker life there is a new holy experiment. Personalities and contexts are infinitely varied, and the Quaker way is not to bring everyone into a common form, belief, or outward life, but to support one another as we seek to orient our lives around a new Center where we are secretly fed by the hidden spring of Love. The call is to find community in faith, not in form. Each one seeks to be deeply responsive to the inward promptings of the Spirit as it makes use of our lives, gifts, and personalities, within our own unique cultural and historical contexts. The practice is to sink down to the spring of life. The promise is that once having found that new orientation, we will have discovered an extraordinary treasure, worth selling everything in order to buy the field that holds it.[10] The experience and testimony of those who came before, and what John Woolman's life and *Journal* teaches so clearly, is that keeping a finely tuned attention to the voice of the Inward Teacher yields a life in which we are inwardly repatterned, given new vision and hope, and brought to clear guidance for our lives. We are released into joy, service, humility, courage, and many other fruits of the Spirit. Such a life always speaks much more powerfully than words.

Promise, Practice, Experience

It is as if my painted roof had been smashed and,
instead of the darkness I had dreaded,
I had found the stars shining.[11]

—Caroline Stephen

Fox and his temperament give a flavor of Quakerism's transforming promise during a period of severe repression in the seventeenth century, and Woolman is a model for a radically faithful spiritual practice in the eighteenth century that yielded a steady and compassionate witness against slavery. Caroline Stephen was a nineteenth-century British Quaker whose writing

10. Matt 13:44.

11. Stephen, "Letter," 450.

helped introduce Quakerism to a wider non-Quaker world. She was a convert from the Church of England who found in simplicity what she had not found in the complexity of liturgical worship. A gifted writer, she is known among Friends as a trusted voice for Quakerism for those outside the tradition, those new to it, and for many of us who have been a part of this movement for a long time but are always in need of clear reminders of what a truly radical call it is to place one's entire life, moment by moment, in the hands of the Living Presence and to make one's life a holy experiment.

Those who come to us from other traditions, or even the merely curious, often ask, "What do Quakers believe?" This should be no surprise since most religious traditions are commonly distinguished by specific beliefs. What is the doctrine or creed; how are the beliefs of this denomination different from others, etc.? These are the usual assumptions that most of us make when comparing traditions. To these questions Caroline Stephen offers only this: "The one cornerstone of belief upon which the Society of Friends is built is the conviction that God does indeed communicate with each one of the spirits He has made, in a direct and living inbreathing of some measure of the breath of His own Life."[12] Everything Quaker is built upon this one essential cornerstone.

What is immediately obvious is that this statement is more of a promise than a doctrine, and it points to practice rather than mere belief. Moreover, it is a promise based on the experience of those who have gone before and have come back with news of what they have found. Caroline Stephen's own direct experience is a moving example of someone who allowed the tradition to carry her to profound personal transformation. Her metaphor of the painted roof is a perfect image of how ego wants to paint the universe with ideological imaginings, and yet when life intrudes, as it inevitably does, our painted roofs collapse and we fall into the darkness of mystery. She writes that she was brought to this point when she "saw no escape, nothing to wish and no reason to expect any good thing."[13] With nothing left to strive for, she fully surrenders into "the good and perfect and acceptable will of God on which my soul could rest with a rest and peace that are better to me than any pleasure."[14] This is the transformational moment. It is expressed in the quaint language of nineteenth-century Quakerism, but it speaks across the generations. There are those moments in which every subtle ego investment is relinquished into the greater mystery. Ego's painted roof shatters and the soul's brilliance can finally shine through.

12. Stephen, *Strongholds*, 26.
13. Stephen, "Letter," 450.
14. Stephen, "Letter," 450.

The language of these early Quakers is steeped in biblical theism. The Quaker approach to Scripture, however, is not to take the language ideologically, as a requirement for belief, but as an invitation, as a promise that leads to practice that leads to experience. For early Friends, biblical language was a call to spiritual life and transformation, to dimensions of Soul that are beyond words. We who hear the promise, and commit to the practices, will have our own adventures in worship and we will also have to struggle with finding words to express the inexpressible. Quaker writers and teachers make use of a great variety of words and metaphors, all of which are pointers toward the mystery and none of which define it.

These writers are like a friend of mine who told me about a mountain spring near where I live in the southern Appalachians. It gives forth an unceasing flow of cold, clear, fresh water and now that I know where it is, I go there often and fill up some large jugs. Sometimes there are others there who are also filling their containers, and sometimes I'm there alone. Sometimes I get there in the bright morning sun and other times I don't get there until dusk. I know that this spring is still flowing even in the middle of the night, in foul weather and fair, and whether or not anyone is there to notice it or to drink from it. I don't know where it originates or how far underground it runs before it breaks into the visible world. It doesn't care whether I believe in it or not, or what I might believe about it. It doesn't care what names I call it, or if I call it anything at all. It doesn't flow because I ask it to, nor does it stop when I ignore it. It pays no attention to the relative merits of those who come to drink, a fact for which I am personally grateful! Before my friend told me about it I didn't know it was there, so didn't avail myself of it. But now I do know, and now I can't get enough. I've never tasted water like this before. Now nothing else tastes as good or fully satisfies my thirst. There is also a fountain that springs forth in the soul. Like Fox, Woolman, and Caroline Stephen, I want to order my life in such a way that nothing hinders my access to the Divine Fountain.

I take hope from these wilderness explorers, these experimenters in the holy, because they show by their lives and their words that just as the body cannot be fed by yesterday's heartbeat, the soul can only be fed by the "direct and living inbreathing" of God. They also make no effort to hide their very real weaknesses and struggles. There aren't any Quaker saints, only vulnerable and obviously very human pilgrims who have decided to trust a promise and persist in the practice. I learn from Caroline Stephen's moment when she saw "no escape, nothing to wish and no reason to expect any good thing" that most of us need to be brought low, like an addict hitting bottom. Now I don't feel so bad about the many times I have crashed into the limits of my abilities. My failures have taught me far more than my successes, and there have been many failures. I have been blessed/cursed with such a fierce determination to forge my own way that my journey has often been made difficult by my stubborness. Give me a heroic journey, a climb to a Himalayan cave; make me a martyr or a saint and then I'll feel like I've achieved something, or earned it. But ask me to be still and rest in Love, and ego has nothing to *do*. Tell me to just relax and trust, and I'm more likely to think you've lost your mind than to take your advice.

I once saw a card posted on a friend's refrigerator that said, "Notice: I am a Quaker. In case of emergency, please be quiet." I wonder what would happen if our first response to a crisis were to be quiet and listen? Would our political crises not escalate to war? We all have our painted roofs. We are addicted to our ideologies. Perhaps if we let them break open, we would not find the darkness we dread, but bright stars shining.

The Peace Testimony

I told them . . . that I lived in the virtue of
that life and power that took away the occasion of all wars.[15]

—George Fox

The raw material that George Fox brought to the holy experiment was that of a very serious and devoted seeker along with a rebellious streak and a fiery temperament. A modern depth psychologist would see in him a very human personality, yet one whose ground and center had shifted in such a way that he experienced a profound sensitivity to the inflowing of new insight, wisdom, and grace. The core features of personality don't change, but they can be integrated in a new way and put to new purposes. The awakened person doesn't suddenly become a saint with none of the usual cracks showing. The opposite is really the case—the light and shadows of personality become *more* visible, especially to the one who carries them. The real awakening occurs when we finally learn fully and humbly to embrace the whole of who we are, shadows and all.

Not long after the dawning of the atomic age, C. G. Jung lectured at the Zurich Psychological Club. A questioner asked him if he thought the world might be able to avoid atomic war. His answer, surprising, profound, was "I think it depends on how many people can stand the tension of opposites in

15. Fox, *Journal*, 65.

themselves."[16] What an amazing response, and how deeply honoring of the importance of inner work! Jung spoke the language of depth psychology, and Fox spoke a spiritual language that was seeded throughout with biblical imagery, yet they are both pointing toward the dynamics of transformation. Fox claimed to have found an amazing Life and Power, one that helped him transcend the polarizing passions that compel us to war. At one point in his *Journal*, Fox states that he passed through the flaming sword that bars the return to paradise and that he had been brought into the state of Adam before the fall. But he also sees beyond the limitations of language when he says, "And I saw into that which was without end, and things which cannot be uttered, and of the greatness and infiniteness of the love of God, which cannot be expressed by words."[17] His profound experiences, dramatic visions, and eloquent words bear witness to a transformed life.

The journals of early Friends show that many of them also experienced profound transformations, and although these Friends did not have the benefit of the language of modern depth psychology, they didn't really need it. The wisdom of the psyche is ancient and appears in multiple idioms throughout human history. It was enough that they experienced the Light of God as an illumination of their inward condition, bringing their shadows and self-deceptions to the searching of the Light. Fox reports that he had visions of all manner of evils and temptations and that these were given to show him that "the natures of these I saw within, though people had been looking without."[18] Margaret Fell, an early convert to the new movement, a major influence, along with Fox, in the early years of organization, wrote that the Light of God "will rip you up and tear you open."[19] These early Friends were relentlessly dedicated to practices that they knew would take them on a radically honest inward journey. They trusted that they would be led to the discovery of that Life and Power, one that would free them of the projected shadows that so often fuel our outward wars. Those same discoveries are reflected in Quaker writings up to the present. Howard Brinton, one of the early directors of Pendle Hill, writes, "If the soul is able to find in the silence union with the peace of God at the heart of existence, then inward peace is secured and new knowledge and power received. The soul, no longer exhausting its energy in conflict with itself, becomes integrated and unified. Hence arises new power and vision for tasks ahead."[20] The soul

16. Hannah, *Jung*, 129.

17. Fox, *Journal*, 21.

18. Fox, *Journal*, 19.

19. Fell, *Epistle to Convinced Friends*, 92.

20. Brinton, *Inward Peace*, 29.

is established on new ground. It is set free *from* the exhaustion of internal conflict and set free *for* creative peacemaking in the outer world.

The Friends' peace testimony is rooted in and sustained by spiritual practices that point toward such awakenings, or what we might call transformations of consciousness. Some confusion entered into the mix, however, with an early document known as the *Declaration of 1660*. This was composed in response to suspicions that Quakers were involved in violent revolutionary movements threatening the restored monarchy under Charles II. The dozen signers of this document, which included Fox, declared Quakers to be "harmless and innocent," thereby seeking to insulate Quakers from the retribution that was being visited upon the revolutionaries. The *Declaration* states, "All bloody principles and practices, we, as to our own particulars, do utterly deny, with all outward wars and strife and fightings with outward weapons, for any end or under any pretence [sic] whatsoever. And this is our testimony to the whole world."[21] It is a statement of absolute pacifism, and it is defended by careful reasoning and appeals to the authority of Scripture. The document achieved its purpose, and the Quakers were spared.

The argument served to help us avoid the king's retribution, but it burdened future generations with having to sort out the true ground of our peace testimony. Is it grounded in the mystical presence of God as expressed in Fox's account of his own awakening? Or is it a principle-based ethical commitment grounded in Scripture and reason? One unfortunate consequence of the *Declaration* was that many later Friends simply posted a framed copy of the *Declaration* in their libraries and adopted a rule of behavior. Principled pacifism became a shadow-creed. For some, it was elevated into a position of such unquestioned authority that it was taken as a defining moral imperative required of all Quakers. From then on, many Friends who participated in war were expelled from the Society. This was not the case prior to the *Declaration*. Fox himself had defended Quakers who fought in the English civil wars.

If the *Declaration* is not taken as a stand-alone document, but is placed in its historical context with its defensive purpose clearly in view, and if it is then read alongside other early Quaker writings, we can see that it was not intended to replace prophetic mysticism with prophetic moralism as the ultimate ground and foundation of our peace testimony. However, the failure to read the *Declaration* in its historical context led to the promotion of a pacifist doctrine grounded in a scripturally based moral argument, one that was then imposed on all future Quakers. This development began to obscure the deeper ground of the peace testimony. As with so many religious

21. Fox et al., *Declaration*, 1.

movements, the outward form became our measure, and the call to inward awakening began to lose its place as the heart and soul of the movement.[22]

Early Friends, however, were unequivocal in their insistence that our form of worship is in service to a radical spiritual awakening, and they anticipated that out of that fundamental repatterning of consciousness would emerge a new creation in which war would no longer be necessary. To some, this distinction between mysticism and moralism may seem like splitting hairs. After all, many who act on principle and many who prioritize an inward transformation are very often engaged in the same outward activities. Does the inward condition even matter as long as the behavior is just? Quakers are longtime fellow travelers with those who practice a Social Gospel based in a moral reading of the Bible, and there are mystics and moralists in all traditions. The lines are not institutional. Rather, they are discerned in the Spirit. The mystic and the moralist often walk alongside one another. But walking alongside must not be confused with walking the same path.

The distinction might look something like this: God put the wind of the Holy Spirit in our sails. Then, having discerned the direction, we started rowing. Then some of us began putting more faith in our oars than in the wind. How difficult it can be to stay finely attuned to the wind, especially when the voices of political certainty and righteousness, right or left, are so fierce and unwavering. How many of us are willing to challenge the established political certainties of our own communities when we sense the Spirit moving in a different direction? What courage would it take to move left from a right-leaning community, or to move right from a left-leaning community, and to suffer their censure if not exile? Quakers are not exempt from these spiritual challenges. Yet, at the heart of our tradition, we hold to no creed, *neither theological nor political*, because we seek the immediate presence and guidance of a Living Spirit whose ways are not our ways, and whose in-breaking Life is often nothing less than astonishing. Quaker witness, if it is to remain vital and authentic, must stay close to the winds of the Holy Spirit.

Quakerism is a holy experiment in prophetic mysticism. With no established creeds, but only the authority of the Spirit, discerned in prayer and

22. Steve Smith, a Quaker and a retired professor of philosophy and religious studies, writes, "What might be called principle Quakerism—a body of attractive values regarding peace, simplicity, integrity, community and so on—is a free-floating belief system that has lost its roots in transforming spiritual experience and thus lacks vitality and dynamic power. In contrast, testimony Quakerism is the authentic fruit of the Inner Christ, that of God within one's own heart—the source from which all else flows." Smith, *Living in Virtue*, 27.

community, it is not surprising that we are constantly in danger of falling into an undisciplined collection of conflicting opinions, passions, and ideologies. At our best we take ego out of the witness and fill it with Light. At our worst we take the Light out of the witness and fill it with ego. Perhaps this is why the history of Quakerism is rife with splits and separations. Our family tree shows so many limbs, branches, and twigs that we look like a poorly tended shrub. This is not a reason for despair so much as a reminder that we humans are messy, unconscious, difficult creatures in desperate need of awakening to that larger Life and Power.

I doubt that I will convince very many Quakers that we are not principle pacifists. The belief is too deeply entrenched in our tradition. I once tried to make the point in a workshop that I was leading. The response was a stunned silence followed by such a hue and cry that I wondered if these avowed pacifists were going to temporarily suspend their principles in order to tar and feather their retreat leader! Fortunately, that didn't happen, but I have learned to tread lightly around this topic. Now, I simply stress that Quakerism is a holy experiment. It thrives or dies on the basis of persistent inner work. Our peace testimony carries the inspirational authority and awakening power of the Spirit in proportion to our own awakening to that Life and Power that takes away the occasion for all wars. The Quaker way is a sacred journey into the wilderness of the heart.

The Bottom of the Disorder (I)

To attempt to do the Lord's work in our own way and to speak of that which is the burden of the Word in a way easy to the natural part does not reach the bottom of the disorder.[23]

—John Woolman

Modern Quakers are the bearers of an ancestral heritage that includes a rich history of quiet, courageous, imperfect, but dedicated souls who, in allowing nothing to hinder their "most steady attention to the voice of the True Shepherd," were led to historic work for religious freedom. That original prophetic witness for liberation persisted through the centuries and grew to address multiple forms of oppression. Quakers were active participants in hiding and guiding enslaved people on the Underground Railroad; we were leaders in movements for women's suffrage, in war reparation efforts,

23. Woolman, *Journal*, 112.

in civil rights movements, in campaigns for the equitable distribution of wealth, in movements for a sustainable ecology, and in many other issues of social concern. Understandably, we are often associated with these efforts, and we often attract new members because of them. That presents us with a dilemma.

The central gift of our tradition lies in dedicated spiritual life and practice, out of which may arise courageous leadings to act in the world. But our new members are not always aware of or even interested in this fundamental core of the tradition. Many have come into the Quaker movement because of what on the surface appears to be a political ideology. But acting from political alignment alone, without first seeking deeper spiritual ground, fails "to reach the bottom of the disorder." I suspect that a modern version of Woolman's phrase, "easy to the natural part," might be "satisfying to the ego." Ego loves ideology, and our communities, like most, drift toward ideological homogeneity. More than a few meetings have lost members over ideological disagreement, and some of our annual conferences have split over issues such as LGBTQ advocacy, rigid approaches to racial justice, and other intensely debated concerns.

Given dedicated spiritual practice, we can break through ego's fears. But when the mystical stream is not faithfully tended, our religious, psychological, and political ideas begin to calcify into more fear-based structures of thought. We are all bound by these thought forms to some degree, which is why we need ongoing spiritual practices to break through them. At their most extreme, calcified structures of thought become ideological cults that generate right/wrong choices—litmus tests for ideological purity. Eventually, our actions are narrowed down to are-you-in-or-out kinds of binary options. Thought forms that are ideologically bound invent gods to give them divine sanction. Sometimes they adopt the gods of tradition and then do whatever trimming and shaping is needed to get them to fit, and sometimes the urgency of the moment displaces all notions of God.

Prophetic mysticism, in contrast, is grounded foremost in a dedicated practice of deep relinquishment in search of awakening. We engage practices that welcome awareness of all that ego has forced into the shadows, the better to surrender into the humbling processes of transformation. When everything is surrendered, all bets are off. We allow for the possibility that the mysterious guide we call God is not bound by our all-too-human rules. Woolman's phrase, "the bottom of the disorder," names a longing to get to the root cause of the disease. His spiritual sensitivity gave him unusual insight into the human condition and helped him diagnose the spiritual disorder at the foundation of our lives.

Again and again in the Quaker journals and other writings the call is to "dwell deep," or "sink down," or "relinquish all," thereby coming into a place of pure surrender where everything of one's own invention is let go so that something new can come. There is purity in the longing. Of course, it is never pure in expression. We are recognizably ourselves, embodied persons with personalities and complexes, so inevitably there is rust in the pipes, but the hidden spring can use even rusty pipes for a pathway into the world. I realize that this is not the most sophisticated incarnational theology, but maybe it will serve for the moment. The essence of our holy experiment is based in a "what-if." Let's show up, bring all our blind and broken places to the table, surrender ego as fully as possible, and then see what happens. There's nothing easy about it. Every time I hear someone refer to the gospel as good news, I think to myself, "Sure. It's great news for the soul. It's terrible news for the ego." The gospel is a promise more than a doctrine, despite centuries of being treated otherwise, and it calls for practice more than mere belief. We touch the bottom of our disorder when we open onto that Life and Power that takes away the occasion for all war, whether internal to a single personality, within our communities, or outwardly in the world.

In the Quaker tradition, as in all others, I find ideologically trapped individuals, but I also find inspiring accounts of living witnesses, those whose lives were transformed and who subsequently lived in ways that shook their communities to the roots by the utter authenticity and power of their presence. A well-known account is in William Penn's description of an encounter with George Fox, where he says, "The most awful, living, reverent frame I ever beheld was his in prayer."[24] Isn't it interesting that in this passage he doesn't bother to tell us the content of the prayer, only that Fox himself embodied awe and reverence. This was the memorable thing, the inspiration. And here is the central and most essential witness of our tradition—that the very experience for which we were originally derided, and from which we have taken our name, is itself the message. The content is secondary. *The quaking itself is the message.* We are created for wonder, for worship, for awe, and for love. I could also say it another way, that we are created *by* Wonder, Worship, Awe, and Love. We become who we are, authentically, when we stand in our own becoming, loved into being, yielding to the very quaking of creation. When we arrange our lives in such a way that nothing hinders our access to the Divine Fountain, then our lives become the witness.

24. Penn, "Extracts from William Penn's Preface," xliv.

PART II

Peacemaking

CAN ONE BE PRAYERFULLY strategic, a calculating contemplative? The strategic activist and the mystic prophet are not always easy companions. Sometimes it's a beautiful fusion, but sometimes they split, and when they do, the mystic wants to act purely from inward leading, without concern for strategy, and the activist wants to plan careful strategies but does not consider inward, spiritual dynamics. They need each other, and a core aim of this book is to find a path to the beautiful and creative fusion. In the first section, we considered the inner world of the mystic, and in this section, we will focus on the systemic and strategic dynamics of nonviolence. Then in the final two sections, having considered them separately, the inward and outward will be rewoven into their original wholeness.

In this section, some history, examples, and strategies of nonviolence are lifted into view because of their power to bring large systemic interactions to light. This section is not a guide to action, although I have included an appendix with a list of excellent resources for those wanting to learn more about building effective strategies for change. This section is rather an introduction to nonviolence as a worldview, an organizing pattern for understanding both personal and political dynamics. The aim of this section is to present nonviolence simply as a model for how the world works, in its fundamental evolutionary drive toward an ever-more complex and integrated whole. There is an underlying *Eros* at work in the deep structures of nature, psyche, and in our shared political life.

The three chapters in this section challenge our habits of thought related to peace and conflict. Our biases are evident in our failure to see the violence in some forms of "peace," and in our failure to embrace the extraordinarily creative and hopeful dynamics in some forms of conflict. Violent "peace," the theme of chapter 4, is deadly and oppressive, whether it appears in the inward or outward world. Nonviolent conflict, the theme of chapter 5, brings hidden violence into view where it can be creatively engaged. Nonviolence is a means of engaging conflict that extends beyond particular social issues into an ongoing work of building nonviolent dynamics into the social structures of deep democracy. Nonviolence is the one form of conflict that violence can suppress but can never finally defeat. It alone can deliver a nonviolent peace, the theme of chapter 6. Here, peace and conflict are no longer polarized but are in a creative dance. They are intimately interwoven as essential creative elements of every transformational event. A thoroughly authentic and creative argument, as every healthy couple knows, taps the deep Eros of loving engagement.

CHAPTER 4

Violent Peace

They dress the wound of my people as though it were not serious.
"Peace, peace," they say, when there is no peace.[1]

THE JOURNEY FROM ZAGREB, Croatia, to Sarajevo in Bosnia and Herzegovina took a circuitous route. We crossed back and forth across political lines, first through Prijedor, a Serb-controlled city in northern Bosnia and Herzegovina, and then to Sanski Most in Bosniac territory, then to Zenica, and finally Sarajevo. I had a window seat on the bus as it took its winding route through mountainous terrain and could enjoy the scenery as we bounced along over narrow roads. The beauty of the natural environment, however, was interrupted periodically as we passed by stark evidence of recent destruction. There were signs of life and hope on the faces of many who were rebuilding and working through the trauma. And there were signs of death and bitterness on the faces of others. I was unable to read the silent histories behind these faces. What assessments do they make of this ill-conceived war, one taken in patriotic zeal at the behest of a Serbian president who lied, distorted history, manipulated fears, and fanned the fires of hatred, a president who was driven by a lust for power and who suppressed dissent? These are people who once lived peacefully together, intermarried, and shared a common land. Now they are divided by traumatic memories of brutality and betrayal. What lies behind these brooding masks? Will they be able to find their way back to peace?

There have been many books written about the breakup of the former Yugoslavia and the war that followed, and many of them lament the lateness

1. Jer 6:14.

of international intervention. UN mediators wavered and hesitated, and issued warnings to the Serbian leaders that never led to action. UN "safe areas" were violated, and as in the case of Srebrenica, became sites of atrocity and mass murder.[2] For three years Serbian forces shelled Sarajevo from enclaves in the surrounding mountains. Early on they hit and burned the National Library, destroying countless volumes, many of them ancient and irreplaceable. Snipers in hillside bunkers shot citizens at random. Then in August of 1995, thirty-seven people were killed in a Sarajevo marketplace by a Serb shell. It was widely reported, along with graphic television coverage, and finally, public pressure forced NATO to respond. Air strikes targeting Serbian command centers, ammunition storage, and sniper positions in the hills around Sarajevo ended the shelling, and convinced Serbian leaders to come to Dayton, Ohio, where a peace accord was finally settled.

What followed was often called "peace," and anyone who has ever experienced respite from such terror and violence would be impatient with my wanting to qualify "peace" with quotation marks or an adjective like "violent." But some words are asked to carry too much freight, and they lose depth of meaning when we ask them to carry burdens they were never meant to carry. Following Dayton, there was a cessation of violent conflict, but for nearly ten years after, it was necessary for NATO to maintain stabilization forces in the country. At the time of my visit to Sarajevo, in May of 2004, there were still soldiers of several nationalities patrolling the streets wearing armbands identifying them as security forces, and their presence was what made it possible to travel in relative safety. However, the war that had been stopped outwardly lives on in traumatic memory.

We long for a future without violence, but until nonviolent structures and systems are widely understood and built into our political arrangements, we are left with the painful necessities created by violence. Nonviolence is gaining ground, in Bosnia-Herzegovina, in Serbia, and elsewhere around the world. But all too often those nascent movements are overwhelmed by relentless brutality. In Bosnia, what was begun and carried out in violence had to be brought to a stop by violence, otherwise it would have continued unabated. Now the fighting has stopped, but there is not yet peace. The beast has merely lumbered back into its lair. Peace will come, but there is still much work to be done.[3]

2. More than eight thousand unarmed Bosniak men and boys were rounded up and murdered by units of the VRS (Army of the Republic of Serbia) under General Ratko Mladic. The massacre at Srebrenica has been ruled a genocide and has been called the worst atrocity on European soil since World War II.

3. Efforts to heal traumatic memory and to work toward forgiveness and reconciliation have been undertaken by a number of organizations, including the Karuna Center

The Beasts of War

Bosnia can teach us about the wild beast,
and therefore about ourselves, and our destinies.[4]

—Peter Maass

Peter Maass isn't the first writer to refer to war and its ravages as the work of a wild beast, or to understand that the beast lives potentially within each of us. The "beasts of war" are archetypal and appear in images and myths across cultures and religions. They can be easily activated in the collective imagination, and shrewd politicians have known for centuries exactly how to stir them to life when it suits their purposes. Generations of grief, fear, and rage, residue of unhealed trauma, are activated in wars of aggression as well as in wars of defense. The rage for war cannot be killed off or defeated, as violent efforts are employing the very means that brought them to life in the first place.

Driven back into its lair, the beast of war can be easily reawakened by an act of provocation, and if that is lacking, old wounds can be surfaced and exploited, and if that fails, a narrative of victimization can be carefully fabricated and propagandized. In our own recent history, we have a classic example of the fabrication of a victim story about a "stolen" election that instigated an assault on the capitol. Former president Donald Trump continues to inflame passions over imagined grievances for craven political purposes. Milosevic reached back six hundred years in order to stir war fever among Serbian citizens, recalling the massacre of Serbs by invading Turks in 1389. The steady stream of nationalism that poured from the Belgrade propaganda machine continued to fuel the fires of victimhood until virtually any act of war was justified as righteous defense.

Chris Hedges, a veteran war correspondent who interviewed people on all sides, noted, "All groups looked at themselves as victims—the Croats, the Muslims, and the Serbs. They ignored the excesses of their own and highlighted the excesses of the other in gross distortions that fueled the war. The cultivation of victimhood is essential fodder for any conflict. It is studiously crafted by the state."[5] The dynamic has been repeated throughout history.

for Peacebuilding. My visit to Sarajevo was to help out my sister, Demaris Wehr, who had worked with the Karuna Center's program and was returning to Bosnia to conduct interviews for a book project. See Wehr, *Making it Through*.

4. Maass, *Love Thy Neighbor*, 273.

5. Hedges, *War*, 64.

Leaders wanting to mobilize collective support for war or even oppression of their own citizens can activate the beast at almost any moment by stoking the fires of grievance, and inflaming the passions of fear and rage.

Left unhealed, generational trauma becomes sedimented into collective memory where it takes on a mythic and unassailable character. Hedges tells of interviewing a Palestinian woman who turned to her two-year-old son and said, "Tell the man what you want to be." The child, already mirroring the expectations of his family, responded, "A martyr."[6] Generations of pain have been narrated in this family and will continue to be until there has been some reckoning with traumatic memory and the overwhelming affect that goes with it. The complexities of the Israeli-Palestinian conflict must be sifted by truth, confession, reparation, and reconciliation. All sides must make a fierce and unbreakable commitment to peace. Two-year-olds are not born to be martyrs.

Fortunately, we are getting better at healing trauma, and we are building a body of research in conflict transformation, and creating programs like Alternatives to Violence and Braver Angels that are teaching us critical skills.[7] In the aftermath of war, healing can occur through truth and reconciliation efforts and many other such programs. These bring the beast out of its lair into the light of consciousness. They are essential to healing. But when we ignore these efforts, the beast merely goes into hiding until the next round in the cycle. Even when violence is used in defense of the oppressed, it is a diseased "cure." There can be no lasting peace until violence itself is unmasked.

6. Hedges, *War*, 68.

7. An especially effective effort in this regard is the *Alternatives to Violence Project*, which as of 2019 is active in thirty-three states in the US and in forty-five countries around the world. It has trained over 1,500 facilitators. AVP works in diverse settings, including prisons, schools, churches, shelters, and many other venues. See https://avpusa.org.

Uncovering that which is hidden

There is very little evidence of warfare between 9000 and 4000 B.C.E., and not a great deal until around 3000, after which it proliferates dramatically.[8]

—Walter Wink

"The domination system" is a phrase that refers to new forms of social organization that arose around five thousand years ago and that created the conditions for the emergence of warfare. Riane Eisler is the cultural historian who first coined the term. Her work is multidisciplinary, reaching across sociology, anthropology, psychology, and theories of social transformation. She contrasts "domination systems" with what she calls "partnership systems." Her terminology has been picked up by a number of authors, notably Walter Wink, who understands her model historically, theologically, and archetypally. To say that domination systems are archetypal is to say that they form an ancient patterning of thought and perception that extends across cultures. Eisler writes that "underlying the great surface diversity of human culture are two basic models of society." The "dominator model" is characterized by systems of "ranking," assigning superiority to some and inferiority to others. Power relations are framed in terms of dominance and submission. The "partnership model" is characterized by egalitarian systems of "linking," interdependence, and shared power and responsibility.[9] She says that partnership models of social organization flourished successfully for many thousands of years until the archaeological evidence begins to show the emergence of domination system models when defensive structures, weaponry, and warrior gods begin to appear around 3000 BCE.

There is no consensus among scholars as to the reasons for this development, but it is clear that it occurred, and that the domination system prevailed. Partnership systems were not extinguished altogether. They still persist in some societies and in a variety of communities, such as in Quakerism, but the domination system is by now so deeply embedded in the structures of Western consciousness, and in most of the cultural systems around the world, that it masquerades as the essential nature of the universe, divinely ordained, and taken as "commonsense" reality. It has become the collective worldview within which we acquire what sociologists of knowledge call our "primary socialization."

8. Wink, *Engaging the Powers*, 36.

9. Eisler, *Chalice and the Blade*, xvii.

Patterns of social organization shape virtually every detail of our lives, certainly our economic and political systems, but also our religious ideas and the dynamics of our inner worlds. Personality formation takes place within a context of background narratives that set the stage for how we come to understand who we are and our place in the cosmos. Sociologists describe primary socialization as a process that defines not only the object world but also the perceiving subject.[10] It is as if we are born onto a stage upon which a variety of actors may play but which, nevertheless, imposes certain limits. There will be patterns of perception, types of interactions, even ways of forming identity that simply will not be possible without changing the backdrop, just as one cannot play *Our Town* on a stage set for *Hamlet*.

"Uncovering," under circumstances such as these, means something far more than merely revealing something that is hidden somewhere on stage; it means turning up the house lights. It means revealing the play for what it is—a constructed narrative that governs the interactions, the perceptions, even the very identities of the actors. We cannot see how insidiously the domination system shapes perception until we set it in contrast to the far more ancient partnership system. A model that I use in my teaching places these two systems side by side.

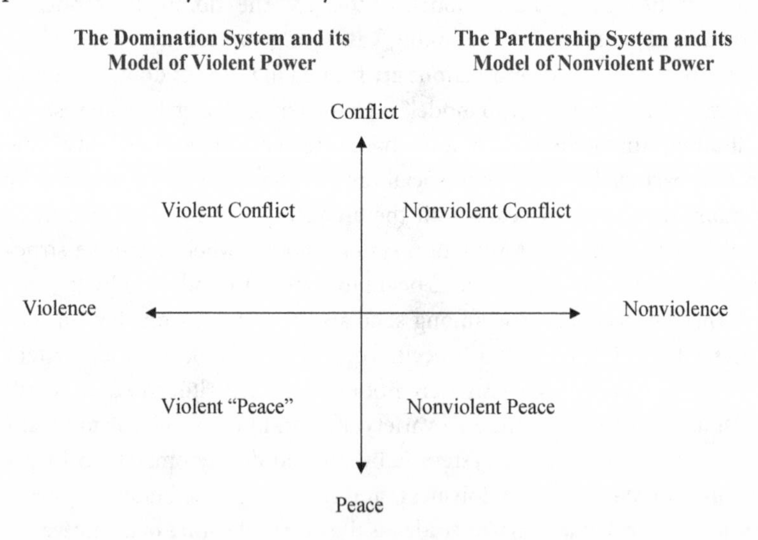

10. Berger and Luckmann, *Social Construction of Reality*, 134–35. The authors comment that "The child does not internalize the world of his significant others as one of many possible worlds. He internalizes it as *the world*, the only existent and only conceivable world, the world *tout court*. It is for this reason that the world internalized in primary socialization is so much more firmly entrenched in consciousness than worlds internalized in secondary socializations." Berger and Luckmann, *Social Construction of Reality*, 154.

In the domination system's model of power, conflict and peace are opposites. Sometimes I cover over the right half of the model to illustrate how limited thought becomes when the domination system is the commonsense world. We are horrified by war, but the domination system offers no other frame within which to imagine a different future because it can only imagine an unending cycle of violence. "Peace" is little more than the suppression of conflict. War ends when one side dominates the other, and the defeated side suffers not only terrible loss, but also displacement, humiliation, and often rape, and even enslavement. Sometimes barely a generation passes before the rage that is buried in violent "peace" explodes into the next cycle. Violent repression and violent revolution are in a tight dance with each one shadowing the other. When the domination system is the only lens we look through, we cannot imagine a world without this dance of war, oppression, exploitation, terrorism, and violent revolution.

Without a dramatic shift in perspective, it is nearly impossible to speak of nonviolence, except moralistically, or in terms of an otherworldly idealism. Nonviolence sounds like foolishness, or passive resistance. Dedicated activists with the best of intentions are tempted to fall back on violence because they think nonviolence is little more than an appeal to the values of love and conscience. In workshops I sometimes hear the objection that nonviolence is foolish, naïve, no match for the boot of oppression. The objection is based in a profound failure to understand its dynamic. Nonviolence is indeed love in action, but not the kind they imagine. It is fierce, militant, and effective love.

In the next chapter we begin to explore the world of nonviolent conflict. How does it work? What new and surprising kind of peace does it bring? Strategic nonviolence works with a different model of how political power works, and once that model is understood, it becomes clear how effective strategies can be built on its foundation. But in failing to gain a critical understanding of strategic nonviolence, some activists are tempted to abandon it and "fight fire with fire." It is a tragic miscalculation. Violent protests play directly into the hands of those who seek control through domination. That is their game and they are very good at it. They will even insert *agents provocateurs* into protest movements to incite violence, thereby creating the pretext and justification for violent repression. Activists who promote violence are simply doing their job for them.

What eventually emerges in the conversations generated by these four quadrants and the radical differences between the left and right halves is an awareness that when we speak of systemic oppression, we are not only talking about our social institutions; we are even more fundamentally talking about habits of perception that are reified in our theological and psychological ideas, habits that have been many generations in the making and are, therefore, deeply sedimented into the collective psyche. Systemic oppression runs far deeper than our social and political institutions. We are trapped by *theo-psychic-socio-spiritual* systems that are embedded in the structures of consciousness. Of course, we can and have done very creative peace work within the horizons of the domination system. It's actually pretty amazing what peace workers have accomplished, even without challenging the deeper structures of consciousness that limit our frames of reference. However, these efforts do not reach "the bottom of the disorder." We need an archaeological dig into the psyche. We will turn to that discussion in due time but before we go there, let's not lose the lessons of violent "peace." We've paid a high price for them.

- Violent "peace" does not resolve conflict; it merely suppresses it, thereby creating the conditions for an ongoing cycle of violence.
- Violence is the domination system's game and its advocates are very good at it. They want political struggles to be played out on their home turf. Consequently, activists who consider violence a realistic option are playing into their hands. They might as well be *agents provocateurs.* They are doing their work for them.
- Violent "peace" is structural violence. Martin Luther King Jr. called it "negative peace." Racism, patriarchy, homophobia, etc., are systemic.
- The domination system is at least five thousand years old, but it is not the oldest, nor is it the original form of social organization. Partnership societies existed for thousands of years before the emergence of warrior societies, and continue to exist in many indigenous societies and in some minority communities in the Western world.
- Structural violence is not only embedded in our cultural institutions; it is embedded in our habits of perception. Generations have been socialized into its distortions. We are trapped by *theo-psychic-socio-spiritual* systems that shape consciousness.

This last lesson is crucial, and is often missed in more politically focused discussions. The domination system has distorted not only our political systems, it is also embedded in our religious and psychological ideas, and in many of the ways we understand spirituality. We will turn to these deeper impacts in later chapters. But for now, there is one more critical issue that needs special attention: The domination system has profoundly distorted our beliefs about human nature.

We have been told, over and over that we, especially men, are innately violent. It is not true. The domination system has taught us to think of gender in binary terms and to think of *the* feminine and *the* masculine, as if these are fixed qualities, with domination system features assigned to the masculine, and partnership system features assigned to the repressed feminine. This language appears in the literature of depth psychology, as well as in theological and spiritual writing that is focused on countering the effects of patriarchal religion. However, the reification of gender, where masculinity is identified with the domination system, fails to fully uncover the deeper roots of patriarchal ranking. What is intended to be a liberation message for women has the unintended consequence of driving the insidious effects of the domination system more deeply into the shadows. The full alignment of men and women for the sake of liberation must include a deeper reassessment of gender, and for this conversation we owe a great deal to communities that identify as nonbinary, transgender, and queer. The language is still emerging, and I won't presume to speak for those communities. However, in my work with men over the years, I have become convinced that our collective work for liberation will not be complete until we free ourselves from a terribly misshapen view of masculinity.

Violent "peace" and the unbearable sorrow of men

In patriarchal societies men are assigned the role of "violence objects."[11]

—James Gilligan

The ideas that violence is instinctual, that humans (especially men) are fundamentally warlike, and that humans have always fought wars are deeply entrenched in our beliefs about ourselves. We see the reluctant soldier as an aberration rather than the norm. James Gilligan is a psychiatrist who has spent over thirty years working with our nation's most violent criminals in the Massachusetts prison system. He notes that violence is almost always driven by desperation to avoid shame. He notes that "masculinity, in the traditional, conventional stereotypical sex-role of patriarchy, is literally defined as involving the expectation, even the requirement, of violence, under many well specified conditions: in time of war; in response to personal insult; in response to extramarital sex on the part of a female in the family; while

11. Gilligan, *Preventing Violence*, 59.

engaging in all-male combat sports; etc."[12] These conditions are narrated in such a way as to produce shame. Shame and humiliation are intolerable. In the internalized and unconscious calculus of the domination system, violence replaces shame with pride.

Prison culture merely reveals what is already present, but suppressed, in the wider culture. The domination system constructs "masculinity" on a foundation of shame. For most men, it is a core emotion, though often deeply unconscious, and the least accessible. Grief and fear are linked to shame, making them also somewhat inaccessible. Anger is the emotion most culturally acceptable for men, being the least linked to shame, and consequently, the shame-linked emotions are often converted to anger. As most men in Western culture have experienced at some point in our lives, any deviation from the expectation of competition and dominance, such as a display of vulnerability, some timidity, or even worse, a display of tears, or walking away from a fight, these behaviors are commonly met with shaming and ridicule. The shaming of men, both by other men and by women[13] is rooted in cultural values that insidiously socialize men for war. As "violence objects," men are conditioned every day to silence our instinct for cooperative relatedness in order to turn us into soldiers capable of killing our brothers.

Despite our deeply entrenched beliefs, social scientists have come to near unanimity in their rejection of the theory of innate violence. These behaviors are socialized and are passed down generation to generation, but they are not innate. It is more the case that boys are not offered any other viable models for what it means to become a man and, consequently, they either find a way to fit the mold or they must endure shaming, rejection, and isolation. Gilligan notes that a major factor that "enormously increases the likelihood that people will respond to feelings of shame by means of violence is that they do not perceive themselves as having non-violent means by which to maintain or restore their self-esteem and self-respect."[14] The issue is the universal human need for respect, not a universal human proclivity to violence.[15]

12. Gilligan, *Preventing Violence*, 56.

13. Women sometimes shame men with statements like "man up," a phrase that suggests that a man is only a man when he is potent, vigorous, and assertive. Girls become women by natural processes, but a male must "become" a man by way of initiation into the rites of an often-toxic masculinity, and then he must continually "prove he is a man" lest he be shamed back into boyhood.

14. Gilligan, *Preventing Violence*, 37.

15. Walter Wink takes a thorough look at the issue of innate violence in the third of his *Powers* trilogy. He writes, "Violence is not, in fact, a constant in human societies. There are primitive peoples surviving even today among whom violence is almost nonexistent. In the Philippines, Africa, New Guinea, and Malaysia there are tribes that are still

Many men are able to live authentically despite enormous social pressures, but sadly, many do not. Nonconforming males suffer an increased risk of depression and suicide. To be born male in a patriarchal society is to either conform or to suffer daily assaults on one's self esteem. However, if enough trust can be established to assure emotional safety, men who are able to step free of the toxic expectations that come with being treated as violence objects reveal a very powerful *reluctance* to engage in violence. Dave Grossman, a military psychologist who has written an extensive study on the nature of killing and what it takes to get soldiers to do it, writes that he has drawn "a novel and reassuring conclusion about the nature of man: despite an unbroken tradition of violence and war, man is not by nature a killer."[16] He cites a well-known study by S. L. A. Marshall on World War II veterans in which he showed that "of every hundred men along the line of fire during the period of an encounter, an average of only 15 to 20 would take any part with their weapons."[17] There have also been a number of parallel studies that he says "all confirm Marshall's conclusion that the vast majority of combatants throughout history, at the moment of truth when they could and should kill the enemy, have found themselves to be conscientious objectors."[18] This presented a considerable problem for combat trainers. In the years between World War II and Vietnam, training focused on overcoming this natural resistance to killing and yielded the result that an estimated 95 percent of soldiers used their weapons in combat in Vietnam. Obviously, rigorous training can overcome our natural reluctance to kill. But human nature, contrary to widely held belief, is not essentially violent.[19] A desire to preserve life appears to be our essential nature.

Military trainers have learned that in order to achieve victory on the battlefield, there is first a psychological victory to be won in the training of combatants. That which naturally resists killing must be vigorously overcome, and, according to Grossman, this is accomplished in three ways. First, through desensitization to the fact that killing is the mission, then

---

preliterate, relatively lacking in gender role specialization, nonhierarchical, and remarkably free of violence. They do not deal with conflict by scapegoating or sacrifice, but by early socialization into cooperation and nonviolence." Wink, *Engaging the Powers*, 34.

16. Grossman, *On Killing*, xiv.

17. Grossman, *On Killing*, 3.

18. Grossman, *On Killing*, xv.

19. William Ury agrees with Riane Eisler, Walter Wink, and many others that only in the very latest chapter of human evolution is there evidence of organized violence. He says that there is "little conclusive evidence in the archaeological record for the story of pandemic human violence during the first ninety-nine percent of human evolution." Ury, *Third Side*, 33.

conditioning the particular behaviors that are necessary to killing so that the behavior is automatic, and then providing a plausible rationalization so that a psychological denial mechanism can be in place to wall off the ensuing horror and revulsion. Grossman calls these three aspects of training "thinking the unthinkable," "doing the unthinkable," and "denying the unthinkable."[20]

It is no accident that young men are especially selected for this training, as the prefrontal cortex, the site of the executive functions such as higher reasoning, further differentiation of ego, and independent judgment, are still in development through the mid-twenties. Add to this the reality that we have few genuine initiation rites and that many fathers, having been socialized into the same domination system, and who also had no initiation into a healthier masculinity, simply pass on a toxic masculinity to their sons. Military training, not unlike becoming a member of a gang, offers an initiation rite that confers the pride of "becoming a man" by breaking down innate compassion and relatedness in order to train young men into thinking, doing, and denying the unthinkable. The domination system shames away anything "feminine" in order to install a toxic masculinity. It damages the soul in order to "make boys into men."

The theory of innate violence is false. Psychologists, sociologists, anthropologists, and political scientists are in general agreement on this.[21] There is an overwhelming reluctance to kill, as shown in the Marshall study. There is a natural trajectory of the soul toward life and relatedness that military trainers must divert and bend back towards killing. As Václav Havel, the Czech poet and playwright who later became president of Czechoslovakia, wrote in one of his essays, "Individuals can be alienated from themselves only because there is *something* in them to alienate. The terrain of this violation is their essential existence."[22] If we can be kept ignorant of this terrain of our essential existence, this *something*, then we can more easily be induced to violate it.

William Ury, an anthropologist who also cites the Marshall study, observed that "the inner resistance to violence is a well-kept secret, for interestingly, when interviewed, each rifleman believed that he was the *only* one

20. Grossman, *On Killing*, 251, 252, and 255.

21. In fact, according to Michael Nagler, "UNESCO convened a seminar of some of the world's most distinguished behavioral scientists to make a public statement on innate aggression. Unheralded, but crucial, the resulting 'Declaration of Seville,' released in 1986, pilloried the popular view that a complex behavior like human aggression could be programmed by our genes and was therefore ineradicable." Nagler, *Is There No Other Way?*, 63.

22. Quoted in Schell, *Unconquerable World*, 196.

disobeying the orders to shoot."[23] This was the case in spite of the fact that nearly 80 percent of his comrades were also avoiding firing their weapons. There is a terrible loneliness in every man who has not yet found his way out from under the burden of internalized shame. Those who are fortunate enough to find a community of brothers who can point the way out of enslavement to the domination system's toxic "masculinity," and who can walk with them through a wilderness of unbearable sorrow, and who can help them find their way to a true partnership masculinity, find that they need give up none of the extraordinary beauty of being male. We are not finding our "feminine side"; we are opening onto a deep reservoir of human qualities that rightly belong to the full gender spectrum.

Awakening, Mourning, and the Great Turning

We are brought down to the dust: our bodies cling to the ground.[24]

Those of us on the privileged side of the domination system's ranking,[25] and those on the oppressed side, have different paths to walk, but our common destination is the restoration of partnership ways of being within an undivided home that is our native habitat. Awakening to the extraordinary depth and toxicity of the domination system is only the beginning, however. The shock of that awakening leads to deep mourning, as we take in the magnitude of suffering it causes and as we begin to see through its lies about human nature, and the extraordinary violence in what it calls "peace."

It is not enough merely to gain an intellectual understanding of the dynamics of oppression. There must also be an inward liberation, a change

23. Ury, *Third Side*, 22.

24. Ps 44:25.

25. Current language about privilege is an example of how our choice of words sometimes obscures more than it reveals. Those who win in the domination system's lottery gain privilege in its hierarchical ranking system. But the "win/lose," "privileged/oppressed" framing is language that further entrenches domination system thinking. Jesus' teaching gets to the deep root when he says, "Blessed are you who are poor, for yours is the kingdom of God" (Luke 6:20). Jesus is not saying that there is some special virtue in being oppressed. Rather, he is saying to the poor, "Consider yourselves blessed. We are all in desperate need of grace, but the poor are more likely to know it." To the rich he says, "It is easier for a camel to pass through the eye of a needle than for a rich man to enter the kingdom of God" (Matt 19:24). He is not saying that the rich are especially bad people. Rather, he is saying to them, "We are all in desperate need of grace, but the rich are more likely to be blinded by very seductive and addictive false gods, making it harder for them to know it."

of heart, and a turning in a new direction. This turning is what "repentance" is meant to convey in the gospel tradition. Our turning, or repentance, initiates a descent into grief and comes to expression in mourning. We resist grief's call into the depths of the body, its pull into the dust where our bodies cling to the ground, but this is the full measure of lamentation, and a true and deep turning cannot happen without it. Awakening must move beyond ego's guilt. The heart must be broken open.

I recommend the brokenhearted life. It is an extraordinary pathway to awakening. Resistance to grief is powerful, but when we find the courage to allow the descent to occur, to give it permission, grief will pull us down into the body and then we can finally yield to the mourning which opens the way to the turning. This realization was brought home to me powerfully the first time I visited the Vietnam Veterans Memorial in Washington, DC.

It was a beautiful spring day, peaceful by anyone's definition, and I had plenty of time to feel the full weight of the long, dark, descending stone that bears the names of over fifty-eight thousand men. I didn't fight in that war; I protested it, but the names on that wall identify men that I consider my brothers. I never judged them, despite differences in political convictions. I reserved all my judgment for the system that made them violence objects, used them up, and then abandoned them. On that spring day, not long after the memorial was opened, I let my hands feel the letters chiseled into stone as I read name after name, and I watched as others came by and lingered, left a memento, or quietly wept. The memorial itself is a physical embodiment of grief. It takes a long, slow descent into the body of the earth, mirroring the way of grief which pulls us down into our bodies. The psalms of lamentation express this powerfully when they speak of souls in dust and bodies clinging to the earth.

My Quaker background and high number in the draft lottery insulated me from that war, but putting my hands on those names erased all difference. One of the most offensive platitudes I've ever heard started to run through my mind: "There but for the grace of God . . . ," and then a feeling that some might call "survivor's guilt" arose within me. But neither the thought nor the guilt brought me any peace. So, I sat and waited, listening for something true, feeling the names more than reading them. And then finally the names became faces and I began seeing brothers, the faces of men with whom I might have developed deep bonds of friendship, shared laughter and searching conversation. I felt my heart open with love and loss, and finally I was brought down into grief. Through such deep sorrow, the way opens to an embodied peace that does not deny difference but finds a deeper unity in our shared humanity. Veterans Day has never been the same for me, ever since that spring day. I understand that many want to make it a day for lifting up heroes and demonizing enemies, but for me it is a day of mourning. I mourn for all men, of all nationalities, for Vietcong, for Nazis, for Confederate soldiers as well as for the Union troops. However vigorously I may oppose the values for which they fought, I see in the souls of men the unbearable wound of being made into "violence objects." Grief has taught me to see with the eye of the heart.

I don't much care for political and moral debates anymore. I hear too much certainty and conviction on all sides, too much polarization, which alerts me to the presence of large shadows, unexpressed doubts, and an unwillingness to expose vulnerabilities. I don't like aligning myself with a side, however much I might be persuaded by its argument. I have a wildly idealistic fantasy that moral discussions and political debates should all be held within circles of grief. No one would be allowed to speak who hadn't first been brought down into the belly of lamentation. Those who grieve can no longer bear shadow-denying certainties and polarized opinions, for they have already heard too many violent words, and seen too much of the self-righteousness that drives shadows into exile.

Ego cannot do the soul's work. We must be brought down into the body's mourning where the soul can finally begin a journey toward the Great Turning, a term which signifies a collective awakening, and a renewed commitment to building a life-sustaining, partnership world.[26] The war beast is fed by grief denied and a hardened heart. Grieving is an act of sanity. After five thousand years of the domination system's lies and distortions, a new world is trying to be born. When we finally wake up to the unspeakable suffering of violent "peace," perhaps then we can to join together in finding another way.

Five thousand years is enough.

26. The Great Turning is a phrase used by various writers, notably Joanna Macy and David Korten. Some emphasize the awakening of consciousness in a spiritual revolution, others emphasize the cultural, political, economic, social, and ecological implications. I believe these are inseparable, which is why I prefer to speak of *theo-psychic-socio-spiritual* systems. For a comprehensive introduction to this worldview, see Korten, *Great Turning*.

CHAPTER 5

Nonviolent Conflict

> Dictatorships are never as strong as they think they are,
> and people are never as weak as they think they are.[1]
>
> —Gene Sharp

In the early months of 1943, the Gestapo arrested the remaining Jewish men in Berlin who had so far escaped arrest because of their "Aryan kin," that is, they had non-Jewish wives. They were taken to a detention center on the Rosenstrasse, not far from Gestapo headquarters. Very quickly the word about what had happened spread to family and friends and a demonstration spontaneously developed in front of the center. It soon grew to nearly six thousand people, and was made up of the wives and supporters of the detained men. The demonstrators could have been cleared away quickly and violently, but the regime faced a dilemma. The public murder of respectable Germans, mostly women, citizens who were identified with the scapegoated Jews not by blood but by marriage, would have severely undermined the regime's legitimacy in the eyes of much of the German population. Joseph Goebbels, Hitler's propaganda minister, decided the risks were too great and ordered the release of the men. More than seventeen hundred were freed. Some, who had already been sent to concentration camps, were brought out again and returned to their families. Virtually all of them not only escaped the camps but survived the war.[2]

1. Sharp, "Dictator's Worst Nightmare."
2. Stoltzfus, *Resistance of the Heart.*

The Rosenstrasse wives saved the lives of their husbands, witnessed to humanity and justice within a few blocks of Gestapo headquarters, and exposed the lie that nonviolence couldn't have worked against the Nazis. It was just one of a number of such nonviolent successes against Hitler. The obvious question then is why was nonviolence not applied more often and more systematically? Nonviolence educator Michael Nagler suggests that perhaps a major reason had to do with the fact that neither participants nor observers had any idea what was happening, and consequently had no idea how to turn it into a systematic program of resistance. This event went by mostly unnoticed simply because it was not recognized for what it was. As he puts it, "You just don't see what's coming at you from another paradigm, even if it's right before your eyes."[3] They had no name for their actions, no strategy, they simply acted spontaneously in a way that put Goebbels in a double bind and forced a concession to their demands. Only later did analysts recognize in this event a series of actions that fit with a long history of civil resistance and then come to understand the Rosenstrasse protest strategically.

It was finally an American political scientist, Gene Sharp, who became fascinated with such events and extensively researched the history of nonviolence and wrote a systematic approach to strategy in a three-volume work.[4] He also wrote numerous articles, additional books, and the monograph *From Dictatorship to Democracy*, which was eventually translated into more than thirty languages and has informed nonviolent actions and even revolutions around the world.[5] Although he was influenced by many pacifists, including Gandhi, A. J. Muste, and Henry David Thoreau, Sharp worked to free nonviolence from its association to pacifism and religious-moral idealism and to make it accessible to a much wider range of activists in search of models for effective strategic planning.

Sharp shows that for thousands of years some form of nonviolent resistance has been used as an effective, if somewhat ignored, alternative to war. Whether due to creative insight or dumb luck, citizens suffering under oppression have awakened to, or stumbled onto the simple realization that even the most tyrannical of governments depend upon the cooperation of the governed. The concept is simple: Governments, even tyrannical ones, depend upon the cooperation and consent of the governed. When citizens withdraw that consent and refuse their cooperation, government is weakened, and if that refusal of cooperation extends broadly and deeply enough,

3. Nagler, *Is There No Other Way?*, 118.

4. Sharp, *Politics of Nonviolent Action Parts 1–3*.

5. Sharp, *From Dictatorship to Democracy*.

the supports that keep even the most brutal of regimes in place can be worn away.

Some measure of this principle is at work in all conflicts, including violent ones. The American revolutionists made use of many nonviolent tactics, such as tax resistance, civil disobedience, the building up of parallel, alternative government institutions, economic boycotts, and the like. Both the French and Russian revolutionists made effective use of nonviolent tactics before descending into the bloodbaths for which they are so well known. Religious freedom movements, anti-slavery campaigns, women's suffrage, labor movements, and countless other conflicts, both large and small have been waged with the single strategic objective of putting pressure on entrenched systems in order to shift the balance toward change. For centuries nonviolence has been used, and quite effectively, although it was often not well understood and frequently overshadowed by violence.

A singular event in 1893, however, initiated a cascade of events that would eventually lead to dramatic growth in public awareness and extensive research into the power of nonviolence. It occurred in a train station in Pietermaritzburg, South Africa when a young and somewhat frail Indian lawyer was thrown off a train for riding in a first-class seat, in spite of the fact that he had paid for and was holding a first-class ticket. Mohandas Gandhi was unceremoniously dumped onto the platform and forced to spend the night in the bitter cold of an unheated train station. The next morning, he wired his contact in Durban, who in turn wired Indian contacts in Pietermaritzburg who came to offer him assistance and told him their own stories of hardships endured because of South African racism. This was the watershed moment. Gandhi vowed to remain in South Africa to address the problem. He stayed another twenty-one years.

What Gandhi learned in South Africa he took with him back to India, where he continued his experiments in nonviolence. His work was both inward and outward, and over the next thirty years he deepened his spiritual practice while refining his political methods in his campaign to free India of British domination. He worked tirelessly, eventually winning India's independence from Britain in 1947, and left the world a dramatic and large-scale example of effective nonviolent struggle, along with an extensive body of writing that would be studied by activists for generations to come. Martin Luther King Jr., deeply influenced by Gandhi, successfully applied nonviolent principles in the American Black freedom movement. Gene Sharp completed his three-volume study in the early seventies and went on to contribute extensively to the literature on nonviolence. Mass nonviolence effectively brought an end to the Vietnam War by the mid-seventies. The anti-nuclear power movements in the US and in Europe have been largely nonviolent. And then, in the last decade of the twentieth century, an astonishingly effective application of nonviolence on an even larger scale was about to unfold. Walter Wink's account underscores the importance of these years:

> Then came 1989–1990, years of unprecedented political change, years of miracles, surpassing any such concentration of political transformations in human history, even the Exodus. In 1989 alone, thirteen nations comprising 1,695,100,000 people, over 32 percent of humanity, experienced nonviolent revolutions that succeeded beyond anyone's wildest expectations in every case but China, and were completely nonviolent (on the part of the participants) in every case but Romania and parts of the southern U.S.S.R. The nations involved were Poland, East Germany, Hungary, Czechoslovakia, Bulgaria, Romania, Albania, Yugoslavia, Mongolia, the Soviet Union, Brazil, Chile, and China. Since then Nepal, Palau, and Madagascar have undergone nonviolent struggles, Latvia, Lithuania, and Estonia have achieved independence nonviolently, the Soviet Union has dissolved into a commonwealth of republics, and more than a dozen countries have moved toward multiparty democracy, including Mongolia, Gabon, Bangladesh, Benin, and Algeria. If we add all the countries touched by major nonviolent actions just since 1986 (the Philippines, South Korea, South Africa, Israel, Burma, New Caledonia, and New Zealand), and the other nonviolent struggles of our century—the independence movements of India and Ghana, the overthrow of the Shah in Iran, the struggle against authoritarian governments and landowners in Argentina and Mexico, and the civil rights, United Farm Worker, anti-Vietnam and antinuclear movements in the United States—the figure reaches 3,337,400,000: a staggering 64 percent of humanity!

To this extraordinary accounting of countries and numbers, he then adds the sober comment, "All this in the teeth of the assertion, endlessly repeated, that nonviolence does not work in the 'real' world."[6]

6. Wink, *Engaging the Powers*, 264.

Experiments in Truth

We should not forget that even evil is sustained through the cooperation, either willing or forced, of good people.
Truth alone is self-sustained.[7]

—Mohandas Gandhi

Obviously, it does work in the real world. But, much as advocates of nonviolence like to point to its successes, especially the dramatic ones like India's independence movement, the American Black freedom movement, and the Eastern European revolutions of 1989–91, there have also been gains that were later lost and outright failures. Even dramatic successes do not guarantee an ongoing and stable peace. Independent India has not been spared its share of violent struggles; institutionalized racism persists in the US, and neither the Eastern European movements nor the Arab Spring movements have completely prevented the return of oppressive governments. The dynamic peace of deep democracy requires ongoing, creative, engaged, nonviolent action. Just as farmers must turn over the soil each spring lest it become too hardened to nourish new life, so also must political systems undergo an ongoing nonviolent revolution of ideas, people, issues, solutions, and sometimes the very structures of government. We still have much to learn, but the astonishing power of nonviolence is now in our collective awareness and many individuals and organizations are working to advance our understanding.[8] At the heart of it all is Gandhi's awakening to the basic dynamic of political power.

What Gandhi began to understand in South Africa, and further refined in India, was that oppression violates a self-evident feature of reality, namely that the urge toward life, equality, justice, and freedom is a force of nature. It can be brutally suppressed but it cannot be extinguished from the human spirit. This is a truth that needs no proof; it is self-evident and self-sustaining. Gandhi found within himself a fierce commitment to refuse further cooperation with injustice regardless of personal consequences. And he realized that if he could find this within himself, he could inspire it in other people, and it was a small step from there to recognize it as a principle of reality: The persistence of evil, in all its forms, large or small, relies on our collective consent.

7. Gandhi, *Essential Writings*, 98.

8. See the appendix for a list of books, articles, and websites on nonviolence.

How radically different this is from our general assumptions about political power. Steeped in domination system thinking, we assume that power is always top-down. In the words of Mao Tse-tung, "power grows from the barrel of a gun." Those individuals or elite groups who control the guns, the resources, and the levers of government are the power holders. According to this model, the only significant feature in the dynamics of political power is the struggle of opposing factions for control.

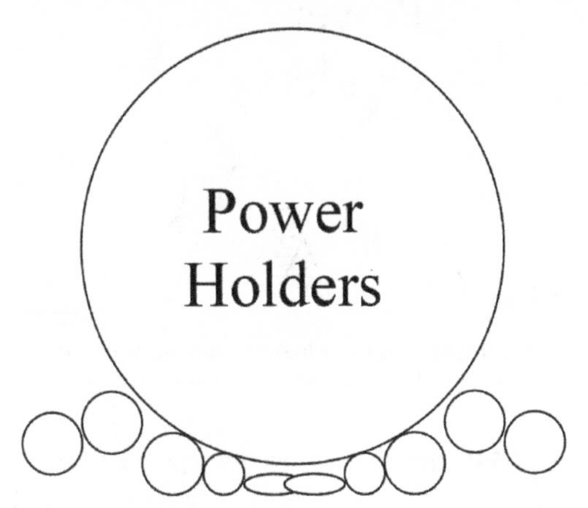

Those without power, the masses, the oppressed, etc.

The domination model of power is the one we live with every day. It is firmly entrenched in our minds and our politics. It is enshrined in our language, and in our religious and psychological ideas. It is insidiously present in our economy, in many of our social institutions, as well as in many family structures. For virtually every client I've seen in practice, it has become the internalized dynamic of relationship with self. It is as if the domination model of power has become the operating structure of the inner world.

However, despite its ubiquity in both the inner and outer worlds, the domination model paints a false picture of reality. The figure above reveals nothing about the true source of power; it is merely an image of oppression. A partnership model of power, on the other hand, reveals something that is much closer to the way things actually are: Power is *granted* to temporary holders who depend upon a collective belief in the *legitimacy* of rule, and on the collective *consent* of the ruled. Any government that loses legitimacy in the eyes of the people, or their collective consent, has suffered a potentially fatal erosion of its power. Oppressive systems are highly invested in keeping these realities a secret. People like Gandhi and King shouted them from the rooftops.

The figure below reveals the hidden dependency of power holders, and the real power that is held by each one of us. Collectively, this power can topple regimes and reinvent systems from the ground up. Inwardly, it can set us free from internalized oppression and reconnect us to our native goodness, creativity, and joy.

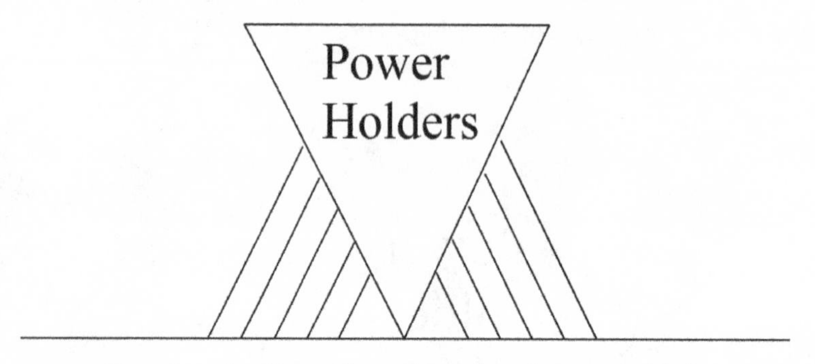

Power base, the citizens who participate in and cooperate with the structures of power and grant authority to power holders

Gene Sharp calls the lines of connection "pillars of support." Imagine any system, from a small family to a large government, and it will quickly become clear how the stability of that system depends upon such pillars. Everything from the willingness of the military to carry out orders, to citizens voluntarily paying taxes, to factory workers continuing to produce goods are what keep power structures in place. In a family, somebody has to pay the bills and somebody has to put food on the table and take out the trash. No religious community would survive if people didn't put money in the collection plate and serve on committees. We eat because farmers grow crops and we exchange goods and services because bankers transfer money. Small towns and big cities depend on transportation workers continuing to drive the buses, and sanitation workers continuing to keep the trash from piling up. These are all aspects of our social commerce that serve to keep our institutional structures in place. This is how it works both for those institutions we want to keep in place and for those we want to dismantle. For highly complex systems the model simply adds more pillars, and draws in supports for the supports.

When those structures become oppressive, nonviolent actors know that if organized action can shift any one of these pillars, even slightly, a tremor is sent through the whole system, and power holders are forced to respond. Imagine you are standing on a scaffold painting your house. Now imagine that someone comes along and starts to loosen one of the supports. That would get your attention. I once offered this image in a workshop and a skeptical participant responded, "Yeah, he would pull out a gun and shoot you! This nonviolence stuff will get you killed!" Indeed. Make no mistake about it. Certainly, Gandhi and King knew this all too well. Gene Sharp expressed impatience with this kind of response and was exasperated that nonviolence would be held to a standard that few bother to consider when advocating violence. Historically, human casualties have always been far fewer in nonviolent campaigns than in violent ones. But if anyone thinks that nonviolence is just about putting flowers in a gun barrel, they should stay home. This is serious business for serious people who know they are putting their lives on the line.

Mobilizing citizens to engage in an economic boycott, or a sanitation worker's strike, or mass civil disobedience may well trigger a violent repressive response. Nonviolent strategists know this and plan overlapping strategies in order to apply pressure at multiple points, sometimes managing to sidestep repression and at other times using the brutality of repressive violence to delegitimize oppressive forces who show tooth and claw. Nonviolence is sometimes called political *jiu-jitsu* or *asymmetrical warfare*. Power holders are often astonished when activists maintain nonviolent discipline even in the face of violent repression, and are at a loss when their violence generates even more massive campaigns. Persistence in nonviolence presents a dramatic contrast with the violence of government repression, drawing mainstream support away from power holders as the veneer of legitimacy is stripped away and their brutality is unmasked.[9]

As the ground shifts under their feet and more pillars are loosened, power holders are eventually forced to the negotiating table. Sometimes, the systems of government are corrupt, and the goal of nonviolent pressure is to cause their collapse. If parallel institutions have been created, in a process that Gandhi called "Constructive Program," then systems that are corrupt, like dictatorships, can be brought down and new governmental structures can take their place. The partnership model of political power helps us see our own essential and inescapable participation in its dynamics. There are by now millions of examples of effective nonviolent actions around the

9. Mainstream support is more likely to shift in the opposite direction when movements fail to maintain nonviolent discipline. In 2020 when mass protests followed police killings of Black men and women, they were almost completely nonviolent. However, some violence erupted on the fringes, and it was precisely this violence that the Trump administration seized upon and amplified in its attempt to build a fear-based campaign on a "law-and-order" platform. This was a classic example of how the street violence of the few was used to mask the structural violence and racism of a president with dictatorial pretensions. The Trump administration was counting on this street violence to ramp up fear. Oppression generates rage, justifiable, understandable, and important. But rage translated into violence is always a strategic disaster.

world and all of them in one form or another make use of the "pillars of support" model.[10]

New perspectives on community organizing, on building effective strategies for change, on methods and types of intervention, on the power of alternative institutions, on the strategic and effective application of civil disobedience—all of these and more are being researched and put into practice. There is tremendous hope here. As awareness of the power of nonviolence begins to reach deeper into our collective life, not only might we finally break the endless cycle of wars, we will begin to internalize its creative dynamic into our own lives and families, even into our ideas about psychology and spirituality. There is a way to end war, and it is within our reach. Nonviolence offers the only reasonable vision of a sustainable future.

Faithfulness, Effectiveness, and Hope

There is something in the universe that unfolds for justice.[11]

—Martin Luther King Jr.

I have emphasized the strategic dimension of nonviolence because strategy is too often ignored in favor of idealistic moral claims. Gandhi and Martin Luther King Jr. were uniquely gifted in their ability to hold both of these together. They lifted up inspiring visions of faith, but they were also careful strategists. We misunderstand them if we only hear the inspiration and not the strategy. Both critics and advocates of nonviolence often make this mistake. The failure to understand strategy leads the critic to think of nonviolence as naïve, whereas that failure leads the idealist to believe that nonviolent change works primarily through an appeal to conscience, or even through purely spiritual means effected by taking on unmerited suffering. Sharp's research is neither naïve nor idealistic. He notes that persuasion alone is the *least* common of the mechanisms of change. By far more often, change happens through some form of nonviolent coercion.

Both Gandhi and King gradually developed an increasingly sophisticated strategic application of partnership power over time. Neither of them, however, ever lost their trust that their actions were consistent with that

10. Swarthmore College now has an extensive database of nonviolent actions, and more are being added as they occur. See Global Nonviolent Action Database in the Appendix.

11. King, "Power of Nonviolence," 14.

mysterious "something" that unfolds for justice. As Jonathan Schell put it, "What Gandhi, Havel, and most of the others who have won nonviolent victories in our time believed and made the starting point of their activity was a conviction—or, to be exact, a faith—that if they acted in obedience to certain demanding principles, which for all of them included in one way or another the principle of nonviolence, there was, somewhere in the order of creation, a fundament, or truth, that would give an answering and sustaining reply."[12] King spoke of that "something" that unfolds for justice in his address, "The Power of Nonviolence," delivered to a packed crowd of Berkeley students in 1957. In that address he places primary emphasis on "agape love" and "winning over" the opponent. The later King begins to sound less idealistic. With the counsel of strategists like James Lawson, Wyatt Tee Walker, Bayard Rustin, Glenn Smiley, and others, King's strategy grew sharper, more discerning, and his faith, though always strong, grew less idealistic. As their visions matured, both Gandhi and King became what might be called Faithful Realists.

Faithful Realism brings together two kinds of hope, the one eternal, the other temporal. Early Quakers, who identified with pacifism, anchored their lives in an eternal hope, and used the phrase "Lamb's War," taken from the book of Revelation, to describe the daily struggle to work for peace in the midst of a painfully compromised world. Just war theorists, on the other hand, unwilling to abandon a duty to protect and defend, see temporal hope as an end worth pursuing even with violent means. No doubt both care deeply about the real world, and both may be sustained by faith, but they are split along the lines of moral ideology. The circles below suggest a way that pacifists and militarists might work together without having to iron out all their ideological differences. Strategic nonviolence is a big tent that has enough room for both principles and pragmatism.

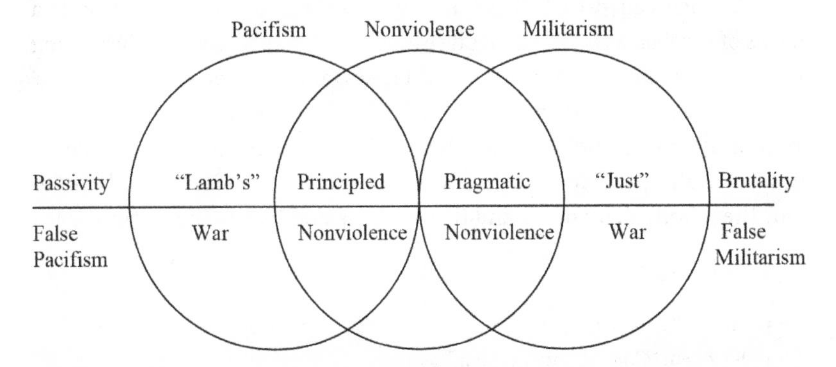

12. Schell, *Unconquerable World*, 207.

When pacifism and militarism are ideologically bound, they are subject to becoming blind to the extremes of their positions. Too much pacifism without the warrior's heart falls too easily into an otherworldly detachment from outcomes. Too much militarism without the pacifist's principles is too easily seduced by domination power. But pacifists and militarists do not have to be implacably opposed. Rather, they can understand that in joining forces in nonviolence, they are calling on different, but complementary energies. Nonviolence requires all the strengths of the warrior: strategic planning, enormous courage, determination, commitment, heroism, and a willingness to suffer and die for the sake of defense, protection, and restoration of a just order. Nonviolence also calls on all the qualities of compassion: a resolute unwillingness to inflict harm, a steadfast holding to the promise of God's healing presence in our midst, a quick willingness to forgive, and a commitment to work toward restoration and reconciliation. Strategic nonviolence holds these energies together in a dynamic tension. The promise of nonviolence is that it sees a holy and possible future already embedded in this present world, and that it responds to the injustices of the present world in light of this holy and possible future.

Gandhi and King held both kinds of hope and lived in the tension between them. Many of us, however, struggle with that tension. Gene Sharp, always the strategist, says that military people understand him better than pacifists do.[13] He is concerned that too much focus on the spiritual or moral aspects of nonviolence will detract from its being taken seriously in the world. Daniel Berrigan, on the other hand, was a priest and a pacifist. He took a nearly opposite perspective: "From a religious point of view, nonviolence is not primarily a tactic. It is a way of living and being and expressing the truth of your soul in the world. Tactics come and go. Tactics now work and now do not work. The gift of faith, as I understand it, is to be able to die well when called to."[14] It is Sharp who writes, "Nonviolent action is a means of combat, as is war. It involves the matching of forces and the waging of 'battles,' requires wise strategy and tactics, and demands of its 'soldiers' courage, discipline, and sacrifice."[15] It is Berrigan who writes, "I think this concentration upon political effectiveness is very often a trap."[16] I can imagine a fascinating and animated conversation between them. I would love to pour them both a cup of tea and then sit back and listen. Then after the tea

13. Sharp, "Gene Sharp 101," 18.
14. Berrigan, "Connecting the Altar," 96.
15. Sharp, *Politics of Nonviolent Action* I, 67.
16. Berrigan, "Connecting the Altar," 96.

is done, I'm sure they would put their ideological differences aside and get to work planning the next action.

We live in a world that is already profoundly compromised by the choices of those who preceded us. We are rarely offered pure options; our choices are always constrained by limits imposed by those who built the stage upon which we are now the actors. Our task is to work at building our constructive program, creating alternative institutions that embed nonviolent principles from the ground up, dismantling the institutions of injustice, and remodeling the stage for the next generation by revisioning our political, theological, and psychological ideas, even our spiritual practices. Nonviolence thrives in that middle circle, in the tension between radical faith and down-to-earth realism. Faithful Realism is not an ideological embrace of one side or the other; it is an ever-evolving *praxis* of contemplation and action within a nonviolent frame that drives transformation.

Nonviolence within a Global Context

> Globalization is inescapable—the question is whether it will be a democratic globalization or a U.S.–led corporate globalization (with thin democratic rhetoric).[17]
>
> —Cornel West

In 1953, demonstrators filled the streets of the German Democratic Republic. They were brutally suppressed by occupying Soviet troops and the East German police. In 1961, GDR troops surrounded West Berlin and began installing barriers between the eastern and western sectors of the city, the first fortifications that would become the Berlin Wall. Citizens looked on in dismay. Protesters in Poland and Hungary demonstrated in 1956, and in Czechoslovakia in 1968. But the forces of oppression were overwhelming. For nearly forty years the Communist regimes in Eastern Europe were monolithic, being firmly embedded in the much larger Soviet system. By the mid-eighties those structures were beginning to show visible cracks that gradually widened into fractures. And then, like the sudden collapse of a weakened dam, a rapidly unfolding series of events led to the fall of Communism in Eastern Europe and the reunification of Germany.

Nonviolence finally broke through the last critical pillars of support in the fall of 1989. Demonstrators again and again filled the streets. The people

17. West, *Democracy Matters*, 22.

just kept coming, despite repression. They prayed and carried candles; they marched and spoke out, and they maintained strict nonviolent discipline. In November of that year, the entire government of the GDR resigned, one in a series of cascading events in Eastern Europe.[18] As one officer later commented, "We had planned everything. We were prepared for everything, but not for candles and prayers."[19]

Much as it is tempting to extol the virtues of nonviolent mass resistance, the reality is that the dynamics of people power are always played out within the context of systems that are themselves embedded within larger systems. Every pillar of support is itself supported by numerous other pillars. Multiple interlocking systems work to keep oppression in place, despite nonviolent resistance, as they did in East Germany in 1953. However, the interlocking nature of oppressive systems is also their vulnerability, as King began to realize in 1967 when he could no longer separate what he called the triple evils of racism, militarism, and materialism. Many within the movement felt that by coming out against the Vietnam War, King would be compromising the civil rights movement. But King saw that the reverse is true. Large systems are interconnected. He saw that a multi-focused strategy would ultimately get deeper into the roots of racism by exposing it as one fruit of an even larger poisoned tree. He saw at least two others, in militarism and materialism, and now, standing on his shoulders, we can see even more. Now we are addressing multiple, intersecting oppressions, and opening our horizons and hearts to our oppression of the earth itself.

Belief in the domination system model of power is itself one of the pillars of support that props up oppressive systems. However, when the people begin to see through the lie; when they begin to understand and to exercise partnership power, things begin to change. Even if oppressors get nervous and escalate repressive measures, even if initial efforts are suppressed, seeds are planted in hearts and minds, and fissures begin to appear in what might have previously looked like monolithic structures. The dramatic nonviolent revolutions in Eastern Europe are a perfect case study. There were profound periods of awakening, and then a series of well-planned strategic nonviolent actions, then the inevitable escalation of repression in the face of nonviolent pressure, and then the ultimate success of nonviolence. The following timeline offers a picture of each of these dynamics as major pillars of support were either weakened or removed. It also shows the incredible momentum

18. For a full account of the shifting forces in East Germany that eventually led to the collapse of the regime, see Bleiker, *Revolution in East Germany*.

19. This comment has been attributed to Horst Sindemann, a central committee member of the former GDR. See Newell, "Nikolai Church in Leipzig."

of nonviolent transformation that finally becomes irresistible when the pillars start to fall.

- 1976: Václav Havel, a popular Czech writer and dissident, along with many others, signs and circulates *Charter 77*, a document critical of the Communist regime, particularly on its human rights violations. Signatories include artists, politicians, lawyers, psychologists, historians, academics, and a variety of other professions.
- 1978: October: Havel's essay *The Power of the Powerless* is published.[20]
- 1978: October 16: The Polish cardinal Karol Wojtyla is elected pope and takes the name John Paul II. Two things happen in Poland on that day, according to a journalist who later wrote a retrospective: "The population broke open bottles to celebrate and the then-ruling Communist Party went into emergency session."[21]
- 1979: May: Václav Havel begins a four-year imprisonment for his role in circulating *Charter 77*. His prison letters to his wife are later published as *Letters to Olga*.
- 1979: June: The new pope gives an address during a visit to his homeland that draws nearly two million people.
- 1980: August: In the course of massive labor strikes in Poland, workers take over the Lenin Shipyard in Gdansk. Lech Walesa, an electrician who had been fired by the regime in 1976 for his activities as a labor organizer, returns to the shipyard and is elected head of the strike committee. Negotiations lead to legalizing trade unions and greater freedoms of expression. Walesa goes on to help form Solidarity, a broadly inclusive confederation of unions that is nonviolent and anti-communist.
- 1981: The Communist regime in Poland institutes martial law. Walesa is arrested and imprisoned. The following year Solidarity is outlawed.
- 1982: In September in the GDR, Christian Führer, pastor of the *Nikolaikirche* (Church of St. Nicolas) in Leipzig, begins holding regular Monday gatherings for peace prayers. In the ensuing years the gatherings grow. New actions are added including pilgrimages, protests, and speeches, all calling for an end to the Cold War.
- 1985: Mikhail Gorbachev comes to power in the Soviet Union. The Soviet system is in serious economic stagnation. Gorbachev embraces

20. Havel, *Open Letters*, 125–214.
21. Dempsey, "Counterbalance to Communists," 4.

glasnost and *perestroika* in an attempt to reform the Soviet bureaucracy and revive the economy.

- 1988: Gorbachev abandons the Brezhnev doctrine, announcing that Soviet troops will no longer be used to crack down in the Soviet satellite nations. He may not have fully realized the extent to which this weakened the East European military establishments.

And then came the cascading of events in 1989:

- May: The numbers of protesters participating in the Leipzig peace prayer demonstrations increase dramatically. Police repression also increases.
- September: All two thousand seats in the *Nikolaikirche* sanctuary are filled and three hundred thousand more protesters are in the streets outside, carrying candles, calling for peace, practicing nonviolence.
- September 11: Hungary abandons a twenty-year agreement with the SED (*Sozialistische Einheitspartei Deutschlands*, or German Socialist Union Party) and opens the Austro-Hungarian border. This creates a "back door" for East Germans whereby they can transit Hungary to the west. By September 14, nearly fifteen thousand East Germans have left the country. This so-called "hole" in the Iron Curtain renders the Berlin Wall irrelevant.
- October: Police repression escalates, and infiltrators from the party, and the *Stasi* (the state security police) occupy seats in the *Nikolaikirche* where they hear calls for nonviolence. The infiltration appears to work in reverse. They are drawn into conversations and finally withdraw with no further arrests.
- October 18: Erich Honecker, the leader of the Communist Party in the GDR, resigns. Nonviolent protests continue all over East Germany.
- November 4: Nearly half a million people protest in East Berlin.
- November 7: The entire government of the GDR resigns.
- November 9: The people gleefully take sledgehammers to the Berlin Wall while East German soldiers look on.
- November 17: Student demonstrations in Prague are suppressed by police.
- November 20: Prague demonstrations grow from two hundred thousand to half a million.

- November 24: The General Secretary and top leaders of the Communist Party in Czechoslovakia resign.
- December: Václav Havel becomes president of Czechoslovakia.

And then, finally, in 1990, Germany is reunited on October 3, and in December of that year Lech Walesa becomes president of Poland.

It would be impossible to point to any one event in this list to account for the dramatic transformations of 1989 and 1990. There are "top-down" structural factors, such as the shifting economic fortunes of the Soviet Union, Gorbachev's decision to abandon the Brezhnev doctrine, and Hungary's decision to open the border with Austria. There are also many grassroots "bottom-up" factors, notably growing public demonstrations and acts of noncooperation. Significantly, there are also critical "inside-out" factors such as the publication of Havel's essay *The Power of the Powerless* that gave many dissidents not only an awakened understanding of the possibilities of nonviolent resistance, but also a new awareness of how deeply the totalitarian politics of fear had seeped into their inner lives. Despite suppression, Havel's essay was widely circulated underground, including crossing the border into Poland and finding its way into the hands of labor union activists. Zbygniew Bujak, an electrician at a tractor factory who became a Solidarity organizer, later commented that reading Havel's essay "gave us the theoretical underpinnings for our activity. It maintained our spirits; we did not give up, and a year later—in August 1980—it became clear that the party apparatus and the factory management were afraid of us." [22] Liberation of the inner world—exposing lies, exorcising fear and learned helplessness—these are as critical in freedom movements as shifting the pillars of support in the outward political world.

The guardians of repression know this perhaps as much as anyone, which is why they predictably practice the politics of fear and intimidation. Certainly, this is a major aim of escalating repression. Yet, powerful "inside-out" factors such as Havel's writing and the pope's visit to Poland in 1979 can knock the props out from under even the most repressive regimes. Once the light of truth begins to dispel the fog of disinformation and propaganda, and once the inviolable dignity of the soul begins to break through fear, and once the people begin to awaken to the real power of nonviolence, the structures of oppression are fatally weakened. After nearly two million people hung on the words of John Paul II, some invisible inward balance shifted from fear and intimidation back toward empowerment and hope. They went home and began to talk about change. Lech Walesa later credited John

22. Bujak in Paul Wilson's introduction to *Power of the Powerless,* in Havel, *Open Letters,* 126.

Paul II with providing much needed inspiration and courage. The political impact of the new pope was not a function of weakening outward structures of oppression but rather inward ones. It had solely to do with inspiration and restoring a personal sense of dignity and power. By 1989, that growing sense of dignity and power had become an irresistible wave. Repression no longer kept people out of the streets, but actually had the reverse of its intended effect. A hundred arrests brought a thousand more protesters; a thousand arrests brought ten thousand more people to the streets, and when two hundred thousand protestors were met with repression in Czechoslovakia, the streets were bursting with almost a half million just three days later.

A very poignant example of this "inside-out" shift is in a story that came out of the Magdeburg peace prayers. Regular peace prayer protests had been growing throughout the GDR for a number of years culminating in the events of 1989. In Magdeburg, a participant later wrote about one of the peace-prayer events of that year: "Members of the youth group, to which my daughter also belonged, gave reports about the events of 7 October. At that time the prayer of one of the young people moved me to tears. He knew that his father, outside with the troops that had surrounded the Cathedral square, stood in readiness for their mission, while he prayed inside the Cathedral. He said, 'I ask God, that never again must a father and son stand so against each other!'"[23] His father, it was later learned, had, at considerable risk, refused to bring his baton, but filled his pockets with bandages instead. In the hearts and minds of this father and son, as well as in thousands of others around the country, the revolution was already an accomplished fact. There remained only the bringing of an inward truth into outward visibility.

Now, as we face new challenges in the twenty-first century, interdependent economic, technological, and political systems have grown into a vast web that makes globalization inescapable. Cornel West makes this obvious point, but also says, "Let us not be deceived: the great dramatic battle of the twenty-first century is the dismantling of empire and the deepening of democracy."[24] A truly democratic globalization will require a mass awakening to the dynamics of nonviolence. Václav Havel makes virtually the same point when he warns of a new kind of totalitarianism and contrasts its aims with what he calls "the aims of life." Life, he says, "in its essence, moves toward plurality, diversity, independent self-constitution, and self-organization, in short, toward the fulfillment of its own freedom."[25]

23. Marx, *Hier konnte jeder reden.*

24. West, *Democracy Matters*, 22.

25. Havel, *Open Letters*, 134.

The structures that oppress are both outward and inward. We inhabit systems within systems within systems. We are globally interconnected, mutually interdependent, and, as Martin Luther King Jr. taught nearly sixty years ago, we are irrevocably bound together in a common destiny. Nonviolence is local *and* global, personal *and* political, inward *and* outward. The power of nonviolence can undermine oppression wherever it is found, unseating our internal dictators as well as those that are outwardly political. There can be and must be an ongoing nonviolent revolution of the soul that parallels our outward freedom movements. Deep democracy begins in a vision of our interdependence, where we understand that our neighbor's well-being is as vital as our own. Nonviolence yields a new kind of peace, an inward/outward partnership peace.

CHAPTER 6

Nonviolent Peace

See, I am doing a new thing! Now it springs up; do you not perceive it?
I am making a way in the wilderness and streams in the wasteland.[1]

HAVING JUST SEEN HOW many "top-down," "bottom-up," and "inside-out" factors influence political transformations, it should be no surprise that even successful nonviolent campaigns are fragile. We have more than a few modern examples of very hopeful nonviolent revolutions giving way once again to violence and tyranny. A sustainable peace that is thoroughly nonviolent and democratic must be vigilant in building nonviolent processes into all levels of influence. As critical as it is to build fully democratic social and political structures, unless there are corresponding efforts in theology, psychology, and spiritual practice, the hidden domination system mythologies that govern our internal structures will resurface in new form.

For many who are committed to working for a just peace, this is an idea that is sometimes not very seriously considered. We may give a nod of assent to the necessity for inner work, and try to make time for it, but for many, the crises of the world are so urgent and compelling that the personal and spiritual are set aside, dismissed as optional, a luxury, or privilege, or even as navel gazing. The bias is in the direction of political action. Reshaping our political institutions into fully democratic structures that reflect partnership values is certainly crucial. Nonviolent political structures provide the "top-down" environments that are essential to a sustainable nonviolent peace. Likewise, engaged citizens who are well trained in the ways of

1. Isa 43:19.

nonviolence and who are committed to ongoing, "bottom-up" advocacy are essential to keeping our institutions healthy. But it is a three-legged stool. "Top-down," "bottom-up," and "inside-out" forces must all be addressed at once; otherwise, the weak leg will cause the whole structure to collapse.

Nothing serves the forces of oppression better than when we collude in their concealment by pretending that we are not infected by them, psychologically and spiritually, as well as politically. Trying to engage the world on behalf of justice without committing to serious and ongoing inner work is like trying to clean up a toxic spill without a hazmat suit. Walter Wink is fierce in his warnings about this attitude:

> The impatience of some activists with prayer, meditation, and inner healing may itself represent an inchoate knowledge of what they might find if they looked within. *For the struggle against evil can make us evil,* and no amount of good intentions automatically prevents its happening. The whole armor of God that Eph. 6:10–20 counsels us to put on is crafted specifically to protect us against that contagion of evil within our own souls, and its metals are all annealed in prayer.[2]

Because I have spent so much of my life studying the dynamics of change in both the outward political world and the inward psychological world, it has been inescapable to me, sometimes even astonishing, to see how similar these dynamics are. It has become obvious to me that there is an oppressive overlay of the domination system, not only in our political arrangements, but also in our minds and hearts. When we consider how to realize the full promise of nonviolent peace, we must pay special attention to this often neglected third leg of the stool. The deeply unconscious narratives that structure our perceptions, thoughts, emotional energies, and behaviors, if left unaddressed, will simply sow the seeds of domination system relational dynamics into the next iteration of our collective family system. What good is it to remodel the house if there are structural flaws in the foundation?

The critical question we must ask is "Who are the gods who govern our complexes, and how are they at odds with the ones we profess?" Our world is saturated with false gods and the many false selves that orbit them, and each of these lives preach and proclaim their gods, if not in so many words, then certainly in the life-narrative that is played out for others to see. Our lives preach to the world. Intentionally or not, we are evangelists for the gods of our complexes. They are addictive and have a possessive effect on our perspectives and behaviors. As every alcoholic family knows, the

2. Wink, *Engaging the Powers*, 206–7.

damage caused by addiction is systemic, not just individual. Everyone in the system is forced to orbit the god at the center of its universe. Some enable it; some become preoccupied with fighting it; some pretend to ignore it; some just do their best to escape. Every position in the alcoholic family is reactive to the idol until it is finally dethroned in recovery.

On the collective level this same dynamic plays out when entire communities or even nations are in orbit around false gods. Psychologically, it is not unreasonable to use theological language in describing them, for the gods of our complexes present a very powerful organizing center for the personality. Paul Tillich, a major twentieth-century theologian who was also a very astute observer of the psyche, offers this insight: "The objects of modern secular idolatry, such as nation and success, have shown healing power, not only by the magic fascination of a leader, a slogan or a promise but also by the fulfillment of otherwise unfulfilled strivings for a meaningful life. But the basis of the integration is too narrow. Idolatrous faith breaks down sooner or later and the disease is worse than before."[3] Tillich came to live and work in the US in 1933 after coming into conflict with the rising Nazi regime. He was starkly aware of the idolatry of nationalism and the religious idolatry of the German churches that had possessed his country. His words speak just as plainly and prophetically to the modern world. Profound evil arises in the shadow of idolatry. I fear we are once again dangerously close to that precipice.

Fortunately, our efforts to turn toward the unconscious, to let our eyes become accustomed to the dark, and to uncover the shadow complexes that operate from concealment, those efforts are met by an answering presence within. Call it God, if you will, or Soul, but by now it should be clear that I use such words as invitations. Find the language that is inviting for you and then trust the process. My language is theistic, but feel free to translate as needed. The promise I offer is that inner work has an Ally, and requires only willingness and the courage to venture into trust. This inner Ally, Friend, Truth, or Light is irrepressible. As the seventeenth-century Quaker Isaac Penington wrote, "Now that which is of God cannot bow to anything which is corrupt in man. It can lie down and suffer, and bear the plowing of long and deep furrows upon its back; but it cannot act that which is against its life."[4] Sometimes I catch myself toying with despair, wondering if all of this kind of talk is more illusion than reality. But I have always found that with patience and persistence, something breaks through.

3. Tillich, *Dynamics of Faith,* 109.

4. Penington, *Inward Journey*, 35.

We know there are many unforgiving and ungenerous people—nothing remarkable there. They are simply mirroring the harsh, domination system world into which we were all born. But sometimes breakthrough moments, such as those that occurred in Eastern Europe in 1989, also occur in individuals and couples who finally break free of internal complexes. The inner Ally is at work in the dark, beyond our immediate view, like an underground spring that finally surfaces. Nonviolence was building for many decades in Eastern Europe before breaking through into visibility in the eighties. Individuals in therapy sometimes feel like they are just slogging along without much progress and then the last tumbler finally falls into place and the lock opens. It's not easy to walk into the wilderness of inner work, trusting nothing more than a promise. It is small wonder that we would rather be enslaved to our complexes than hazard a journey through a desert. But let's see what happens if we do.

When we take the principles of nonviolence into the inner world, a model appears that holds much of what psychologists have already learned about the psyche while also opening a view that shows the internalization of domination system structures. Following Jung, the model shows that the mature psyche must ultimately find a way to bring ego into meaningful relationship with Soul, but the model also adds the intriguing suggestion that nonviolence might point toward some critical practices that serve to break the possessive hold that the domination system has on our habits of perception.

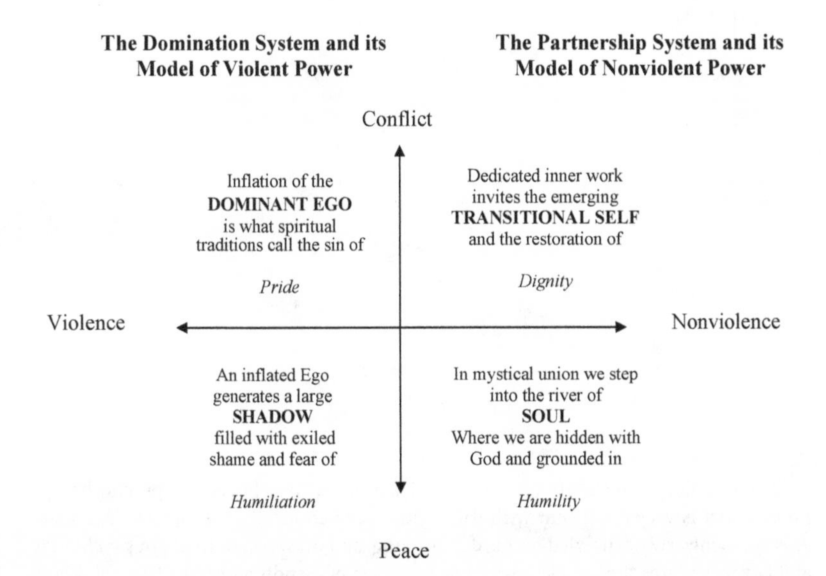

Note that all the dynamics of violence and nonviolence are also at work in the inner world. What is oppression in the outer world becomes repression in the inner world, and sometimes depression as well. The overvalued ego generates its exiles as surely as a dictatorship generates refugees. The cycle of violence with its dance of repression and revolution is also evident in our internal conflicts and battles.[5] Regardless of where we are in the intersectional scheme of political privileges, one who becomes increasingly practiced in inner work will not long tolerate a divided community, either in the inner or outer world. Therapy that listens to the soul should come with a warning label: "Listening to the soul will generate spiritual restlessness and profound dissatisfaction with oppressive systems in both the inward and outward life; it will open your eyes and let you see through the self-serving ideological rhetoric of politicians, profit makers, and many of those who claim to speak for God."

Psychotherapy and religion can offer extraordinary pathways to liberation, but they are also potentially dangerous because, while their original intent is to serve the soul, all too often they merely domesticate it. Many psychotherapies and religious practices are steeped in habits of thought that are shaped by the very forces that must be overturned. When psychotherapy and religion can once again listen to and *care* for the soul rather than try to *save* it, or force it into adjustment to an oppressive world, they will have been restored to their true mission. Let's look at how theology is similarly infected.

5. For a deeply insightful, even radical approach to a liberating psychotherapy process that is very consistent with this model, see Schwartz, *Internal Family Systems Therapy*. Schwartz acknowledges his debt to Jung, and draws on both depth psychology and family systems theory. He does a masterful job of blending insights from both and offering a method for "self-therapy."

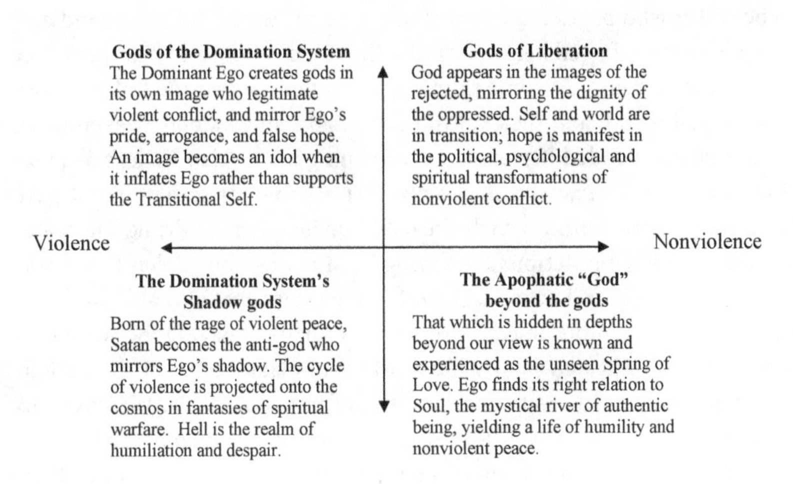

Theological ideas have psychological consequences. Conversely, where we are in our psychological development will have a big impact on what sort of theological ideas we will find most compelling. If we overlay the two four-quadrant models, the one psychological, the other theological, it becomes clear how each mirrors the other. The psychology of religion, however, goes beyond simple mirroring. Some theological images can impede psychological development, and burden it with oppressive ideas. And some psychological processes can generate a crisis of belief, especially if one has been spiritually formed in institutions that teach a domination system theology.

From the perspective of Soul, the issue is not belief vs. disbelief, for either one can be a station on the journey toward greater health. Either one can also function as further entrenchment in a defensive stance against growth. Some images and ideas serve the soul and others oppress it. From the perspective of Soul, the most important feature of theological images, ideas, and religious practices is their illuminating and awakening power. The goal of nonviolent theology is to make a deeper communion possible. We need clear, open, honest, nonviolent theological ideas, conversations, and religious practices to show us where to find the Hidden Spring, and then once we've learned to drink from its clear waters, we can have a more fluid relationship with the words that got us there. Religious language functions uniquely in this way. More poetry than science, the best teachings are narratives, parables, and metaphors, and the best God-talk is the kind that awakens.

I find a wonderful story about the language of awakening in the life of Helen Keller. With no sight, no sound, and no language, she submitted to her tutor who pressed the letters of the word "water" into her hand and then alternately shaped her mouth into the vocalization, and held her other hand under a pump. At some moment this utterance became linked to her experiential world, and the explosion of insight and sudden awakening of consciousness flooded her with overwhelming joy.[6] Helen Keller's acquisition of the word *water* didn't just give her a name for something; it gave her a social world within which she could invite others to drink. The water itself was no less mysterious for having been named, but Helen Keller was transformed forever. Likewise, the infinite mystery that we call "God" will never become a simple objective referent by virtue of having the word *God* appended to it. But we who use the word as an invitation rather than a definition are seeking to create communities of transformation. We utter this word because we are thirsty, not because we really understand anything.

Unfortunately, too many of us try to drink the word instead of the water. Nikos Kazantzakis chastises himself for this and, calling himself a "nanny goat," says, "you feel hungry, but instead of drinking wine and eating meat and bread, you take a sheet of white paper and inscribe the words *wine, meat, bread* on it, and then eat the paper."[7] We can't feed on theology, but neither can we ignore the reality that it is human nature to think about ultimate things. Inevitably, we seek language, thought, and words for mysteries that we know are beyond words. We long to know and be known through the medium of language. Theology is more art than science. It thrives on metaphor, expressions that remain open-ended and full of tension, affirmations that are shadowed by negations. Religion serves best when it opens the horizons of Soul and we awaken to joy.

6. For an amplification of this story and its link to the awakening power of language, see Van Buren, *Edges of Language*, 50–52.

7. Kazantzakis, *Report to Greco*, 190.

Prayer Is Political

> To become aware of the metaphors that govern basic perspectives is, among other things, a political act, for the possibility of change both at the personal and public levels depends upon consciousness of hidden metaphors.[8]
>
> —Sallie McFague

If there were a single spiritual practice or set of beliefs that worked for everyone, we all would have been awakened out of the nightmare of the domination system a long time ago. Something deeper than simple agreement is needed. I write personally, sharing my own journey and personal convictions, not because I want to prescribe creedal beliefs and practices for others, but because I want fellow travelers on this journey toward depth. I'm a Jesus-loving Christian, and that path has sustained me, and brought me out of some very dark places. But many Christians are under the spell of a Christianity that has been overtaken by domination system gods, so I often find myself walking alongside delightful fellow travelers from other traditions, or no tradition, who live outside the margins of the Christian world. With them I find what the Quaker Thomas Kelly found, those who "welcome us authoritatively into the Fellowship of Love."[9] True community is not tribal, based in sameness, or theological agreement, but in something deeper. On the surface of these relationships, we might find a challenging, or even fiercely engaged disagreement. Kelly says that he has sometimes found in these communions with others people "with chilly theologies but with glowing hearts."[10] For those who drink from the well, disagreements of mind, culture, and experience always dissolve into the deeper agreements of Love.

Tribal agreement is more likely to support my illusions than to help me along the way. Diversity of belief, practice, and experience is a problem only when tribal loyalty is our ultimate commitment. There are many paths, practices, and beliefs, and any of them can be drawn into ego's program for self-salvation. When prayer or other kinds of spiritual practice merely rehearse a fixed ideology, they fail to interrogate the hidden metaphors that govern basic perspectives. The ideology becomes the god, and its practices

8. McFague, *Metaphorical Theology*, 55.

9. Kelly, *Testament of Devotion*, 79.

10. Kelly, *Testament of Devotion*, 81.

are more likely to support the dominant ego than they are to invite the shadowing of ego as it moves toward the transitional self. Such prayer is obviously political in its covert support of domination system theologies and identities.

For those willing to question their tribal loyalties, however, diversity is of great benefit because it brings the tensions that drive ego toward the transitional self. Our shadows are exposed in our polarizations, and a commitment to diversity forces ego to yield to deeper ground. A truly healing spirituality, regardless of form, is one in which we engage practices that invite the nonviolent overthrow of internal dictators and the structures that keep them in place. The best spiritual practices are those that awaken consciousness to its illusions, bring hidden metaphors to light, and expose the gods embedded within our ideologies. Such work is also obviously political in its search for the inward/outward transformations of both self and world. They open the eye of the heart so that we can see and dethrone our idols.

But a caution is in order. Some practices are appropriate for the first half of life precisely because they support the ego, and others work better for the second half of life because they can help the well-established ego begin its descent into the transitional self. Spiritual direction must take into account each client's personality organization before recommending practices or beliefs. It is far better to listen for the metaphors that shape the narrative and to notice which ones serve and which ones impede an unfolding developmental process toward psychological and spiritual maturity. Better to engage process more than content. I live and work near Asheville, North Carolina, a town that has an extraordinary diversity of religious belief and practice, from New Age to conservative Christian. I have clients all across that spectrum, many of whom endorse beliefs and practices that would never work for me, but clearly serve and support the unique journey of that person. Conventional wisdom has it that spiritual direction and psychotherapy should not overlap, and that is certainly appropriate when practitioners of one discipline are not trained in the other. But the separation is artificial. Practitioners are inevitably involved in both worlds, trained or not. It would be better, consequently, to either thoroughly train in both disciplines or to work closely with other practitioners across disciplines so as to have good consultation or to make wise referrals.

Prayer, like theology, has political as well as psychological consequences. We can no more separate ourselves out of the inevitably political human community and the wider ecological community in which we are embedded than we can pretend that we are not formed psychologically or influenced by theological ideas. Once we become aware that we are held within and by metaphors and narratives that govern basic perspectives, and that the horizons of our perception can be opened up by working to make them conscious, a new kind of prayer becomes possible. We begin to see that each inward stance of the self has its gods, as well as its rituals and practices designed to keep that stance secure. But, if we have the good fortune to have been cracked open either by beauty or suffering, and sometimes both, then we have gained the priceless blessing of getting a glimpse into our personal and human condition. There is no prison more confining than the one we don't know we're in. Coming to an awareness of how trapped we are is painful, but it is the essential and necessary condition for our liberation. Prayers of the heart are never just rehearsals of an ideology; they are pleas for transformation.

The Bottom of the Disorder (II)

Go into yourself and explore the depths from which your life flows.[11]

—Rainer Maria Rilke

The domination system has become sedimented into the psyche as surely as it has been in our political structures. It is like the compacted soil that lies anywhere from a few inches to several feet under the surface that farmers call "hardpan." It is resistant to the penetration of roots, forcing plants to settle for a shallow root system and depriving them of the nutrients that live deeper in the soil. A dear friend, a retired farmer who puts up with my calling him "a farmer-mystic," once wrote a short essay about the inner life, which he titled, "Set Your Plow Deep."[12] The easier path is to raise the plow and skip over the hard places, but the wise farmer shifts down and lets the plow do its job. Likewise, in the inner life, our roots want to go much deeper into life-giving depths, but after years of getting by with a shallow root system, we may not even realize that greater depth is possible. We take the domination system as the true ground, the harvest is diminished, and we never imagine that a greater and more abundant life is possible.

Like abused children, we inhabit a limited and traumatic field of perception, forced to see through its lens.[13] Healing trauma does not come by

11. Rilke, *Letters*, 16.

12. Marvin Shrock, "Set Your Plow Deep." Unpublished essay.

13. The use of "we" is always problematic, especially when the writer is like me, "Pharaoh's child" (white, male, etc.). Those who do not share my privilege inhabit a different "we," and many who see the world through the eyes of oppression, already know a great deal about survival through partnership systems. However, I believe the

way of forgetting, but by growing the house of consciousness. Living under the burden of unhealed trauma feels like living in a small room with no windows, whereas healing feels like traumatic memory is finally held with compassion in a much larger room filled with light. Transformational practices support healing by breaking through hardened structures that limit perception, and by opening awareness onto a relational world that overcomes isolation. Unfortunately, for many, a partnership world that is alive and fertile, a relational world of compassion, is far outside the horizons of consciousness.

Fortunately, there are underground movements that have always gone into the depths from which life flows. Celtic Christianity, with its earth-based spirituality, thrived on the margins of the Roman Church. Even those who didn't fully escape the conscription of Christianity into the Roman Empire spawned many groups and practices that sought to grow up through the cracks in empire's oppressive overlay. The desert mothers and fathers, underground movements such as the Beguines, countless mystics over the centuries, Quakerism which rose in seventeenth-century England, and many other individuals and movements have broken through the trance of the domination system. A sustainable nonviolent peace finally becomes possible when more and more of us are willing to engage practices that break open the psyche's depths into greater life.

Given that we are formed within systems that are embedded in our everyday language and in the cultural habits of perception that have been centuries in the making, we need what I think of as meta-practices, that is, practices that support a critical awareness of how our participation in religious traditions and their disciplines, or in many cases, a choice not to participate in any traditions or disciplines, either further embeds daily perception in unconscious metaphors or raises them to conscious awareness where they can be noticed, discerned, then either more fully embraced or discarded. Meta-practices can be brought to any religious tradition, or to secular worldviews, to any type of prayer or meditation, and to everyday habits of thought. There are probably many such practices, but I would like to recommend four:

1. *Develop a sensitivity to language and metaphor:* Break the habit of literalism and learn to hear the metaphors and narratives of everyday speech and in everyday experiences. They reveal the underlying patterns of experience. What can be said in any language system, and more importantly what *cannot* be said, reveals a lot about the dominant

"we" in this chapter is mostly warranted, at least for North Americans steeped in the competitive individualism that has become extreme in "our" culture.

assumptions of that world. Language shines a light on certain aspects of experience and obscures others. What can be named is what can be known and elaborated in the imagination. That which has no name remains obscure.

As an example, I offer a dilemma that appears in the peace literature where there has always been a lot of discussion about the word *nonviolence.* For many, the word is inadequate because it names something by what it is not. Various alternatives have been proposed, such as "Soul-Force" and "Truth-Force," but they are the equivalent of "heaven," a word with so little reference in the imagination that the word evokes little more than harps and golden streets. Hell is much more highly elaborated in the mythic imagination; it is a Technicolor world, full of fire, risk and taboo, whereas heaven is all pastels and clouds. Hell is the world we know, violent and traumatic. It is the world we make movies about and continually reenact in a collective repetition compulsion. Like traumatized children we don't know any other world and consequently suffer a poverty of imagination when it comes to words like *heaven.* Until lived experience funds the linguistic imagination, it's probably better just to call it "non-hell." Likewise, I prefer to stick with the inadequate, but commonly used term *nonviolence.* The dilemma itself is a commentary on language and culture.

Sensitivity to language, metaphor, image, and narrative is greatly helped by finding poets who awaken you and who are able to name things you know but have never had words for. Let them hold your familiar experiences in unfamiliar images and let new words, images, and narratives reshape how you hold memory and anticipation. See if you can find your own poetic voice and see how creative language and metaphors offer new wineskins that can hold new experiences. Let the invitation of new images and narratives become the new house of consciousness. Find the metaphors and narratives that help you allow your traumatized mind, body, and spirit to be held in compassion.

2. *Commit to regular dreamwork:* Dreams are the narratives offered up by the unconscious every night. The dream speaks in its own language and over time we can learn to hear what it wants to say. Every dream comes in service to our awakening, and invites us to new ways of being in relation to the unseen forces that shape the unfolding world. The imposition of a theory, or a rush to interpretation too often silences the voice of the dream. Cultivate a "beginner's mind" in relation to the dream and learn to hear it in its own native tongue. I find it helpful to notice dreams as they appear in a series over time, as if there is

an ongoing narrative that is picked up again each night. I choose to believe that all dreams are valuable and that the agency that produces them, the Dreamer, is in service to our growth and well-being. I see the Dreamer as an essential conversation partner in my clinical work and in my own ongoing growth. Often, if my client and I miss the mark in hearing a dream, a subsequent dream sets us straight. Likewise, if we are on the mark, subsequent dreams then take us further on the journey. Every now and then there comes what Jung called a "big dream" that is life transforming.

Dreams also sometimes speak of collective forces that are far beyond the concerns of the individual psyche. They bring inspired, important, and sometimes amazing perspectives that open onto the collective unconscious in ways that can be transforming of whole communities. Such dreams are reported throughout the Bible and other sacred literature around the world. Dreams have guided modern scientists to new discoveries, and indigenous peoples to medicinal plants, soldiers to safety, and communities in search of healing and reconciliation. Dreams of lost loved ones have come to many people in such vivid ways that it is an easy leap to see them as visitations. Ancestors and guides have appeared in dreams at critical moments. One inspiring example comes out of a research project at Monticello. The researcher dreamt that "a Black woman with a terrible condition of low-blood sugar came to tell her she had a responsibility."[14] In the context of her work, the researcher heard the dream collectively and discerned that the dream figure's healing would come as they began a search for a lost burial ground for slaves. "Another participant in the research dreamed a Black man called to her: 'We will not rest until you find out.'"[15] The burial ground was eventually found to be under a parking lot and there are now annual remembrances that honor the dead. May they rest in peace.

3 *Live relationally and imaginally:* We all talk to our computers and cars anyway, so instead of being embarrassed about it, why not bring a relational sensitivity into all of our encounters with all of the natural world, which includes not only our fellow humans, but also those fellow creatures that we presume to be inanimate. Practice what Sallie McFague, in another of her many extraordinary books, calls a "Subject-Subjects" model and "The Loving Eye," as opposed to a "Subject-Object" model

14. Lorenz and Watkins, "Silenced Knowings," 4.

15. Lorenz and Watkins, "Silenced Knowings," 4.

and "The Arrogant Eye."[16] Indigenous people have for centuries engaged the natural world as animate, seeing all creatures as endowed with Soul, and taking lessons not only from the animal world but also from insects, trees, rocks, and everything under the sun, in a deep sensitivity to the Living Spirit in all of creation. A relational way of seeing supports a partnership way of being. It resists habits of objectification which are a product of the domination system. The objectification of the world supports our exploitation of it.

Living relationally invites compassion. Make it a daily practice. Let compassion open in your innermost being and then let it encompass memory and anticipation. Learn to hold your busy mind in quiet compassion. Let your heart expand to family and neighbors and out into the wider community. Let compassion stretch beyond your comfort zone until it holds the other, the enemy, or the politician you love to hate. This is where many of us get stuck, so it is important to remember that compassion does not undermine your discernment; it actually sharpens it and grounds responsive action in wisdom. Keep widening the circle of compassion until it extends to all of creation.

Opening to a relational way of seeing and being shifts identity out of its isolation in the individualized self. Loneliness is a tragic feature of the Western, isolated self. But a self-in-relation that is embedded in a world of subjects is beautifully companioned by a teapot as well as a blue jay. When loneliness becomes a peaceful solitude, we find ourselves in a new kind of relation with our fellow humans. Less burdened with fears and dependencies, we are more grounded in an ability to love and accept the other as they are, with no need to change them into someone more to our liking. There is an amazing joy in seeing the beauty of the Divine in all creatures, all beings, and in all things.

4. *Listen to the Body:* Western habits of splitting mind, body, and soul have taught us to do most of our living from somewhere above the neck and shoulders. We treat our bodies like we treat nature, as objects to be manipulated, ignored, or abused. Consequently, our bodies are forced to carry the disowned stories, feelings, and scars of our personal and collective wounds. Like dreams, our bodies can be messengers from a world outside our conscious awareness. If we learn to listen to the body's wisdom, we can open onto wonderful new horizons for awakening and healing. As I will describe in a later chapter, I am convinced

16. McFague, *Super, Natural Christians*, 32–39, 67–117. It's all in the comma between "Super" and "Natural," a comma that overturns centuries of egos elevated *above* nature, and restores us to our mutuality with and embeddedness in nature.

that the bodies of white people carry hidden wounds that come with being inscripted into racism. A core but often-neglected feature of our efforts to heal racism is discovered when we reconnect to our bodies. Those who inhabit Black bodies and female bodies know this all too well. But those of us who inhabit Western, white, male bodies, not all of us, but many, have deeply internalized the domination system's rejection of the body. For many white men, the disowned body carries our unhealed grief and shame.

Overcoming the objectification of the body restores our severed connection with the earth, from which we are formed and to which we will return. Learning to listen to and respect the body as subject is key to healing many intractable problems such as our disordered relation with food, other substances, and each other. Our Western habits of objectification of the body leave us with no place to find Soul or the Divine except in transcendent, otherworldly realms. Listening to the body as subject freshens the religious imagination and restores us to a sense of the immediacy of the Divine in this present moment, in this breath, and this heartbeat.

These meta-practices, developing a critical awareness of language and metaphor, committing to dreamwork, learning a relational way of seeing, and learning to access a whole-body way of knowing are all crucial pillars of support for a new consciousness and a new kind of participation in our collective structures. Conversely, literalism, ignoring the dreamtime, objectification of nature, and disowning the body, are all pillars of support for the domination system. Our loss of these practices has led to the impoverishment of language and dulling the imagination, whereas rediscovering them awakens the mind and heart to the possibilities of nonviolent peace.

The domination system and its gods are raging now. They always do when new life begins to break through. We are at a critical juncture in our evolution where we must make a decisive choice for nonviolence. The gods of domination will always yield a seething, unstable, resentment-filled, violent "peace," a smoldering cauldron slow cooking the next terrorist attack, or act of nihilistic despair in a mass shooting, or a full-scale violent revolution. But the real meaning and true essence of revolution is not armed rebellion, but a continual turning over, a constant renewal. It is the fertile and vital process of any healthy democratic system. One might even understand the democratic process itself as an ongoing and self-renewing nonviolent revolution, one that is vigilant in confronting social institutions that have become oppressive while also working to sustain those that truly serve. This is neither a liberal nor a conservative view, but rather one that seeks to conserve the best and overturn the worst of our social structures. Thriving democracies are living systems that are sustained by outward structures, freshened by bottom-up nonviolent engagements, and populated by individuals and communities that practice the inside-out revolutions of awakened consciousness. In the Beloved Community, the one we once regarded as an enemy will be seated at our elbow. The last shall be first, and the prodigal comes home. Those who drink from the well are reconciled in the agreements of Love. This is finally the meaning of nonviolent peace: God's house is not divided.

PART III

Inward Activism

Transformational work is hard. For all of our good intentions and committed efforts, we are nevertheless limited by a common belief that only outward, visible activity makes a difference. This section deepens the conversation begun in the last chapter, and considers inner work as a psychological, political, and theological process.

Chapter 7 explores "Nonviolence for the Soul." Bringing along the perspectives of strategic nonviolence developed in the second section, we now turn toward the inner world and see how very similar dynamics are at play there. The journey to psychological healing and integrity is illumined in new ways when viewed through a nonviolent lens.

Chapter 8 works with nonviolence as it impacts the particular experience of those who are born to systemic privilege. How does political and economic privilege impact our inner development? The traumas of oppression are well researched, but the traumas associated with being schooled in the ways of privilege are not well understood. The journey to political healing and integrity must include healing for Pharaoh's child, as well as for those who suffer under the domination system's oppression.

Chapter 9 brings a nonviolent perspective to *theodicy*, the term theologians use to refer to our reflections on the problem of evil. Whether professionally trained or not, we are all foxhole theologians when brought to the existential edges of our lives. How are we to think of the Divine Presence when confronted with the brutality of oppression, and if we call this "evil," as we certainly should, then what do we mean by the term and how are we to understand its existence? Thinking about these questions is just something that humans do, and our theological ideas have psychological and political consequences.

CHAPTER 7

Nonviolence for the Soul

[Love] is a noble calling for the individual to ripen, to differentiate, to become a world in oneself in response to another.[1]

—Rainer Maria Rilke

Samantha is a client who had cycled through several previous therapies and was not helped by any of them.[2] I could see pretty quickly why the usual approaches of therapy didn't work for her; she had the look of someone whose ability to trust was on its last legs. I've never cared much for books by therapists who describe their work with clients in ways that make the therapist out to look brilliant and heroic. So, just to be clear, I take no credit for the way that the work with Samantha unfolded. She called me because she had not worked with a pastoral counselor before and spirituality was important to her, so she clearly hoped that I had something that her previous therapists did not. I told her that I had more or less the same training they had but since they had not helped her, and I had pretty much the same tool kit, I wasn't sure what we would do. No matter. She insisted that she wanted to work with me because she had heard that I am someone who prays. That touched me and stirred something within that I have come to recognize as "a leading," so I said I would agree to work with her on one condition—that she understand that I don't have any remedies that she hadn't already tried, but that I would listen deeply and respectfully, and I would certainly pray.

1. Rilke, *Letters*, 56.

2. Not her real name. Many other details are also changed to disguise her identity, though none that impacts the essence of the story and the power of her work.

Given that she had already had so many disappointments in therapy, it was clear to me that this last effort needed to be a very different kind of journey. I proposed that I would offer reflections only if she asked, and even then not as interpretations but only as possibilities. Her part in the collaboration would be to listen within herself for her own words, and when she did invite me to speak, to listen for how my words either brought her into deeper alignment with herself or pulled her off course. That suited her just fine; she even seemed grateful for it, so off we went into what I was convinced would be a joint venture in helplessness.

Samantha's story was horrendous and heartbreaking. She talked and I listened. Only rarely did she want to hear from me, so I kept my thoughts to myself. She would come for her weekly session and struggle to find words for what she wanted to say, and then when she had no more to say we would just sit together in the quiet of my office with no sound other than the occasional car going by outside. For me, the silence was usually fine, even familiar, a Quaker meeting for two. But for her the silence was often difficult. Sometimes she would get up and leave early. At other times the silence was difficult for me too because it brought my helplessness sharply into my awareness. This was hard to bear, especially when her story evoked my outrage on her behalf, or sorrow or deep compassion. But I remembered a story from one of Parker Palmer's books where he tells of his experiences with depression. He was dean at Pendle Hill at the time, and there were various people there who offered advice and wanted to help, all to no avail. But there was one man, a quiet Quaker elder in that community, who would come regularly to see him and, saying very little, would simply massage his feet.[3] That story sustained me in my work with Samantha. It gave me permission to not know anything, or to be "helpful" in any tangible way. I was responsible for only what I had promised—to listen and to pray. As Parker puts it, "By standing respectfully and faithfully at the borders of another's solitude, we may mediate the love of God to a person who needs something deeper than any human being can give."[4] In prayer, I released Samantha into the care of a love and wisdom far greater than my own, a love that could feed her soul from the inside.

Bit by bit, her story unfolded. With each new layer I was grateful that I had kept my mouth shut when we were in the previous layer. I would be convinced that I was beginning to understand something profound about her condition, when suddenly she would pull back the curtain and the whole narrative would be set within a much larger frame. She was on her own

3. Palmer, *Let Your Life Speak*, 63.

4. Palmer, *Let Your Life Speak*, 64.

archaeological dig, not trying to figure herself out so much as just following the trail wherever it led. Her dreams became richer and more elaborated, and also somewhat more inscrutable. Great! Dreamwork! Now being in territory I thought I understood, my tireless hope that I might actually turn out to be helpful was once again sending up flares. But here too I was helpless. She never indicated that she wanted conversation about her dreams; she just wanted to share them. We were deep in the wilderness and neither of us had any idea how we were going to find our way out. Gradually, I learned to be grateful for my helplessness and finally stopped wishing I had opened a hardware store instead of becoming a therapist.

Then one day, after about three and a half years of our work together, she pronounced herself healed. And, indeed she was. The heavy cloud of fear and depression had been gradually lifted and was finally simply gone. Nothing much had changed outwardly. She still had a miserable job and a heartbreaking of a marriage, but something deep and significant had shifted within. It was as if she had reached the bottom of her own disorder, and like the prodigal, she "came to herself"[5] as it were, and she was able to get up from that place and begin the journey home. Some needed changes in her outward life came relatively quickly and efficiently, and she would check in with me periodically, just for the moral support, but the day soon came when it was clear that we were done. She thanked me sincerely and credited me with far more than I deserved, and then left. I got a postcard about a year later saying that she had moved to San Francisco and was doing well.

Samantha could have quit her job and her marriage and moved to San Francisco without going through all the bother and expense of giving therapy another chance, but she still would have brought herself along for the journey. As Jon Kabat-Zinn says, "Wherever you go, there you are." Somehow, she intuited that it wasn't her outward life that was the source of the problem; it was that she was not at home within herself. The real work was following the trail into the wilderness within, maintaining fidelity to what was true, in the plumb-bob sense of "true," not in any interpretive sense of "true." Then once she found her way home to that, the rest just took care of itself.

The paradox of therapy for clients is that they can't do their work in isolation, but neither can they do their work if someone else is trying to do it for them. The paradox of therapy for therapists is that the theories and techniques that we've spent so much time and money learning how to master are all useless if we haven't also learned to lay them aside and just stand in awe of the mystery of the soul.

5. Luke 15:17.

The Soul in Therapy

The soul is like a wild animal.[6]

—Parker Palmer

Sitting with Samantha was like waiting for a unicorn. I could sense her fragility, her mistrust, and her hypervigilance. Sometimes a spontaneous fantasy would pop into my mind that a five-year-old version of my client was sitting on the couch next to her, watching us both and listening closely, wondering if she would be heard, and if she would be safe. Sometimes I could feel the terrible weight of Samantha's self-loathing bearing down on her. At other times I would simply sit in awe of the courage it took for her just to show up week after week, and I saw in that courage a soul struggling to break free. My silence became a very interesting discipline for me in that it required a severe relinquishment of my habit of looking for the healing moment or insight in some outward exchange between my client and me. With Samantha, my outward contribution consisted almost entirely of being attentively present, listening deeply, on rare occasions sharing a reflection at her request, and in keeping my promise to pray. What she did not see, and did not need to see, was the intense inner work that was sometimes required for me to sustain this discipline.

Not only in therapy but also in everyday life we are constantly, and unconsciously, filtering our perceptions of each other through our own experiences. With Samantha I had ample opportunity to find mirroring or reactive parts within myself. Her wounded child would evoke both my own wounded child as well as a rescuer. Her self-loathing would evoke my own inner critics and a fierce defender. Her courage would inspire me to embrace more deeply my own fears and my determination to keep growing. My task, however, was simply to notice these internal states as they passed in and out of my awareness, but not to engage Samantha from any of their perspectives, and to receive whatever state she was in at the moment with a prayerful acceptance. Holding my own inner states in compassionate awareness, resisting the pressure to act, and listening for the deeper stillness within, was the essential discipline required in order to host the soul's work, both within myself and in my client.

This requires a kind of double attention, an inward and outward awareness that supports the stance of the transitional self, an engaged but non-reactive witness. By holding this tension within myself, a tension between

6. Palmer, *Let Your Life Speak*, 7.

my own internal states with their pressure to act, and respect for the soul's unfolding mystery, allowed me to bring the better angels of the transitional self into the room, and implicitly to invite a similar stance in my client. The healing happens in "the between," in the relational space where both participants can enter into a dynamic of discovery. Ego loves certainty, knowing, agency, feeling useful, important, and helpful. Sometimes clients who are terrified of their own uncertainties expect therapists to rescue them. Some even demand it and quit therapy if they don't feel better quickly. Sometimes therapists who are terrified of their own uncertainties expect this of themselves. But the soul wants something else, and we must be willing to suspend all our certainties, all of our expert helping techniques in order to hear what the soul wants. Care for the soul requires a willingness to be a wilderness explorer, to stand in the tension between ego and Soul, between knowing and mystery.

There were two people in the room, when I worked with Samantha, both of us with egos and shadows, and both of us working hard at finding a way to be in a healing relationship with the whole self. Here is where the nonviolent model is helpful for psychotherapy. If I put two of my four quadrant diagrams side by side, mirroring each other, it would be clear that all sorts of pairings of part-selves are possible, most of them leading down blind alleys. The most harmful of those pairings would consist in two people unconsciously engaged from shadows. The healing constellation, however, requires a therapist who is disciplined in inward listening. The therapist's most important task is to maintain the inward discipline of staying grounded in Soul.

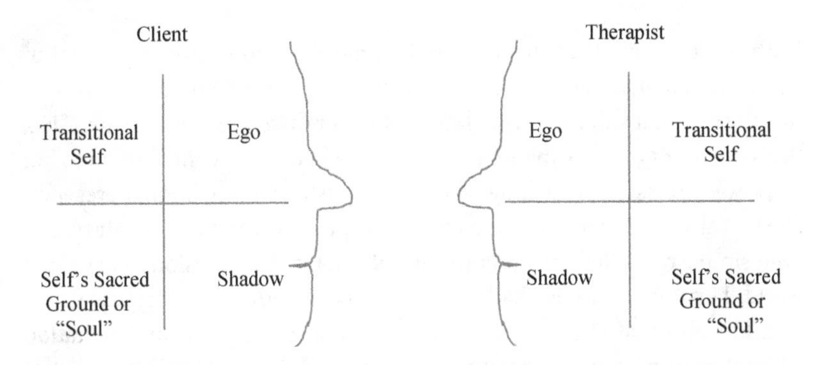

I'm convinced that if I had even once broken our agreement and had tried to dispense my pearls of wisdom, the whole therapy would have come to a quick end. My ego-need to feel useful would have taken over and the unicorn would have fled. James Finley says that the true self (or what I am here calling the "transitional self") is like an intensely alert gazelle: "One distant footfall of the false self sends him into unreachable obscurity. One breath of self seeking, one trace of the false self's acrid wiles and the true self becomes the nobody that is not there."[7] Fortunately, Samantha convinced me of my helplessness at the first visit and from then on my work was all on the inside. She didn't want my wisdom; she wanted my helplessness, that plus my willingness to be *male* and trustworthy at the same time, a rarity in her experience. What she needed most from me was someone who could keep a campfire lit while she went deep into the wilderness in search of her native habitat, or what Václav Havel calls "the terrain of authentic existence."[8] Her last thread of hope turned out to be someone who was willing to just shut up and pray. Deep in the wilderness Samantha found something within herself that I could never have given her, and once she had grounded herself in that she could take a stand against her internal dictators. Finally, the oppressive, internalized regime was overthrown, and she simply got up and walked out of her prison.

The Ideology Trap

I feel suddenly wary.
Everything within me is about to be named, boxed,
contained and controlled.[9]

—Annie Rogers

With most of my other clients there is somewhat more trust, less fragility, and consequently, the work can be much more conversational. I can trust that my part in it will meet with honest assent or dissent, an "Ah-ha" or a "No, that's not it." But with Samantha, it was clear that my best contribution to her work was precisely my willingness to relinquish a conversational presence. She had already experienced too much interpretation and commentary, and even simple reflection, however insightful, felt like an intrusion in her inner world. Fortunately, I have had some experience with the wilderness in my own life, and that allowed me to entertain uncertainty and disorientation without becoming overly anxious. I understood that getting lost is part of the deal. We do this work, not in order to find out what we already know, but

7. Finley, *Merton's Palace of Nowhere*, 92.
8. Havel, *Open Letters*, 148.
9. Rogers, *Shining Affliction*, 99.

precisely to lay down what we know so as to discover something new. Had I been unwilling to get lost, I would have gotten anxious every time I lost my ideological compass, which was pretty much every session. My anxiety would have driven me to try to get Samantha back into the familiar territory of my own favorite psychological theory. For all of our good intentions, we therapists too often fall back on our theories and techniques because they help *us* feel useful, not because they particularly serve our clients.

Annie Rogers, in therapy herself while training to be a therapist, was profoundly attuned to how her first therapist initially invited her into a welcoming space that gradually became ideologically bound. As that problem deepened, Annie found herself forced to choose between her therapist's ideas and interpretations over her own inchoate, embodied knowing. It was as if a truth lived inside of her that desperately needed a trustworthy relationship that could welcome it, and be a non-intrusive host for it. Only in such a relational space could her truth find its way into speech. As Annie went deep into the wilderness, her therapist became anxious and suddenly retreated behind the screen of her theories. Fleeing the uncertainties and risks of the wilderness, the therapist effectively left the room despite remaining physically present. Suddenly abandoned, left with no one willing to join her in trusting her own knowing, Annie could not find the safe, accepting, and non-judging presence that she needed in order to begin to hear her own voice.

Fortunately, she eventually found another therapist who was not afraid of the wilderness. Annie writes that with him, "I found words, or rather, words found me. Words that I hoped would unlock an incomprehensible story pressed against my ears and came out into the room."[10] Trust is what invites the soul out of hiding. Interpretations, techniques, and theories, however insightful, are of little use without it. As Annie herself later wrote, "What has been wounded in a relationship must be, after all, healed in a relationship."[11] The very site of the deepest wound is invariably the vulnerable and trusting heart. Reweaving its broken threads is finally the determining factor in healing.

Yielding to the processes of transformation means loosening one's grip on false-self structures so that we can enter a transitional space where something new can be born. At some point in our lives, most of us need someone who can be trusted to keep track of where we last left the self we know, while we go in search of the deeper self that we hear calling us into being. We therapists sometimes are just coat racks. It is as if our clients are saying

10. Rogers, *Shining Affliction*, 135.

11. Rogers, *Shining Affliction*, 256.

to us, "Here, hold this self for me while I go look for a bigger one. Don't lose track of it, I may need it to go home in." To be worthy of that much trust we must understand that we are not healers. We are explorers in the ways of Soul, willing to offer a relationship that we hope will create the optimal conditions for the psyche to heal itself. It is essential that we make our peace with this reality, for if we see ourselves as the source of healing, we will fall into the ideology trap, and not only will our clients begin to feel "named, boxed, contained and controlled," we too will be boxed in by our having assumed responsibility for a sacred mystery. Then all of ego's fears about competence and worth will be activated, and we will no longer be able to offer the genuine, compassionate, and humble presence that trust requires. However well trained, however schooled in the latest techniques, we must always remember that there is a unicorn in the room, an extraordinarily shy creature, who is exquisitely attuned to the relative safety being offered in the relational field.

The unicorn doesn't care about our theories. All kinds of insights, dreams, difficulties, and problems get explored in therapy, but what finally heals is beyond theory and technique, and beyond anyone's grasp or ability to control. The therapist's most important task is to learn the ways of the wilderness so as to sink down into the depths of the hidden spring of healing and to surrender to it. This is the core discipline that makes a living relationship with the unconscious possible. The essential skill is an ability to be sufficiently self-aware to be able to suspend one's own wishes, needs, and projections so as to allow the relationship itself to tell us what it wants and needs in order to feel safe enough to heal. The therapist who can let go of theory, ideology, and technique, so as to surrender to these depths becomes a "wounded healer," or more accurately, one whose own wrestling with wounds has drawn ego down into Soul sufficiently to open onto the archetype of the Healer that can then be activated in the two souls who have engaged this work together. The "cracked open" therapist becomes a living bridge to these depths, useful and necessary only until the client finds this hidden spring within herself. Then the temporary bridge can be laid down, even forgotten.

Every venture into therapy creates a relationship, unrepeatable because the two personalities involved are unique, and dynamic because in order for healing to happen, both personalities must grow. The therapist who is accustomed to venturing into the wilderness is not afraid of uncertainty, or at least is willing to tolerate the inevitable anxiety that goes with having no idea what to do or say next. The therapist must develop a profound trust in Soul, as it comes to expression as the Inward Guide. Where there is an emerging transitional self, struggling to break free, we can trust that the work will be helped by the Inward Guide. Soul is already nonviolent, so must be approached nonviolently. We build an alliance with the emergent self, anchored in Soul, both within ourselves and in our clients, so that the internal shift can begin to take place, and the client can find new ground within.

Finally, being fed from their own internal springs of hope, clients can begin to find an authentic voice and power to withdraw consent from internal dictators, and to build internal structure on new ground. The work must ripen. It has its own timing and pace. Ego gets worried about processes it can't control, and the temptation to serve ego's fears rather than wait in Soul-time for an unfolding process is common. This can happen on either or both sides of the relationship. Trust is a mutual investment and must be carefully attended.

Again, the unicorn is exceedingly shy. Perhaps I was the beneficiary of Samantha's earlier work with other therapists because she came to me after having played out her mistrust with them and was finally ready to tip the scale toward trust. Or, maybe they were like Annie's first therapist, and they fell into an ideological trap, retreating from relationship, hiding behind theory. I had no way of knowing the hidden dynamics of this earlier therapeutic history; I only knew that I was stepping into the river at this unique point in her life. To attend the soul nonviolently is to pay careful attention to how trust is either growing or retreating in the relational field. My advice to beginning therapists: Learn the ways of wilderness. Respect and trust the soul. Don't pick unripe fruit.

The Relational Self

I never had, and still do not have, the perception of feeling my personal identity. I appear to myself as the place where something is going on, but there is no "I," no "me." Each of us is a kind of crossroads where things happen.[12]

—Claude Lévi-Strauss

We all inhabit space relationally and embodied, but many of us have lost sight of the interconnected, relational field that is all around us. Not only traumatized clients, but also many others who live with a "borderland"

12. Levi-Strauss, *Myth and Meaning*, 3–4.

consciousness,[13] are exquisitely sensitive to the relational field, and immediately sense any disturbance within it. Our brains, indeed our whole bodies are wired for relationship. We are embedded in the natural world, as are all animals, along with every rock, tree, and star. We are in the thick of it, wired into the whole swirling cosmos as intimately interwoven as the smallest insect and the most massive black hole. However and wherever we locate the self, we are all uniquely and intimately "a kind of crossroads where things happen."

Most models for the self in Western psychology lose this sense of dynamic interchange, because we habitually locate the self in a sealed off interiority, and we imagine it to be more of a thing than an event. For most of us, it is a surprise to learn that other cultures do not share our modern, Western assumption that the subjective self is located in interior space, separate from the exterior, objective world. Even our own culture at an earlier time did not share this assumption. Robert Romanyshyn, a teacher, writer, and psychologist in the traditions of Jung, says that to us it is a novel idea that the "self which is more or less experienced as an interior reality on this side of our skin somewhere more or less behind the eyes gazing out upon the world—that self is a historical invention."[14] Its conception may have been many centuries ago, but its birth, its decisive emergence into Western cultural history was during the cultural transition we call the "scientific revolution." It was then that the world increasingly became an object to be observed, and the self underwent a corresponding retreat into interiority. Many writers, from a variety of disciplines, comment on this development. Here is Owen Barfield:

> Whatever it is that we ought to call our "selves," our bones carry it about like porters. This was not the background picture before the scientific revolution. The background picture then was of man as a microcosm within the macrocosm. It is clear that he did not feel himself isolated by his skin from the world outside him to quite the same extent as we do. He was integrated or mortised into it, each different part of him being united to a different part of it by some invisible thread. In his relation to his

13. Jerome Bernstein describes "borderland consciousness" as an evolutionary shift that compensates for the overspecialized and detached Western ego: "I am talking here of a profound, psychic process in which the very psychological nature and structure of the Western ego is evolving through dramatic changes." Bernstein, *Living in the Borderland*, 9.

14. Romanyshyn, *Technology as Symptom and Dream*, 65.

> environment, the man of the middle ages was rather less like an island, rather more like an embryo, than we are.[15]

As the world became de-animated and objectified, what remained of subjectivity and any experiencing self was sealed up in an interior prison, where it could only look out onto a world from the position of a detached observer. Self and world were no longer mutually infused, but were estranged partners. The relational self was cut off and driven into exile. The observing subject was consequently "forced to carry the experienced world inside itself either as illusion or as something merely subjective."[16] Inevitably, this leads to an unbearable loneliness and sense of separation, a cosmic alienation. The "invisible threads" of relationship have been severed. We have fallen into a terrifying isolation in the midst of an impersonal universe.

Under these conditions, a self that is mortised into the universe seems appealing. Yet for the medieval person, there were equally terrifying consequences associated with the embryonic self. Merger states inevitably give rise to separation efforts because we all have a terror of absorption into the other, or possession by the other. The relational self must hold a critical tension. On the one hand, there is an inevitable separation anxiety that arises with the newly differentiating self, and on the other, there is a merger anxiety that rises when the boundaries of the self are too permeable. Under optimal conditions, the growing child enjoys the ongoing, trustworthy relatedness that is required in order to overcome separation anxiety and achieve the developmental landmark of "the capacity to be alone."[17] This aloneness is bearable precisely because of a deeply internalized sense of safe and loving relatedness. Throughout the life span, the differentiating adult requires ongoing connection. We all need closeness without merger and distance without abandonment. Secure relatedness is a necessary condition for true individuation.

Across world cultures, there is a wide range of conceptualizations of the self, with some more sociocentric, and some more individualistic. The extreme sociocentric self is a precipitate of the group, and has no meaningful existence apart from the group. Exile is a death sentence, not only for reasons of physical survival, but more fundamentally for reasons of psychological survival. Exiled from the group, the sociocentric self ceases to exist and it is common in such cultures that one who is exiled soon dies, even when there is no immediate physical cause. In Western culture, the individualistic self predominates, and in the US, for males especially, that

15. Barfield, *Saving the Appearances*, 78.

16. Romanyshyn, *Technology as Symptom and Dream*, 69.

17. Winnicott, *Maturational Processes*, 29.

attitude has morphed into an extreme subtype of *rugged* individualism. For this type, survival is a lonely and heroic journey, and being absorbed into a group is the death sentence.

The transitional self is neither absorbed into the group nor disconnected from it. Having escaped the bonds of the internalized domination system, it sees with partnership eyes. The transitional self is a *relational* self that is both differentiated from and transformed by its relationships within community. The transitional self is dynamic, and stands in relational tensions with regard to its own interior states and with regard to its outward engagements. The transitional self is a wilderness self, for it must become accustomed to being thrown again and again into its dark nights where it must die to both its outgrown identities and its false gods.

Ego, shadow, and self with all its adjectives—false, true, and transitional—are all terms that appear across multiple disciplines, and that take on different meanings in different contexts. Not surprisingly, confusion abounds. I offer my four-quadrant model because it shows the common dynamic of the inward psychological world and the outward political world, and for its clarification of terms. It also shows that when a new orientation is finally gained in the transitional self, it becomes possible to withdraw consent from our inner dictators, and an internalized tyrannical regime can be overthrown. Here it is again:

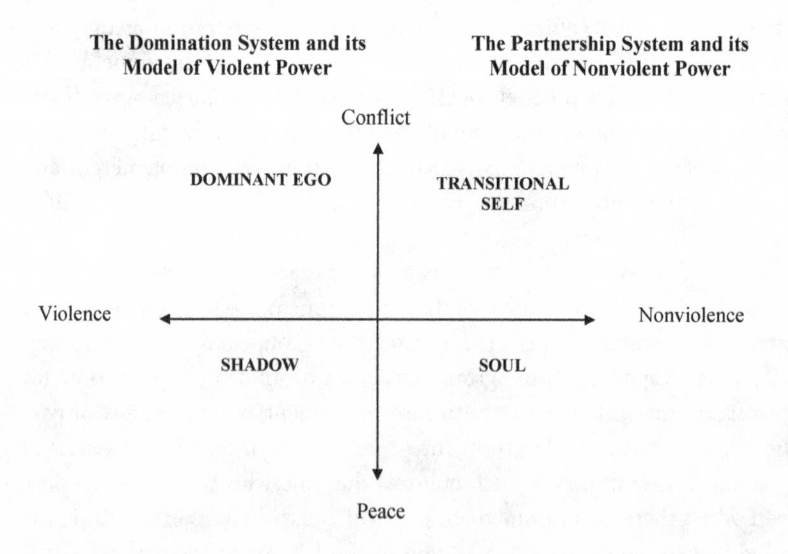

Given that the vast majority of us have been born into domination system cultures, it is inevitable that internal structure would mirror its dynamic. Some version of ego and shadow is probably present across cultures, but Western culture is more extreme in our splitting the inner world into "parts." Ego is the personal, conscious identity, and shadow holds all that is unconscious, positive or negative, that is rejected by the ego-ideal and forced into hiding. Together they form an interactive complex that mirrors the domination system's dynamic of struggle between repression and revolution. Many of us achieve a kind of violent "peace" in the inner world through vigorous repression and other defenses whose sole purpose is to keep shadow from coming into consciousness or at least under tight control. Ego's defenses work well to keep us functioning for the most part, well-adjusted to the surrounding culture. But it's a tenuous balance and various common problems ensue, from projection of shadow onto another or onto a scapegoated group, to an inward condition in which one's life energy is exhausted in keeping up the inward battle. But even when these problems are not present, what good is there in being well adjusted to a sick culture, or in gospel terms, to gain the world and lose the soul?[18]

The drive to shift ground from the ego/shadow complex to the transitional self doesn't come to everyone. But for those who take up this inner task, the call may be spiritual; it may be a midlife crisis, or it may be some intractable problem—a depression, addiction, relational crisis, a trauma or confrontation with mortality. The challenge then is to find the container that can safely hold the dying of a false-self construction while entering the wilderness. At their best, spiritual communities can play this role. A dear friend, a good therapist, regular practices such as prayer, meditation, time given to the arts, or even regular hikes in the woods—all of these and more can provide the transitional space needed for this work. The journey, however, is not merely from the false self to the true. I find this language misleading. I believe it is more accurate to say that the journey moves from the false self to the transitional self—leaning away from the false and toward the true but still a work in progress. We also sometimes speak of the true self as *the* soul. But here again I believe we are better served by the term *transitional self.* We might say that *the* soul stands on the riverbank, but Soul is the river. Or, we could also say that the transitional self is a bridge that spans between the ego/shadow complex and Soul. When the bridge is well established and maintained, for example through regular spiritual practices, traffic can get safely back and forth.

The transitional self is fluid, dynamic, and open. It continually works at showing up, being *true,* in the plumb-bob sense, and listening. And then we step into the river. Soul is the confluence of two loves. For Christians,

18. Mark 8:36.

when we step into the river, we are "hidden with Christ in God."[19] It is "the place where something is going on," or "a kind of crossroads where things happen." Soul is where interior depth opens out onto the world, where we begin to discern the interiority of all things. Our everyday perception sees inward/outward distinctions, but in Soul these distinctions disappear. The world is ensouled, and the Divine Light illumines it all. Conscious experience of Divine union, however, is fleeting because such experience requires some differentiated self to stand apart from union. So mostly we stand at the threshold, staying *true,* listening deeply. And then, finally, in contemplative union, the self disappears into God when it falls into and through Soul into the Divine flowing forth of all being. When the Beloved draws me into union, I disappear from myself and only awaken later when once again I am sitting by the window waiting with my longing. I set a place at the table of my heart, light a candle, and pour the wine. I don't know when or how the Beloved comes, but the candle has burned low, the wine has been drunk, and a sweetness lingers in the air.

The Nonviolent Soul

What would the world be, once bereft
Of wet and of wildness? Let them be left,
O let them be left, wildness and wet;
Long live the weeds and the wilderness yet.[20]

—Gerard Manley Hopkins

The modern house of Soul has been undergoing extensive renovation for nearly a hundred years, ever since the first cracks were discovered in its Cartesian foundations. The postmodern soul is finally escaping its interior prison. Jung's break with Freud was perhaps the beginning of this renovation project.[21] More recently Jung's student James Hillman announced his project of "returning soul to the world,"[22] and others taking ecology as their lens began developing an eco-psychology that completes the project of liberating

19. Col 3:3.

20. Hopkins, *Poems,* 89.

21. Jung's *Modern Man in Search of a Soul* was an early formulation of a post-Freudian and correspondingly postmodern intuition of Soul beyond the borders of Cartesian interiority.

22. Hillman, *Thought of the Heart,* 89–130.

Soul from its exclusive association to human interiority.[23] Soul now belongs to every dimension of creation. As Thomas Moore writes, "Ultimately, then, the fields of psychology and ecology overlap, because care of the world is a tending to the soul that resides in nature as well as in human beings."[24] We awaken to the animate depths of the world.

The animate, interconnected, relational world is nonviolent. That is not to deny the obvious. There are predators and prey. As David Abram says, "There are things out and about that can eat us, and ultimately will."[25] It is rather to take our usual assumptions about what is violent and what is nonviolent and reframe them in terms of relationality. Some pacifist writers, reflecting on the nature of war and peace before Gandhi, King, Gene Sharp, and the immense advances in understanding nonviolence that have emerged in the latter half of the twentieth century, believed that any use of coercive force is violent. Scriptures such as "Do not resist an evil person" and "turn to them the other cheek"[26] were read through a pacifist lens rather than a nonviolent lens. They were actually brilliant teachings about double-binding the aggressor, classic nonviolent action, but the pacifist interpretation continues to obscure this meaning.[27] If our definition of violence boils down to any use of coercive power, then by this definition, nature is bathed in violence. But violence must not be understood primarily as a function of coercive power, but rather as power taken out of its relational and ecological context. In human interactions, coercion is not inherently violent. Parents physically restrain their children from running into traffic, and societies physically restrain criminals from causing harm. Indeed, strategic nonviolence works with systemic power in ways that force oppressive power holders to make changes against their will. In nonviolence, as in nature, coercive power is in service to ecological forces. We humans invented violence as an instrument of domination.

The domination system distorts, even annihilates relatedness. Domination power ultimately worships itself. When domination power is valued

23. See Roszak et al., eds., *Ecopsychology.*

24. Moore, *Care of the Soul,* 270.

25. Abram, *Becoming Animal,* 6.

26. Matt 5:39.

27. See Wink, *Jesus and Nonviolence*, 15–16. Wink points out that the Scripture specifies the *right* cheek. No one would ever strike with the unclean *left* hand, so to be struck on the *right* cheek means that someone *back-handed,* and therefore humiliated, the victim. Turning the other cheek would present the *left* cheek to the aggressor, making it impossible for him to continue to humiliate in this way. The passage isn't about being submissive; it's about standing up for one's dignity, double-binding the oppressor, and nonviolently forcing a shift in the relational dynamic.

over relatedness, one's capacity even to perceive, let alone honor and respect Soul is progressively diminished until the other is reduced to a mere object, without subjectivity, sentience, or value. The domination system's violent extreme ultimately sacrifices all relatedness to power. The partnership system, on the other hand, makes relatedness the primary lens through which it sees the world and everything in it. As we gradually recover our partnership ways of being and seeing, the vast injustices of the domination system can be reversed, and the right use of power can be restored to its native habitat. As we recover our ability to inhabit a relational world, we will finally again see the earth, indeed the whole cosmos, as participant in Soul, endowed with subjectivity and filled with the Light of God. We are the purveyors of violence, not nature, not Soul.

Nonviolence brings power into the service of an ecological sensibility and restores relatedness to its position of ultimate value. Yes, there are things out and about that will eat us. But they are in service to the ecological Soul, and our fear of them is rooted in our attachments to constructs that hold us apart from Soul. Let them go. Fall into Soul. The related, ensouled world has ecological magic in it. Our fear makes us more vulnerable than our actual embeddedness in nature. When we can once again learn to live embodied, as nature lives, at home in the wilderness, our senses awaken to nature's speech and we step into a way of relational being that invites a wide-awake presence within which we act as it is given to act, as we are inwardly led, and we hold stillness when action is not given. When we enter the wilderness where nothing has yet been named and the hidden unity of things can once again come into a felt sense of life, we are stepping into the nonviolence of Soul. We are safe there. For we are as much the tiger as the tiger is us. There will be a holy communion in our meeting, a true *encounter.* All things will be rightly ordered within it, perhaps a greeting of two solitudes that "protect and border and salute each other." And, perhaps, our death, our "last-minute friend,"[28] for life and death are just two of the many faces that Soul wears in the world. We too are creatures of the wilderness and are subject to its ways. *Long live the weeds and the wilderness yet.*

28. Dom Christian de Chergé, *Testament*. Prior of the Abbey of Our Lady of Atlas, a Cistercian monastery in Tibhirine, Algeria, Dom Christian anticipated that he and his fellow monks would be targeted and executed during the Algerian Civil War. In his *Testament*, he speaks to his eventual executioner as "my last-minute friend." He says, "in God's face I see yours," and "may we meet again as happy thieves in Paradise." Dom Christian and six other monks were killed by rebels in 1996.

CHAPTER 8

Pharaoh's Child

In all their exoduses and liberation plots,
I'm Pharaoh.[1]

—Anonymous

Pharaoh was once an innocent child, as was Moses. Had they been born into a true partnership system, they might have been friends. Instead, one was born to institutional privilege, systemic power, and racial supremacy, and the other to oppression. One held people in bondage and the other freed them. The story has God "hardening" Pharaoh's heart, but that's a domination system theology. I prefer to believe that the witness of God within Pharaoh was persistently saying to him inwardly what Moses said to him outwardly: "Set my people free." Had he known he could listen for an inward call, he might have freed the Israelites and devoted his energies to restorative justice. But he never knew to listen. He was told he was a god, and that others had to listen to him, not that he was woven into an ecology of love and justice. Many of us born to systemic privileges in the modern world are captive to the same delusion. But there is a groundswell of awakening.

I am Pharaoh's child. There are multiple, complex, and intersecting social locations involving race, gender, class, age, sexual orientation, gender identity, physical ability, and many more such descriptors that benefit some and exclude others, but I am Pharaoh's child across the board. Whether I want them or not, my social location gives me advantages and benefits every

1. Coffin, *Courage to Love*, 5. Coffin is quoting from a conversation he had with an anonymous WASP who was feeling left behind.

day, and I am spared the indignities and burdens that others suffer. If being Pharaoh's child summed up my identity, I would have no reason to invest my energies in seeking justice for others, but fortunately it does not. I am also God's child. Unlike Pharaoh, I was born into a religious tradition that tells me that there is an Inward Teacher and Guide, a Holy Center that can be felt and followed, and that will bring me home to an undivided fellowship of Love. To call my condition "privilege" is to describe a social and economic reality, but it is a small and inadequate word. It makes my condition sound like winning the lottery. It is in fact a terrible wound to the soul.

Being a child of Pharaoh *and* a child of God sets up a division within me, and when I seek the peace of God, often what I find instead is restlessness.[2] I was formed, schooled, and socialized in a world that taught me assumptions and attitudes that run directly counter to the witness of God within me. Listening for and following that witness has been a journey that brings me to conviction as much as comfort, to a searching Light that exposes both my idols and the internal ego states that worship them. It is as if God is on an inward nonviolent campaign for my freedom, seeking to overthrow my dependence on the false securities of privilege so as to ground me in a new order with a new center.

It has taken me decades to see how this might be so. When I first began learning about racism in my adolescence, one of the first writers I read was James Baldwin. Even though I barely understood what I was reading, I got enough of it to see that my world was full of people who cried for peace when unrest amplified, but not for justice when things were quiet. The more I read, however, the more I understood that Baldwin was writing about much more than the politics of racism. He was also describing our inward condition. I was shocked to read such a bleak assessment of white people. Baldwin did not accept Elijah Muhammad's belief that all white people are devils, but his diagnosis of white Americans was almost as severe. If there was any hope for us, and Baldwin left that an open question, it would come only if we could learn to see ourselves in the mirror that he was holding up: "The white man is himself in sore need of new standards, which will release him from his confusion and place him once again in fruitful communion with the depths of his own being."[3] Now, more than fifty years later, after a lifetime of following an insatiable longing to be "in fruitful communion with the depths of [my] own being," I have come to be grateful for honest mirrors.

2. For a fuller discussion of this theme see Snyder, *Spirituality of Restlessness.*

3. Baldwin, *Fire Next Time,* 97.

Baldwin was certainly not the only, nor the first writer to name the sickness in Pharaoh's soul. W. E. B. DuBois, Richard Wright, bell hooks, James Cone, and many others have raised prophetic voices that fell on deaf white ears. This is old news for people of color and many others who must navigate the underside of privilege, and this chapter may contain nothing new for readers for whom this description fits. If you are someone who is weary of listening to white peoples' feelings, processes, and growing pains, then you may want to just skip this chapter. But if you're like me, if you're Pharaoh's child, then I hope my story will be of some use. There is certainly much within depth psychology and spirituality that speaks universally to the human condition, but this chapter will mostly address a psychology of whiteness, and how privilege impacts and shapes the inner worlds of white people.

Because privilege is a condition that is deeply embedded in the systems and structures of our communal life, it inevitably impacts our psychological and spiritual formation as thoroughly as it does our political life. The domination system thrives on separating, ranking, privileging, and oppressing, and all of that is as much in the inward psychological world as it is in the outward political world. We must learn to be "once again in fruitful communion with the depths of our own being." The structures of the white psyche must be set on new ground as surely as our outward political systems must be restructured to reflect an ecology of justice. When it comes to spirituality, we must be especially discerning. The Spirit leads with both comfort and discomfort, consolation and restlessness. We must learn to discern when the comforts come from the Spirit and when they come from privilege. We must also learn to discern when the restlessness comes from the Spirit and when it comes from ego. Our political ideologies are not reliable guides. We must go deeper. Learning to listen to the white body and its shadows is key.

Becoming White

White America's first racial victim is its own child.[4]

—THANDEKA

Central Florida in 1961 was mostly orange groves and cattle ranches. My mother's uncle gave us shelter when she took my brothers and me and left the family home in Indiana. Thrust into the Deep South, a land viciously segregated, with palmetto bugs the size of walnuts, my brothers and I found

4. Thandeka, *Learning to Be White*, 21.

ourselves in a world of whites-only drinking fountains, segregated waiting rooms, and movie theaters where all the Black kids had to sit in the balcony. The Indiana elementary schools I had attended so far were integrated, but Florida was still resisting the 1954 *Brown v. Board of Education* mandate to integrate schools. Jim Crow was everywhere, and as deadly as the alligators in Lake Tohopekaliga. This was a new world for me and I asked questions I wasn't supposed to ask. My new teachers made allowances for me, since I was from "up North," but I quickly caught on that I wasn't supposed to question or even talk about these things.

It's an odd feeling, to be granted something special, that you don't even know is special, until you see that others aren't allowed to have it. Then the gift comes with somebody else's suffering shadowing it. Shadows can be denied, repressed, and covered over with tight-lipped smiles, but they live on as a burden in the inner world. I was too young to grapple meaningfully with these experiences but now, as an adult, I feel an immense sadness not only for the Black kids who had to hang back until they were let in through a side door of the movie theater but also for the child I was then, invited to go in through the front door. What was I supposed to take away from that? Silenced by the taboo of talking about it, I absorbed wordless meanings by way of meaningless words. Conscious knowing and language are linked, so meanings conveyed through wordless, embodied gestures become a forbidden knowledge that lives on in the body, but not in the conscious mind where it might be subjected to questioning and doubt. I was invited in through the front door of the theater with welcoming smiles that spoke of superiority and privilege, but that in fact masked a brutal assault on the soul.

After a few months, my family's drama unfolded in a way that led to my brothers and me being returned to my father in Indiana and I reentered a school system where the racism was just as vicious but not as blatantly visible. From there my adolescence was lived out in the context of a tumultuous decade. As the sixties unfolded, there were assassinations, an escalating war and increasing anti-war sentiment and protests. There was a growing civil rights movement, the upending of cultural norms, and a series of racially motivated murders and bloody confrontations. In the midst of this Martin Luther King Jr.'s voice soared prophetically. I paid attention whenever he was in the news. I had never heard preaching like that. His words and intonations seemed to rise from some great invisible reservoir of hope, and when he spoke, I felt an answering fire within. All of this I held secretly within my heart, for I sensed that there weren't very many people around me who would understand. But some cracks were developing in my white world, and the light that seeped through began to feel more like a river when he spoke.

I couldn't have described it that way back then. It was a gradual awakening, something that can only be seen in hindsight, and even then, only provisionally, for awakening is an ongoing, emerging process. It all finally broke open for me in the early months of 1968. I was in my last year of high school and working a part-time job at a shoe store. One Saturday afternoon, I took my break across the street at a drugstore soda fountain. I sat in a booth and a few minutes later a Black woman slipped into the seat across from me. I had never seen her before so I said, "Hi. Do I know you?" She leaned toward me and snarled: "You blue-eyed devil!" I was stunned. She kept on: "You were standing on the corner when I came by and you called me a n*****." I protested. "No I didn't. I wouldn't do that!" But she wouldn't hear it: "Don't you *ever* say that again." She was about to explode and I could tell she had only given me a small taste of the rage that was in her, but she held back from saying anything more and after a moment got up and left me alone in my booth, protesting my innocence to myself.

I wanted to defend myself. I wanted her to know that she had the wrong guy—that I wasn't like that. But somewhere inside I knew that someone who looked like me *was* like that; some white guy had spat the "n-word" at her. Did it really matter that she took me for him? At least that was what I assumed had happened. Maybe it didn't matter to her whether she had the right guy or not; maybe her rage over a thousand insults finally spilled over and all she needed was a white face and blue eyes to light the fire. In any case, once I got over my wounded pride, I began to feel more deeply for her. Something in this experience and in Martin Luther King Jr.'s speeches seemed to create an opening toward repairing something within me that I didn't know was broken. I realized that I had just experienced a hint of what she had to live with every day. No one had ever before called me a name based on my race, much less my eye color. I was nearly eighteen years old before I gave much serious thought to my own racial identity. Now I know that this fact alone is *prima facie* evidence of my racial privilege.

I now know that this unknown woman gave me a painful but important gift in her anger. I was introduced to her world, one that clashed sharply with mine, and I suddenly saw my whiteness in her eyes. This anonymous encounter was not between two people with a history; it was bigger than that. It was our national conflict in microcosm, Black and white. To her, I was white supremacy and entitlement personified. But to me, she was pure pain, agony personified, and a dignity that was saying "Enough!" She showed me something I desperately needed to see. If I was as she said, "a blue-eyed devil," and not the child of God that my Quaker community affirmed, then my soul was in mortal danger. She told me, not directly, but essentially, that "white," as it was constructed in the world I inhabited, meant something toxic. Her anger was the shock that finally cracked the shell.

There was never any discussion of racism in my family, and it was this very silence that began my socialization into whiteness. Given no words, no awareness, no recognition that anything was amiss, there was an implicit normalizing of my white world, and a centering of whiteness as normative for all. Racism was seeded into my emerging consciousness in being taught "color blindness" and a "respect for others" that concealed systemic racism by reducing it to prejudice. With no alternative world, I had no way to stand apart from, to name, to reflect on, or to understand racism as a systemic disease, erupting more visibly to me in Florida, but just as virulent, if less visible to me, in Indiana. In the absence of conversation or any sort of critical inquiry, I concluded that racism was in the Deep South, but not in Indiana.[5] And with that assessment, I had no way to see that it was also, increasingly, within me.

This is what I mean by *becoming white.* We are each born into a cultural world that offers pathways for identity formation. Some honor the soul and others split off aspects of experience that cannot come alive in language in such a way that invites conscious integration, leading to sequestered parts that become increasingly inaccessible to consciousness. Becoming white, for me, meant far more than just getting most of my DNA from white ancestors; my whiteness came with a full package of privileges, attitudes, and ways of being in the world that are woven into the very institutions and structures of our shared life. None of this was named out loud to me as a white child. It was simply *embodied*, assumed, accepted without comment, and I was expected to inhabit this whitened world without question.

Then during my eighteenth year, a watershed year in our nation's history, for the first time in my young life, I consciously and painfully saw my whiteness in somebody else's eyes. Given a blunt awakening to the racism that was all around me, and that was embodied for this woman in my white skin and blue eyes, I began to notice more explicitly that when I looked in a mirror, I saw a *white* person. Until then I was just a person. Other people, who were not white like me, needed an adjective. Preachers, teachers, friends, even babies, if they were Black, were identified as such.

5. Years later I learned that Indiana and the surrounding midwestern states were the sites of over 250 acts of racist terrorism, including the infamous 1930 lynching of Thomas Shipp and Abram Smith in Marion, Indiana. Marion is less than twenty miles from my grandparents' farm, yet this event was never mentioned in family stories. It is highly unlikely that Quaker farmers would have been present at this atrocity, but it is disturbing that this event didn't register as significant enough to be passed on as an occasion for learning.

Now I'm embarrassed at the arrogance of that convention, one in which I participated without so much as a blink of awareness.

The Body Doesn't Lie

> Our maps of the world are encoded in the emotional brain, and changing them means having to reorganize that part of the central nervous system.[6]
>
> —Bessel van der Kolk

We take in through our bodies what words aren't allowed to say. But we can listen to our bodies and struggle to find words that bring forbidden knowledge to light. This was the work that Samantha did so courageously, described in the last chapter. Now when I do similar work for myself, when I try to feel my way back into the child body to see if I can feel the feelings of those early experiences in Florida in 1961, a queasy sensation rises in my gut, almost as if I had been secretly poisoned. I can also locate a physical sensation that feels like something tearing apart or breaking off that seems to be associated with the moment that I took in a message of superiority and was forced to split off compassion.

Suddenly I was divided within myself with one part glad for a choice seat in the theater and another part lost in a powerful grief that had to be denied. Some part of me, torn from its native habitat of relatedness and love, chose to preserve my membership in a white community rather than risk censure and rejection from the very people I depended on for survival. I'm not sure it is even reasonable to call it a choice, for choosing requires some conscious awareness of alternatives, and children learn to inhabit the world that powerful adults around them present as *the* world, the only possible world. The immeasurable cost of being a white child in the brutal apartheid of the Deep South in the early sixties is incomparable to that of being a Black child, but it is no less damaging to the soul. An essential part of my nature, that only wanted to love and connect, had to be vigorously suppressed. It's an odd and very sad feeling. Maybe it's like survivor's guilt, or the grief that comes when an innocent love is rendered impossible. I can almost see the light dimming in my child soul as that deeper and truer part of my nature slipped behind a repressive fog of denial. Then back in Indiana, as adolescence unfolded, the combination of my confrontation with a Black woman's

6. Van der Kolk, *Body Keeps the Score*, 131.

rage and Martin Luther King Jr.'s relentless hope opened up my world and began to let some of the light back in.

Teaching children to believe they are superior to their peers and entitled to privileges denied to others is child abuse. Being forced to carry the collective shadows of racism in an inchoate, unacknowledged and unarticulated, forbidden knowing, I had no way of understanding what was happening and no words that could help me sort it out. Now I do have words: It was soul trauma. Privilege damages the soul, and the white child suffers when taught to embrace it. Yet, unless we widen the lens through which we see how white people are inducted into racism to include forbidden knowledge held in the body, and damage inflicted on the soul, naming the white child as a victim of racial trauma may seem like an attempt to create a false equivalency with Black suffering, or a bid for sympathy, or an avoidance of responsibility. But when we understand the soul to be our essential connection to an eternal ecology of love and justice, we can clearly see that privilege damages that connection. Understanding privilege as soul trauma can inform our approach to healing racism. White consciousness can finally begin to move away from being frozen in guilt, shame, fear, and defensiveness, toward an awakening to our own need for soul repair.

Another way to frame this would be to say that the soul trauma of racism is for white people what war trauma is for some veterans. War trauma is also sometimes referred to as "moral injury."[7] Like adolescent soldiers, we are caught up in collective forces that inexorably sweep us into violence before we even know how we got there. Only later, after some of the training wears off, do we begin to suffer from an awakening of conscience. We who benefit from the privileges of systemic racism may not be as immediately and visibly immersed in the horrors of injury and death as soldiers in a war zone, but the violence is no less real. We just use our privilege to insulate us from awareness of the consequences of a system that stacks all the cards in our favor.

Bessel van der Kolk is a psychiatrist who has done considerable trauma work with war veterans. He writes, "No matter how much insight and

7. I have never liked this term and I know that many veterans don't like it either. It is burdened with individualistic assumptions and tones of judgment. Militarism actually trains recruits to activate the very states that the *Diagnostic and Statistical Manual of Mental Disorders* identifies as symptoms of PTSD. Military training psychologically restructures the moral universe of trainees in order to prepare them for war, and then expects them simply to change channels when they return home. Those we label as suffering "moral injury" have almost always done nothing more than be good soldiers. It would be more accurate to say that the moral responsibility lies with the system that trained them, used them, and then abandoned them, a system for which we are all responsible.

understanding we develop, the rational brain is basically impotent to talk the emotional brain out of its own reality."[8] Fortunately, there is abundant and well-documented research that says that regular spiritual practices can bring profound healing to the whole of our being, including rewiring neural pathways in the brain. The journey begins with a return to the body, where forbidden knowledge is held. From there we can begin the journey back to our native relational habitat, and to our soul's longing for the aesthetics and intimacies of the heart. A case could be made that all oppressions begin in disowning and objectifying the body. When we reject the white body that carries the hidden wound of privilege, we are schooled in also rejecting all the Black, brown, yellow, and red bodies that are forced to carry the scars and wounds of oppression.

Guilt, Fear, Shame, Rage, Grief

If we don't wrestle with anger, we never get to the heartbreak.
And if we don't get to the heartbreak, we don't get to the healing.[9]

—Lama Rod Owens

More and more white people are reading books on racism as we are being shocked into awareness by police violence, mass incarceration, and by the stripping away of the mask of racism in high places during the Trump administration. White religious congregations, especially those in the progressive stream, are forming study groups and trying to discern how best to ally movements for Black freedom. All of this is obviously important for understanding history accurately, uncovering everyday brutality, and the ongoing, multigenerational work of galvanizing a broad, multiracial movement that can work nonviolently to build a just society. However, there is a piece to the puzzle that is missing in some of these study groups and in some of the books we are reading.

When I read books that place a heavy emphasis on political analysis and the moral imperative of political action and give little attention to the dynamics of the inward transformation of the heart, I worry about the hidden energies that are animating all this anti-racism work. I certainly don't worry enough to discourage the work itself! An exclusive focus on the inward is no better than an exclusive focus on the outward. But I do want

8. Van der Kolk, *Body Keeps the Score*, 47.

9. Owens, *Love and Rage*, xiv.

progressive white readers to notice and work with the inner states that are unavoidably activated as we learn more about racism and our own complicity in it. I especially want us to challenge the implicit assumption that guilt, fear, shame, rage, and grief are appropriate means of goading people into action. These states are terrible motivators for sustained commitment. They burn hot for a while but ultimately exhaust the soul. We need a radical nonviolent spirituality that grounds us in the more sustainable energies of love and dignity. Guilt, fear, shame, rage, and grief are emotional energies that are difficult guests in the inner world but they come bearing gifts if we are willing to learn from them. If we engage them with compassion, we will find that we need a constructive program of soul repair. We all need this, but I am addressing white readers in particular.

Healing soul trauma gets us to the spiritual root of the problem. Failing that, the symptom will simply resurface, endlessly replicating itself in new forms. Soul repair requires a sustained uncovering, and an ability to wrestle, like Jacob with his night visitor, until we find the blessing in the wound. We are like archaeologists digging through layers of ancestral tragedies and horrors, and we must not recoil from each uncovering but rather bring the light of consciousness into our collective shadows. These intense emotional energies can and do provide fuel for change in the outward political world, but they are like volatile agents that must be deeply understood and handled with care. A first step comes with understanding that racism operates most insidiously from concealment in the unhealed soul traumas of being conscripted into white supremacy.

Our inner worlds hold the secret core of the wound. We break through to the blessing when we discover that guilt, fear, shame, rage, and grief are shape-shifters. Held in the fierce grasp of love and compassion, they soon reveal their true nature. Some are conversions from other, deeper emotions; some are secondary emotional states, reactive to primary ones that feel too threatening; and some are primary emotions that rise from our native humanity. We wrestle not to defeat them nor to surrender to them, but to uncover the face of Love that will either transform them or reveal them to be one of Love's many incarnations in the world. Just see if you can notice within yourself, for example, the differences between a prophetic rage that is fueled by love, a violent rage that is fueled by fear, and a defensive rage that is a mask for shame.

For people like me, engaging these inner states is a spiritual journey that is not one of ascent but rather of descent, a journey into the woods, and then down the ravine into the river of God. I must turn away from the well-lit house of a consciousness that is shaped by privilege. A deeper awakening can't be reached from inside the narrow walls of that world.

Inside the house of privilege, spirituality is often defensive, a bypass of the deeper work of transformation. Sometimes it is presented as a spirituality *of* privilege, where the outward gains and advantages of one's life are presented simply as God's favor, or the well-earned fruit of one's labor, but never as the result of having hit the privilege lottery. Sometimes it is presented as a spirituality *above* privilege, anchoring ourselves in an otherworldly realm that transcends this one and its problems. And sometimes it is presented as a spirituality *against* privilege in which we take a moral stand for justice that, while undeniably important and true, engages in a performative stance where ego takes on an ally identity and wears progressive credentials like a badge. These are all substitutes for genuinely transformational practices. Spiritualities *of* privilege, *above* privilege, and even those that stand *against* privilege, all render us blind to the wound of privilege. They all disown the white body and its forbidden knowledge.

The gods enthroned in these spiritualities offer salvation through a denial and repression of the soul wound. Even moral outrage, however much we may agree with its political analysis, can be one of ego's masks. Each of these defensive spiritualities elicits the devotion of those of us who want to cover over the privilege wound rather than heal it. However, when we can get deeper in, excavating the richness that is outside and beyond the walls of ego's defenses, then we can find a new center that allows for a spacious, compassionate, and generous container for the energies of guilt, fear, shame, rage, and grief. When we do our soul work, we discover the soul's capacity to "sit in the fire"[10] with even the most difficult states. But I cannot arrive there unless I directly address the apartheid in my own white psyche. We are created for love and connection, but when the threads of connection are severed by the wound of privilege, a wound that lives in the deep background of consciousness, then those threads of connection can only be restored by spiritualties that empower deep shadow work.

Let's look at how the model illumines the white psyche, and how radical spiritualities can move us from domination to partnership, and from violence to nonviolence. It is especially important to see how white supremacy is fueled by a fear of humiliation. We cannot move from humiliation to humility unless we can also move from white pride to white dignity. Just as a beautiful masculinity can emerge out from under the toxic masculinity of patriarchy, so can a beautiful white dignity emerge out from under the toxic distortions of racism. We come home to self and other. We drink from a common well.

10. For a profound exploration of inward/outward anti-racism work, see Mindell, *Sitting in the Fire.*

The White Psyche

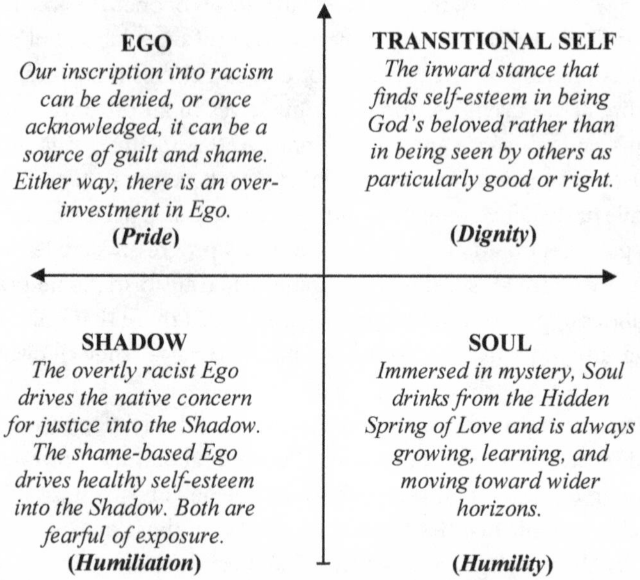

EGO *Our inscription into racism can be denied, or once acknowledged, it can be a source of guilt and shame. Either way, there is an over-investment in Ego.* **(*Pride*)**	**TRANSITIONAL SELF** *The inward stance that finds self-esteem in being God's beloved rather than in being seen by others as particularly good or right.* **(*Dignity*)**
SHADOW *The overtly racist Ego drives the native concern for justice into the Shadow. The shame-based Ego drives healthy self-esteem into the Shadow. Both are fearful of exposure.* **(*Humiliation*)**	**SOUL** *Immersed in mystery, Soul drinks from the Hidden Spring of Love and is always growing, learning, and moving toward wider horizons.* **(*Humility*)**

White pride can be expressed as the overtly racist ego that drives our native longing for right relatedness into the shadow. Or, it can also be expressed as the "innocent" ego ("I'm not racist! I'm one of the good ones!") that drives unconscious racism into the shadow. Either way, the shift toward the transitional self allows ego and shadow to be held in conscious awareness. Dignity and humility are wonderful dance partners, whereas pride is always in need of shoring up, always defending against its fear of humiliation. The white psyche that cannot take the inward stance of the transitional self must drive all of our more difficult states into the shadow, where they fuel either a reassertion of white supremacy or a prickly defensiveness. Either way, white guilt, fear, shame, rage, and grief must be consciously processed. When driven into the shadow, they feed and amplify the tensions of violent "peace." In the sixties those tensions had grown to explosive proportions.

A few months after the drugstore encounter, a tragic event occurred in my hometown. An arms store with an overstock of gunpowder in the basement, a gas leak in an underground supply line, and a spark all came together to ignite an explosion that leveled a block and a half of the downtown area. It was another Saturday afternoon and I was again at the shoe store. Our building, just at the edge of the perimeter of the worst of the destruction, remained intact, but the blast knocked us off our feet and all the glass was blown out of our display windows. Foolishly I picked myself up and went outside to see what had happened, but quickly came back in when bricks and boards began raining down in the street outside. Forty-one people were killed and many more injured. I was one of the lucky ones. Just minutes before the blast I was headed out the door to walk to a bakery to get some snacks for the staff when I was stopped by a customer who had just come in and needed a clerk. Ten minutes later, the bakery was gone. It was April 6, 1968, just two days after the assassination of Martin Luther King Jr.

The two events were unrelated but there were rumors among some of my classmates that they were connected. Black rage thickened the air in the aftermath of the assassination, and riots were spreading across the country. Chicago, Washington, DC, Baltimore, Detroit, Kansas City, Pittsburgh, and other cities erupted in violent protests. The country felt like a powder keg, so when a literal powder keg exploded in our town, it was not surprising that some people looked into the rubble and saw a Black fist raised in the air. When the cause of the explosion was finally established, the rumors subsided, but we along with the rest of the country were on high alert. Revolutionary violence was in the air. In cities where white complacency and denial persisted, explosive conditions were further inflamed. In cities where officials and other public figures named the truth of racial injustice, offered genuine expressions of grief and rage over the assassination, and called for peaceful protests, violence was largely averted. Dignity, humility, an honest ability to name the truth of racism, both personal and collective, are among the fruits of persistent shadow work, and they are powerful healing agents.

We see with the eyes of our inward condition

Do you have eyes but fail to see, and ears but fail to hear?[11]

Two days before the downtown explosion, I was riding with my father on our way to a production of the Richmond Civic Theater. We had the radio on in the car, and the WKBV announcer interrupted the music to bring a special bulletin: "Today, in Memphis Tennessee, civil rights leader Martin Luther King Jr. was shot. He was pronounced dead at St. Joseph Hospital." He went on with his report but I couldn't hear anything else. Grief welled up and I fought to keep down my tears. My father didn't say anything memorable, just "that's a shame." He wouldn't have tolerated my tears so I kept them behind clenched teeth. We went on to the theater without another

11. Mark 8:18.

word and I sat through the play embarrassed by the intensity of my emotion. I was in agony, but nobody else seemed upset. I wondered if something was wrong with me. I wanted them to cancel the play. I wanted my father to say something. I wanted to go to our Friends Church and find the pastor or someone else there to talk to. I wanted to release my agony into lamentation, to rage into the air, to grieve. But my white world was going on about its business as if nothing had happened.

I often reflect on why my father and I responded so differently to this event. Years later, in a moment of shared reflection, I made the observation that he turned eighteen years old in 1930, and I turned eighteen years old in 1968. A light came on between us then, when we could both see how embedded we were in attitudes shaped by national crises, and by forces so much bigger than either of us could understand, much less manage at such a young age. His World War II generation was so patriotically shocked by my generation's rebellion, and my Vietnam generation was so self-righteously blaming of his. I certainly claim no moral superiority to my father. Moralistic judgments are the child of individualism, and I don't see myself, or him, in those terms. Now, all these years later, with my father long in his grave, I know that he would be hurt and feel unjustly accused by allegations of racism. His way of seeing the world was consistent with what many white Quakers and some other well-meaning whites of his generation thought of as "generosity," but was really paternalism. He employed people from the Black community in our home and in his place of business and was conscientious about paying a fair wage. Yet, he remained blind to the systemic suffering of the very people he prided himself in helping. For him, racism was a sin that individual white people perpetrated on individual Black people by calling them names or refusing employment or service in a restaurant. He thought of himself as a good person who wanted to do the right thing. We never discussed racism at home. There was no need. That was a problem for other people. In his mind, we were innocent of such things.

But I am of a generation that burned draft cards and broke rules. I entered adolescence as a kid just trying to navigate a confusing and upended life, but I left it forever changed. During the first years of high school my friends and I sometimes talked about social issues, but mostly we were just kids wanting to have fun before going off to college. Or Vietnam. Those who could afford them drove muscle cars while the rest of us drove Corvairs and VWs. We sang along with The Beatles and Bob Dylan. But we also went swimming at our segregated country club. Then in 1968 two more assassinations and a downtown explosion finally shattered open our segregated minds.

If I look through the lens offered by the systemic model of nonviolence, then I believe it would be accurate to say that by the time my father and I arrived together at that moment, riding in that car and hearing that news bulletin, the systemic forces that were shaping my way of seeing those events were already profoundly different than those shaping his. We each saw those events through the eyes of our inward condition.

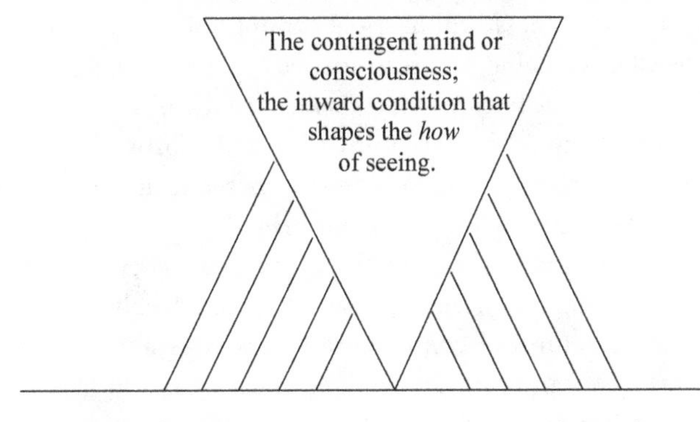

Inward systems

- Organic/genetic factors (brain)
- Developmental factors (mind)
- Individual trauma experiences
- Introjection of outward systems

Outward systems

- Social location (ranking)
- Cultural isolation vs. diversity
- Social trauma experiences
- Projection of inward systems

The pillars of support holding anyone's inward condition in place are multiple and varied. Some are visible; most are invisible, especially to the individual who is shaped by them. Those listed above are just some of the most obvious ones, but an exhaustive list would be nearly endless. Consciousness is fluid, dynamic, and ever adjusting to the shifting forces that influence it.

We are all embedded in interconnected systems, yet we assume that we can somehow stand apart from the relational fields we inhabit. The individualistic, isolated self, imagined as something sealed off and lifted out of its relational field, is the supposedly singular self that we subject to moral judgments. I cannot rank myself or my father on a moral scale because I know that some of the pillars of support propping up my racism were kicked out from under me, whereas the pillars of support propping up his were never seriously challenged. Not only were we shaped by different developmental factors and unique family-of-origin dynamics, we also lived through different social traumas. His adolescence was shaped by economic collapse and breadlines; mine was shaped by assassinations, riots, an ill-conceived war, murdered Black children, and a series of confrontations such as the Bloody Sunday attack at the Edmund Pettus Bridge.

What we see is shaped far more profoundly by *how* we see than it is by what is actually in front of us. We never simply see; we are always seeing *through* some unconscious perspective that shapes perception. Jonathan Haidt, in a fascinating study of how people make moral decisions, concludes that we are not the advocates for truth that we imagine ourselves to be. Rather, we are more like lawyers arguing for a position that was already formed outside our awareness, within tribal communities where we locate our sense of identity, belonging, and security. We argue passionately for positions we believe to be true but are in fact formed for reasons that we barely understand.[12] Our seeing is shaped by invisible and mostly unconscious forces much more than we realize. Very few of us see reality as it is. It is more the case that we see with the eyes of our inward condition.

When we understand that we are caught up in a legacy of countless generations of a domination system that has long been deeply sedimented into the everyday structures of consciousness as well as into the institutions of this world, we can begin the work of uncovering and healing the soul wounds of racism, and multiple other forms of oppression. We can build new institutions with an awakened heart. Reaching the bottom of the disorder requires transformational practices. Inward activism brings an unsettling but extraordinary awakening: Our perception is provisional and inevitably distorted. Seeing this, we can finally begin to take a new inward stance in relation to our own mind.

Recovering heart, returning to Soul

Racism is a heart disease.[13]

—Ruth King

For Pharaoh's child, radical spirituality in all its forms and practices must hold a tension between the comforts of love and the discomforts of having our ego ideals decentered and challenged. The balance between compassion and confrontation is what holds the most promise for retraining the emotional brain.[14] I needed the shock of being confronted with an anonymous

12. See Haidt, *Righteous Mind.*

13. King, *Mindful of Race,* 1.

14. Some years ago when I was working with domestic violence offenders I quickly learned that I needed to find a way to love them before I could effectively work with them. For a description of this work see Snyder, "Violence and Nonviolence."

Black woman's anger, and I also needed to hear Martin Luther King Jr.'s generosity toward my white soul. When I am confronted with my unconscious racism, I have learned to say two things: "Ouch," and "Thank you." Both are important. "Ouch," because it hurts, and that must be acknowledged. "Thank you," because it's probably true, and that too must be acknowledged. I feel no loss of dignity in either one. I may be Pharaoh's child, but I'm also a child of God. I can be confronted and loved at the same time.

I have learned that this work is best done with white allies. Some people of color are willing to do both the loving and the confronting. But many are understandably weary of tending to white growing pains and the struggles that go with decentering the ego. It is tempting to think of those struggles as evidence of "white fragility,"[15] but that is an unfortunate term in that it fails to capture the psychological and spiritual nature of the wound of privilege. By misnaming the disorder, it misdirects the remedy. We can navigate these passages more effectively if we treat privilege as a soul wound. Likewise, political correctness, for all of its well-intentioned cries for justice, too often fails to rise to the challenge of genuine healing, and may even cause harm. Ideological politics serves the same dynamic as ideological religion, and I regard the politically correct much like I do Christians who want to create cults of the doctrinally correct. I love Jesus and I long for justice, but I object to the packaging. I am a student of transformational change and I know that ideology won't get us there.

Our true home is in the ecology of just being and being justice, just mercy and merciful justice. When all of who I am can be held with compassion and surrendered into the mercy of God, then I can fully embrace my pale skin and my ancestral heritage with all of its mix of heroes and horse thieves, abolitionists and slaveholders, without seeing "whiteness" itself as being inherently flawed.[16] When I finally learn to see with the eye of the heart, I can follow more faithfully the Quaker admonition to "speak to that

15. Diangelo, *White Fragility.* The book is packed with helpful insights but the title and much of the content is *essentialist* in that it casts "fragility" as an inherent feature of white people. A more helpful frame would place "fragility" on a continuum with "resilience," terms that represent a spectrum of psychological resourcefulness. White people can certainly be prickly and quick to defend, but we are also capable of deep resilience when we tap the resources of Soul.

16. Human beings like me inhabit "whiteness" as a social construct, and do so differently in different contexts. Some "white" Europeans, for example the Irish, were originally considered "non-white" once they emigrated to America. My use of the term here must be contextualized as *North American, twenty-first-century* "whiteness" in order to be clear that I'm talking primarily about the racing of privilege, in the United States, with our history of the enslavement of Africans and all its sequelae over four hundred years.

of God in everyone." We don't presume that the Divine is always visible or even recognized by the one in whom it dwells, but we do presume that the hidden Spring flows unceasingly and is available to anyone who wants to come and drink from it.

No matter how entangled, mired in, and dependent we have allowed ourselves to become on systems of injustice, no matter how compromised or unconscious, we cannot be fundamentally altered in our true nature. Spirituality for Pharaoh's children requires a return to our original and eternal nature, where we can be brought "once again into fruitful communion with the depths of our own being." In clearing our access to the Divine Spring, we welcome God's nonviolent revolution of the soul. We may at times despair of ever being restored to our place in the ecology of being, to right relatedness in the family of God, but as Martin Luther King Jr. told us, "We are caught in an inescapable network of mutuality, tied in a single garment of destiny."[17] In the end God has put us on this earth to love each other. If we can stand in the fierce heat of that love together, then we can trust that we're going to come out all right.

17. King, "Letter," 290.

CHAPTER 9

Praying for the Devil

Yes, life is beautiful, and I value it anew at the end of every day,
even though I know that the sons of mothers . . .
are being murdered in concentration camps.[1]

—Etty Hillesum

For many people, it isn't only suffering that nips at their heels like a stray dog but actual evil that descends like a hawk, digs in its talons, carries them off, and then drops them into a hell that only humans know how to create. All suffering is not evil, but all evil creates suffering. Natural disasters, misfortune, sickness, death, these belong to life's unfathomable ways, but they are not evil. There is something unnatural about evil, unnecessary, not belonging to nature or to life, but to our uniquely human capacity to willfully stand over against values of beauty, community, justice, and love, even to actively seek their destruction, and in concert with others to create systems, institutions, structures, and whole cultures around a collective devotion to greed, power, and domination. I am persuaded by Walter Wink's assessment that what we call "evil" is a kind of spirituality that congeals around a collective devotion to domination and idolatry.[2] As one can feel the spirit

1. Hillesum, *Interrupted Life*, 96.

2. Wink writes, "I speak of 'demons' as the actual spirituality of systems and structures that have betrayed their divine vocations. I use the expression 'the Domination System' to indicate what happens when an entire network of Powers becomes integrated around idolatrous values. And I refer to 'Satan' as the world-encompassing spirit of the Domination System." Wink, *Engaging the Powers*, 8–9.

of sacred spaces that have been prayed in, so can one also feel the spirit of places devoted to power and greed, and one can feel the spirit of places where great evils have been committed. One does not have to believe in disembodied demonic spirits to account for it. Evil is rather a grave illness of the collective psyche, passed down the generations, with a disorder of the soul at its core.

Etty Hillesum's diary is such a powerful witness precisely because it was written with the certain knowledge that her life would come to a brutal and untimely end at Auschwitz. She wrote of "living in utter peace and quiet."[3] She wrote that "sometimes the most important thing in a whole day is the rest we take between two deep breaths, or the turning inward in prayer for five short minutes."[4] Her writing is excruciatingly honest in her "cosmic sadness" over the evils around her. But, she says, "If you have given sorrow the space its gentle origins demand, then you may truly say: life is beautiful and so rich. So beautiful and so rich that it makes you want to believe in God."[5] She has fallen through the bottom of that sadness into an inexpressible peace. Prayer enabled her to find life to be beautiful, even in the midst of evil's terrifying ways.

What we do with our suffering and how we understand God's presence in the midst of it takes on an even greater urgency when confronted with the unmasked face of evil. Etty Hillesum was able to stay open, inspired, and grounded, and that enabled her to stand confidently, trusting in Life in the midst of death. But for many of us such trust has been terribly damaged by bad theologies that lead to unsustainable answers or to the rejection of faith altogether. When the general culture is overtaken by materialism, and theology no longer makes sense, there is no one left to care for the soul. Living mythologies of good and evil fall behind the veil of our modern type of rationalism. Prayer, if we pray at all, feels like throwing petitions at an empty sky.

When mythology becomes just a collection of quaint stories that long-dead people once believed, the world no longer has any way to address the hidden forces of evil within its own institutional shadows. A reduction of good and evil to political forces, or to individual psychology, fails to push the horizons of perception far enough open to allow us to see and address the collective shadows that congeal into institutional forms that consume, exploit, and destroy lives. A living mythology of good and evil allows us to step into a story that allows us to see how *theo-psychic-socio-spiritual*

3. Hillesum, *Interrupted Life*, 92.
4. Hillesum, *Interrupted Life*, 93.
5. Hillesum, *Interrupted Life*, 97.

systems, or what Scripture calls "principalities and powers," operate from behind the veils. We have looked at domination system dynamics and how they impact our politics and individual psychology, but we must also look at our collective religious ideas to see how all these come together to constellate an actual spirituality of evil. This work is essential for the emerging world. If we dismiss mythology as nothing more than the superstitions of so-called primitive people, then we have rendered ourselves illiterate in the soul's native speech.

The Imago Dei and Its Shadows

You have heard that it was said,
"Love your neighbor and hate your enemy."
But I tell you, love your enemies and pray
for those who persecute you.[6]

It was a hot summer day not long after my eleventh birthday when my mother announced that we would be going to Florida to start a new life. She told us that we mustn't tell anyone our plans, especially our father. She told me that evil spirits were about, and I believed her because she told me her dreams, and what I heard sent shivers down my spine. The day came when my father left for New York to meet my sister who was returning home from a college year in France, and my mother took advantage of his absence to quickly pack up my brothers and me and flee the family home. A plane ride, a stay with a great uncle I had never met, and then finally we were settled in a small central Florida town, ensconced on the second floor of an old and musty apartment building where the iron fire escape wobbled because one of the legs had rusted off. One night, alone in my bed after more of my mother's tales about evil spirits and regaling me with her nightmares, I felt the demons crowding in on me. Shadowy figures felt menacing and oppressive and all I could think to do was to say out loud, "In the name of Jesus, leave me alone!" To my amazement, they were suddenly gone and I fell asleep.

As an adult, I now know that my mother had fallen into a paranoid psychosis from which she eventually recovered. Her breakdown led to her being flooded by the unconscious, both personal and collective, as if in a waking nightmare. At the time, barely eleven years old, and having no

6. Matt 5:43–44.

perspective other than the one that came with the stories my mother told me, I had no choice but to see the world as she had constructed it. She had grown up in a small country church, conservative, Bible-based, and leaning strongly toward literalism. She suffered multiple childhood tragedies, losing her father in a coal mine explosion, and then her brother who fell off the running board of a car. Her shattered world had no narrative that could support healing. It was framed entirely in literalized images of good and evil. My mother never had any therapy. But she clung to Jesus like her life depended on it, which it probably did, and this practice became the path she followed back to sanity. It was courageous work and it sustained her for the rest of her life.

My mother's breakdown and eventual recovery can all be well understood within the frames of modern psychiatry and psychology. But what about those demons? A medical explanation for my mother's condition does not account for my experience. Who or what were they? Where did they go, and by what power was I, as a small and frightened child, able to banish them so quickly? Now I'm all grown up and curious. Is there *anything* anywhere in creation that is separate from or unworthy of love? If we are to pray for our enemies, why not pray for the devil? Might there be something like *collective* shadow work that parallels the kind of spiritual growth we are called to as individuals? How deep can intercessory prayer go? We pray for friends and family. Can we also awaken to spiritual practices that support our collective freedom? Are there hidden spiritual dynamics that we can access for the benefit of the whole?

Our modern Western culture gives me only two options for understanding my childhood encounter with a palpable sense of the demonic, and I don't find either one remotely satisfying. One is the mythic-literal, which would simply take those events at face value and assert that those presences were real and Jesus cast them out. But I am resistant to that idea for a number of reasons, the main one being that I really don't want any of the extra baggage that comes with that literal of a worldview. That world seems too limited to me. I agree with Walter Wink's critique of Frank Peretti's novel *This Present Darkness*, when he says, "The view of evil is scary but finally trivial; his demons are simply imaginary bad people with wings, and the really mammoth and crushing evils of our day—racism, sexism, political oppression, ecological degradation, militarism, patriarchy, homelessness, economic greed—are not even mentioned. It is simply Pentecostal political naïveté writ large on the universe."[7] The mythic-literal view renders the larger systemic view invisible.

7. Wink, *Engaging the Powers*, 9.

My second option is the scientific-reductionist view in which my childhood experience is explained away psychologically. Perhaps my heightened state of fear activated protective defenses and I was able to take a stand against induced terrors that I had projected into imagined figures in the room. This view would hold that my "demons" were a fantasy projection of personified terrors, out-pictured into the room so as to activate a "Jesus-defense." Life's realities are intolerable, so we unconsciously locate ourselves in comforting narratives that make the intolerable tolerable, and that give us some illusion of control in the face of unbearable helplessness. Perhaps my suggestible childhood psyche had simply imagined monsters in the closet and then engaged in some magical thinking. But I'm resistant to this idea as well. Even now when I recall this experience, I know there was something in it that was more than just fantasy. Something more than just my personal psyche was activated.

My mother's spiritual formation was held firmly in the grip of an all-powerful and inscrutable patriarchal god. Her church's response to the terrible and tragic losses of her childhood was "The Lord gave and the Lord hath taken away."[8] How can a child trust a god who lets both a young father and a brother die tragic and untimely deaths? The religious imagination that unquestioningly accepts traditional notions of God cannot possibly resolve such an unbearable dilemma. Just as the parental imago of an abused child must be split in two, thereby preserving one to love and trust and leaving the other to fear and hate, so also must the domination system's gods be split. The *imago Dei* of my mother's inner world had split off an immense shadow that flooded her when her defenses were broken down.

This splitting of the God image did not originate with her, of course.[9] Everyone who shares in the legacy of Western monotheism stands in the stream of a long history of attempts to reconcile experiences of evil with an all-good, all-loving, and all-powerful domination system god. Originally mythologized as an emissary of God, the *Satan*, or adversary, eventually fell into a polarized split and became an anti-god, the CEO of evil.[10] In most of Western Europe, throughout the Middle Ages, the devil was an agent of pure evil, often depicted in iconography and paintings as a lurid monster, a demonic tempter no longer in service to God but dedicated to undermining God's purposes wherever possible. Christian spirituality was obsessed with

8. Job 1:21 (KJV).

9. Jung struggled with the problem of God's shadow throughout his career. See his *Answer to Job*.

10. Biblical scholar Elaine Pagels notes that the Hebrew root for Satan is *stn*, which means "one who opposes, obstructs, or acts as adversary." See Pagels, *Origin of Satan*, 39.

spiritual warfare, warding off evil, exorcising it when necessary, and engaging in severe ascetic practices designed to protect the soul from infection.[11]

Donald Kalsched, a Jungian analyst who has done extensive work with trauma survivors, notes that "the word 'daimonic' comes from *daiomai,* which means to divide."[12] That which is originally whole falls into split off parts when traumatic events overwhelm the psyche's ability to hold such experiences within a narrative container. Kalsched notes that "The antonym of diabolic is 'symbolic,' from *sym-ballein,* meaning 'to throw together.'"[13] Neither my mother nor I had the benefit of that understanding when we stepped into a shared perception of the demonic, but we both accessed spiritual resources that held the tension and supported healing. That which is thrown apart, *dia-ballein,* is restored to its original wholeness through symbolic participation in mythic narratives that can hold the unbearable tensions of good and evil. Many within traditional religions are able to fully inhabit their religious narratives, giving them a pathway to reweave that which had been split off. My mother's return to stability was eventually the gift of her vivid sense of an ongoing relationship with Jesus, whom she saw as having intervened for her, thus insulating her from evil. Jesus was accessible to her, despite the excruciating circumstances of her life, whereas her inscrutable, abandoning, abusive god was not. She could imagine joining her sufferings to Jesus' suffering on the cross, thus also sharing in his resurrection, and in this practice, she found a path to the transitional self with its more inclusive horizons. My mother had a living mythology that gave her a *symbolic* narrative within which the *diabolic* split could be overcome.

My mother's resurrection spirituality was a *participation* story. She didn't make the kinds of distinctions between the literal and mythic that I find necessary. She believed it and trusted it and that was enough. She knew both the cross and the resurrection from personal experience. Eventually she could not only find her lost loved ones in the resurrection, she could also find the lost and traumatized parts of herself. She grew into a vocation as a teacher and artist and credited Jesus for everything that came to her, above all life itself. As an adult, when I eventually pursued my academic studies, she was supportive, but she was also somewhat concerned that I felt I had to think so hard about things that to her were simple and obvious truths of the heart. She had been "saved" as a child, then again as an adult when Jesus came to her rescue. Years later, as she lay dying, my brothers and

11. For a thorough history of the evolution of the mythology of evil, see O'Grady, *Prince of Darkness.*

12. Kalsched, *Inner World of Trauma,* 11.

13. Kalsched, *Inner World of Trauma,* 17.

sister and I had gathered around her hospital bed. She was in and out of awareness, and quite agitated. I opened my Bible and read to her from the eighth chapter of Romans, and also the Lord's Prayer, and all the stress just drained out of her. The story served her well throughout life and became the bridge for her transition into death. She relaxed into a deep sleep and died later that night.

The Divine Fire

For our God is a consuming fire.[14]

My childhood experience fell into the background of memory as I grew into adulthood, and then resurfaced when I was in chaplaincy training at a state mental hospital. I encountered many people whose inner worlds were quite bizarre, some enchanting, but mostly frightening and miserable. I got my heart broken over and over by caring for people who inhabited such terrifying worlds. One evening after a particularly trying day, I was exhausted and needed sleep but couldn't let go of the sorrow I felt for a young woman on my unit who had thrown herself on the floor screaming and crying in desperation. Later, at home in my bed but unable to sleep, I prayed out loud, "How can it be this way? What kind of world is this where some suffer horribly and others don't? Why them and not me?" Finally, I was able to sleep. And then came this dream:

I go into the basement of my house where I find a heavy trap door embedded in the concrete floor of the basement. I hadn't known it was there. I open it and descend into a sub-basement where I find a huge furnace. I peer in and see Fire. It is immense, perhaps infinite, all-consuming. I grasp the handle on the heavy cast iron door and slowly pull it closed. Then I hear someone saying, "That's the difference; you know how to close the door."

I'm astonished by these kinds of experiences. They are unsettling but also oddly comforting. It's as if I have a conversation partner in the depths of the unconscious who comes in my dreams, sometimes reassuring, sometimes disturbing, but always helpful and always with a perspective that is a jolt to my waking consciousness. I note with this dream that it doesn't actually answer the big questions about good and evil, or about why people suffer in general, but it does give me an image: Some know how to close the door; others don't. What does that mean?

14. Heb 12:29.

As with most dreams, this one lends itself to multiple possibilities. My first response was to see that the dream named the obvious reality that those with better defenses, neurological and psychodynamic, are less likely to be overtaken by the contents of the unconscious. But I already knew that, and dreams rarely tell us what we already know. Dreams want amplification and deepening, an exploration of the narrative, so as to invite a new perspective and a new stance. Then I began to hear the dream as an invitation to see commonality rather than difference. I may have a better grasp on the door, but we share a common fire. Jungian scholars Ann and Barry Ulanov write that there are two kinds of madness. There is the kind that is overwhelmed by the unconscious and the kind that fails to access its energies altogether.[15] Who is truly mad, the patients who can't adjust to an insane world or those who can? When is throwing oneself on the floor wailing in lamentation a symptom to be medicated and when is it the purest form of sanity? I know that some mental illness is based in genetic inheritance and brain function, so I don't want to blur all distinctions between the various illnesses. But to presume that everyone who is in the hospital is there for reasons that are purely internal to the individual is to blind oneself to all manner of external forces such as family dynamics, systemic injustices, grinding poverty, unresolved trauma, poorly conceived religious ideas, and socially induced despair. I went back to the unit the next day with a deep appreciation for the reality that we are all in this together. Perhaps this young woman and my other fellow pilgrims on that unit needed to get a better grasp on the door, but maybe I needed to let mine open a bit more. Maybe we're all just trying to get close to the Divine Fire without getting burned.

But the amplification of this dream is only beginning. What about that fire? Is it the fire of hell, or the fire of God? Is it pure potential, an image of passionate heat that can be the driving energy for either violence or love? Is it the alchemist's fire, the primordial heat of transformation? Is it the "big bang" fire of creation, the furnace of life itself, and is my dream-fire an image of my direct participation in the animation of my being, my little bit of personal stardust? The dream image does not come with an interpretation attached. There are no explanatory footnotes. It is a gift from the unconscious, and it is up to me to discern what to make of it.

It is helpful to remember that the Divine Fire is a "*mysterium tremendum et fascinans*,"[16] in the words of Rudolf Otto, the German theologian who probed deeply into the phenomenology of religious experience. He says that the numinous may sweep one into states of profound awe and

15. Ulanov, *Healing Imagination*, 43.

16. Otto, *Idea of the Holy*, 12–40.

worship. He adds that it also "has its wild and demonic forms and can sink to an almost grisly horror and shuddering."[17] Otto's insights parallel those of archetypal psychology. Jung insisted on the autonomous nature of the psyche. Otto makes a nearly identical statement when he says, "The numinous is thus felt as objective and outside the self."[18] I find this hard to dispute, given my experiences. But there is a fine line between phenomenological psychology and metaphysical assertion. Some of Jung's followers have been much too bold in their assertions because of a failure to care adequately for this distinction. James Hillman's study of war is a case in point. He makes the unwarranted declaration that "There is no practical solution to war" and "War belongs to our souls as an archetypal truth of the cosmos."[19] This sort of unsupported claim in the guise of phenomenological psychology leads to what I call archetypal*ism*, or archetypal fundamentalism.

This metaphysical leap is not necessary to make the central point, which is that falling into the grip of archetypal forces has a possessive effect on consciousness. We can become enthralled by the gods of war, and Hillman insists that we not fail to see how thoroughly we can be overtaken, how blinded we can be when Ares or Mars defines the horizons of consciousness. Not only war, of course, but all manner of conditions are functionally states of possession, if we understand that term to mean that we are driven by unconscious forces. Uncovering the mythic depths of war and violence brings these forces to consciousness, where they can be unmasked, reassessed, and deprived of their possessive power. A more persuasive view of the true nature of archetypal forces comes from René Girard, another widely read author whose theories have influenced many scholars across a variety of disciplines.[20] Girard was a French literary critic, philosopher, and anthropologist who offered the view that violent warrior mythologies arise *because of* violent human behaviors. They are the collective psychic *products* of war and violence.[21] This reverses Hillman's view that the gods are

17. Otto, *Idea of the Holy*, 13.

18. Otto, *Idea of the Holy*, 11.

19. Hillman, *Terrible Love of War*, 214.

20. For a thorough review of Girard's hypothesis regarding the origins of violence see Bailie, *Violence Unveiled*.

21. "Myth," as I used the term in the first chapter, dances with "mystery" and invites participation in sacred depths beyond naming. "Myth," as Girard uses the term, *silences or mutes* sacred depths, providing ideological cover for violence. When Girard says that Christianity "de-mythologizes" archaic religion, he means that it uncovers and confronts the idolatry of violence as enshrined in religious narratives that reify human social arrangements. Both Hillman and Girard would be much clearer if they would preserve a distinction between these different uses and meanings of the term "myth." Then Hillman would not have to be so implacably opposed to Christianity and

irrevocably woven into the cosmos. They are indeed driving forces behind war and violence, but their power is in their remaining unconscious, not in their inherent nature.

I am agnostic on the question of the true metaphysical nature of the gods enshrined in Greek and other mythologies, as well as on the true nature of the figures that appear in dreams or visions. Perhaps some of them are personified projections of the unconscious. Perhaps others are precipitates of the collective psyche. Or, they may be beings in their own right, and the psyche can open onto realms that are both angelic and demonic, as well as a world of spirits and ancestors. All of that is fascinating, but those are questions to be debated by others more invested than I am in answering them. My concern is how do we engage the personified representations of the hidden forces that are often driving individual and collective behavior. Whatever their essential nature, these psychic appearances are penultimate. I resist the temptation that is all too common among archetypal psychologists to give too much authority to the appearances. In Gil Bailie's rendering of Girard's work, he puts his finger directly on the core weakness in archetypalism when he writes, "By mystifying human violence and attributing it to the gods, archaic religion endowed a certain form of physical might—usually the most powerful form—with metaphysical significance."[22] The gods are not worthy of that much power, nor must we engage them with the awe that deifying them demands.

Rudolf Otto avoids this weakness by using language that is more cautious than Hillman's or that of other archetypal psychologists. When he says that "The numinous *is thus felt as* objective and outside the self [emphasis added],"[23] his *as-if* language allows me to encounter the appearances *as* living, autonomous beings, but without the feeling that I am engaging a being whose power and authority is beyond question. There is a mutual engagement, and I bring my own authority to the shaping of our relational space. As with any relationship, we are responsible for the stance we take. If we are to bring an authentic voice to the conversation, we cannot avoid the necessity to be clear about where and how we ground ourselves, perhaps especially in the inner world. To do that confidently and with clarity of thought and conviction we must engage the interpretive function that is essential to our nature. Passive or active, conscious or unconscious, we are

Girard would not sound like he is promoting Christian exclusivism. Both archetypal psychology and Christianity are "mythic" in the first sense. However, both can also easily fall into an ideological hardening of the "myth" into an inflexible form that no longer dances with "mystery." When they do, inevitably, they become polarized.

22. Bailie, *Violence Unveiled*, 7.

23. Otto, *Idea of the Holy*, 11.

all meaning-makers, and we incarnate our gods. Therefore, we must choose responsibly. I have made my choice. I choose to see a Holy Fire in that furnace. It gives me both heat and light—passion for living and illumination for the journey. That stance grounds me as I encounter figures in dreams or in the active imagination, and it gives me authority to learn from them as well as to declare boundaries when needed. It was present with me as a child, and continues to inform my life. I reach for it every day and especially when I encounter situations that call for that greater Love that casts out fear.

I do not seek to impose my interpretations on others, but I do ask my clients to unearth and question the inherited narratives that currently inform their lives, and I want to know how their sufferings and illuminations serve the transformational process. Robert Kegan, a developmental psychologist who has observed processes of transformation across the life span, says that "something cannot be internalized until we emerge from our embeddedness in it, for it is our embeddedness, our subjectivity, that leads us to project it onto the world in our constitution of reality."[24] Kegan's observations apply equally to our collective human development. Thresholds of transformation at each stage are characterized by what he calls a "natural emergency," that is, a crisis of emergence occasioned by being confronted by life's dilemmas in such a way that they cannot be resolved according to one's current way of constructing the world. One cannot solve a problem with the same mind that created it, as Einstein famously said. Kegan's version is, "Any real resolution of the crisis must ultimately involve a new way of being in the world."[25] The transitional self is that stance that invites our emergence from an embeddedness in a self-world construction that has become too small.

To pray for the devil is to unmask and name the archetypal figures, images, energies, and beliefs that animate our narratives about evil, and then to stand in relation to them with the authority of Love. Our crisis of emergence calls for a field hospital staffed with a critical care team of intercessors, prophets, mystics, theologians, teachers, writers, depth psychologists, nonviolent activists, poets, musicians, visual artists, gardeners, rebels, citizens, advocates, and any other profession under the sun that supports the transformation of consciousness. Practices that bridge the tension of opposites, allowing the ego and its shadows to be compassionately held by the transitional self, bring nonviolence into our spiritual lives. The nonviolent soul incarnates a nonviolent God, reimagines theology, dethrones the domination system gods in the religious imagination, in our personal and collective psychology, and in our politics. Conditions of extreme polarization

24. Kegan, *Evolving Self*, 31.

25. Kegan, *Evolving Self*, 41.

generate a natural emergency that can fall into breakdown and war, or they can drive an evolutionary advance toward lives that hold a creative tension among multiple perspectives. There is an emerging inward/outward revolution. We are evolving narratives that welcome diversity, and invite all the fertility, creativity, and aliveness of a thriving ecosystem.

Nonviolence and the Power of God

Without telling themselves so, the founders of the theological tradition were accepting and applying to deity the tyrant ideal of power.[26]

—Charles Hartshorne

There is still much work to do. Many rightly reject domination system theologies, but are then left floundering without any vital religious mythology that can ground them in an alive and creative faith. Others cling to traditional expressions of faith but are trapped in the unresolvable dilemmas posed by their undeniable awareness of evil. There are few things more heartbreaking for me as a pastoral counselor than to sit with a client who shares a story of great suffering, tragedy, loss, or mind-numbing betrayal, who then asks, "How could God let this happen?" Of all the domination system's distortions, the notion that God is a controlling patriarch is one of the most damaging. As if our human tragedies aren't painful enough, just when we are most vulnerable, bad theology piles on an excruciating crisis of faith and robs good people of an ability to pray. I know that my client's question is a cry of the heart, and not a request for a theological discussion. Compassion is called for, so that is what I try to offer in these moments. We will deal with the theological damage in due time. Inevitably, when I am home again at the end of the day, I have to work with my anger at the church for causing so much harm. Many of the very institutions that exist to offer solace, comfort, inspiration, and hope have fallen to the domination system, and too often commit spiritual abuse on top of all the other kinds of abuse that we humans inflict on each other.

Given this heartbreak, I insist on two assertions: The first is that *theology's fundamental purpose is to make prayer possible again*. To do this work well, it must *awaken* and not merely inform. Theology is not unlike depth psychology, whose core purpose is to invite a meaningful conversation between the depths of our being and the mystery of the universe. Theology's

26. Hartshorne, *Omnipotence*, 11.

insistence on proposing "God" as its first gesture of speech is to make a particular demand on the universe. Not unlike the demand in an infant's first cry, prayer is a relational gesture flung into the night sky in full anticipation that there will be an answering voice, a waiting Breast offered to our hunger. Theology insists that the risk of that cry is worth taking. It begins with a bold assertion. The Quaker scholar and mystic Rufus Jones stated it plainly: "The Divine Other whom we seek is also seeking us."[27] Any theology that makes prayer possible again bets everything on that promise.

My second assertion is this: *Theology must begin with theodicy.* Given that theology is a discipline that invites critical conversations within a community of the hopeful and the wounded, and given that the spiritually hungry among us bring urgent questions about good and evil, theology must reflect on the possibility of the real existence, love, goodness, and power of God, given the reality of evil. Any theology that cannot or will not address theodicy in a meaningful and convincing way will lose its audience. The community will simply stop listening. Our everyday lives call us to address critical issues of oppression and even the survival of the planet. Faithful people need a religious imagination that can sustain a wholehearted capacity to pray with passion and trust, to draw strength and courage from our spiritual disciplines, and then to act in the world with confidence that "the principalities and powers" cannot continue to exercise their possessive power once they are unmasked and we withdraw our consent.

But theodicy, as it has been expressed within traditional religious thought, is a four-legged animal that always limps on one leg: God is real; Evil is real; God is love; God is all-powerful. This animal can't walk on all fours. You can argue for atheism and then there's no more animal to worry about. Or, you could limp on the second leg and join forces with Christian Scientists and some New Age metaphysicians who insist that evil is not real; it doesn't exist. God is All, and everything that we call evil is pure illusion. I have tried on atheism but found that I'm like Joanna Macy, who says, "I was a failure as an atheist, because I could not cure myself of praying to a god I no longer believed in."[28] For me, prayer is my connection to Life. I can no more give it up than I can breathing. I also tried on Christian Science, but I don't seem to be capable of denying the reality of something that seems overwhelmingly obvious to me. The third leg on the theodicy animal is the one where many traditional, classical theologies focus their attention. This leg asserts God's reality, the reality of evil, and God's power, and then attempts to explain how "allowing" evil to occur is actually a loving act. But I

27. Jones, *Double Search*, 11.

28. Macy, in *Rilke's Book of Hours*, 2.

can't walk on that leg either. That seems like saying it is loving for parents to "allow" their children to run in traffic. Too often that reasoning is defended with an illegitimate default position: "It's a mystery." Indeed, reality is mysterious, but it is an abuse of the term to draw it into the service of an ideology. An all-powerful god who *creates* evil and then *allows* children to suffer and die from its tortures is an abusive, cruel, tyrant god. I once stood on a mountaintop and cursed that god, daring "him" to strike me with lightening. I survived.[29] If I am an atheist in any sense, then it is in relation to this god. The patriarchal, tyrant god *does not exist*, except in the imaginations of patriarchal tyrants and those who have internalized their oppression. Of that I am convinced.

That leaves the "all-powerful" leg, and as we have seen, nonviolence radically reframes the nature of power. I'll let Gandhi's statement first quoted in chapter 5 and repeated here show how this can open up new understandings of the nature of good and evil.

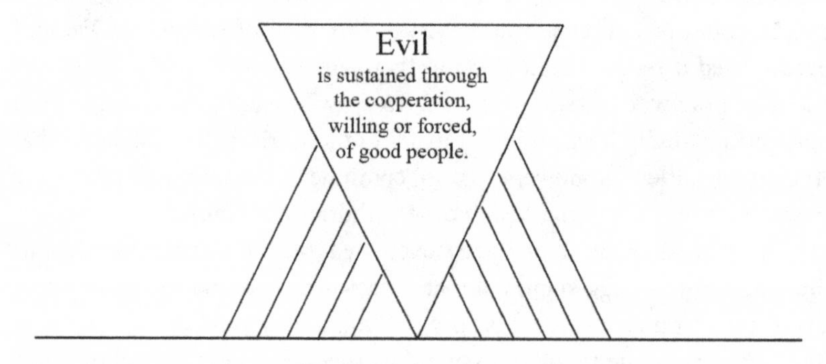

So far we have looked at a systemic model of how nonviolent power actually works, both politically and psychologically. Now let's see how it can

29. A number of months into the sanctuary of my monastic year, an image of a starving child whose picture was on a missionary flyer drove me to a mountain top where I poured out my grief and rage toward God. The sheer immensity of human suffering, in war, oppression, abuse, and countless other contexts, all seemed to flow together in that moment. I threw down my indictment, calling God a criminal and bully, a slumlord and rapacious abuser. I flung it all at the sky and told God I'd go to hell with this child before I'd go to "his" heaven, and that I'd suffer his damnation before I'd endure another day of his tyranny. To my surprise, I was not incinerated on the spot, but released from an inner burden, even flooded with a lightness of Spirit I had never experienced until that moment. My domination system god finally died on that mountain. For a fuller account of that story see Snyder, *Quaker Witness as Sacrament*.

also reframe theology. Gandhi understood that the problem of good and evil is not a question of opposing powers. Evil is rather the consequence of our collective willingness to keep it in place. Evil is not self-sustaining. Only Truth, a term that Gandhi used as a synonym for God, endures in a way that is independent of our cooperation. Note that he did not say that evil is not real, only that its pretense to *independent* reality is a lie. He wrote that evil "has no separate existence at all, but it is only truth or good misplaced."[30] At first glance, this sounds a great deal like the Augustinian doctrine of the *privatio boni*, or the privation of the good. However, for Augustine, the privation of good is "allowed" by his god for a greater purpose, which inevitably tangles him up in confusions about power.

Gandhi is saying something quite different. Evil, in all of its concrete and devastating manifestations, is not allowed, or in any sense willed, or even created by a god who might have created a different kind of world but chose not to. Rather evil persists because we have not awakened to a self-sustaining Truth that empowers us to dismantle evil's structures in the collective psyche as well as in its outward political systems. We have fallen under the spell of the domination system and believed its lie, one that has very real consequences in the world. Walter Wink puts it bluntly: "Paradoxically, those in the grip of the cultural trance woven over us by the domination system are usually unaware of the full depth of their soul-sickness. It is only after we experience liberation from primary socialization to the world-system that we realize how terribly we have violated our authentic personhood—and how violated we have been."[31] A lie believed collectively over many generations becomes concretized in the systems and institutions built upon it. Gandhi's God is an accessible Truth in the innermost ground of our being. The domination system god who stands outside of creation and either wields or withholds controlling power does not exist, except in our collective religious imagination. Gandhi's nonviolent God is both the deepest interiority of creation, and its encompassing whole. The domination system is a vast lie, a multigenerational, world-entangling lie whose power rests entirely in our unconscious consent.

Many theologians object to reframing God's power, the fourth leg of the theodicy animal, but their objections are the result of having failed to understand nonviolent power. I agree that theologies that envision a power-*less* god must be rejected. Supine surrender cannot in any reasonable sense be the Divine response to evil. There are various versions of this god but they are all still trapped in the domination system's assumptions about power.

30. In Mathai, *Mahatma Gandhi's Worldview*, 68–69.

31. Wink, *Engaging the Powers*, 73.

There is, for example, the version of a god that models self-sacrifice as the path to salvation. There is also a version that considers all power of any kind to be evil and, therefore, its god eschews all power for the sake of love. These gods might be mildly comforting but they are not much help. Then there is the cosmic moralist god who is unable to act except through the faithful. We are called to moral obedience. This god sounds a lot like a client I once had who felt that his only access to power was to get others to feel guilty so they would give him what he wanted. I have never found any of these gods even remotely persuasive. For me, none of them invite wholehearted prayer. I am a confirmed atheist in relation to all of them.

But Gandhi's God, that Truth which alone is self-sustained, pulls the pillars out from under the domination system, in both its inward and outward dimensions. Taking dynamic nonviolence as a model for God is to step into an organic, interrelational metaphor where the Divine is seen as working within the ecology of being. Then there is no distinction between the nonviolent revolution of the heart and nonviolent revolution in the world, for transformational processes are at work in both my deepest interiority where I open onto the Divine Presence that indwells the whole of creation, and in the larger systems that I inhabit. Inward activism and outward prayer become a seamless whole. The awakened heart is guided into a sacramental life that doesn't split them. It loves and serves and acts because that is its nature, and it is not exhausted in its efforts because it is fully awake to life's beauty, creativity, and joy, even in the midst of evil's terrifying lie and the vast systems that support it. The awakened heart simply gives what it receives. It acts vocationally, as it is called and led. We participate in a vast ecology of gifts. Like Etty Hillesum, the awakened heart will feel the "cosmic sadness" that comes with knowing evil's brutality, but also like her, we will not presume to carry it as a burden. It is not ours to carry. We will give sorrow its place. We will accept our full measure of all the emotional energies that visit, but then we will rest in our breathing and turn inward for moments of prayer. There, in the soul's quiet communion, we step into a river. We can release our suffering into those currents of Love. We can receive its inflowing of wonder, and we can be restored to joy.

PART IV

Outward Prayer

EVEN IF THE PHRASE "Inward Activism" is new, for most of us, it makes intuitive sense. We get it that some form of intentional, persistent, dedicated inner work is essential to transformation. But the phrase "outward prayer" is more of a stretch. In another time and culture, the adjective would be unnecessary, even redundant. But modernity has fallen into an ever-deepening split between the inward and outward. Exiled to interiority, prayer has been torn away from its native habitat in the body where it comes to expression in our gestures, speech, and outward actions. Rescued from its ideological entrapment and reimagined as conscious participation in the sacred wholeness of being, prayer becomes an open doorway to the source and substance of a sacramental life.

Having been unraveled from whole cloth, can prayer once again be woven back into peacemaking? The next three chapters look beyond the habits of thought and perception that limit the horizons of modernity, especially as expressed in Euro-American styles of consciousness. In these reflections on Jesus, healing, and truth, I bring into view how domination system constructs have distorted the picture, and wonder aloud about what kind of amazing world we can inhabit if we learn to live from a profound sense of our interrelatedness. On our way to that wondering, it helps to know how we got to where we are, to learn how Jesus was co-opted by empire in the fourth century, what healing looks like outside the bounds of Western consciousness, and how truth became the spoils of a bad divorce in the seventeenth century. We are shaped by ancient forces that we no longer see. Bringing them into view again might help us reawaken to our original wholeness.

CHAPTER 10

Jesus

Where Jesus lives, the great-hearted gather.[1]

—Jalāl ad-Dīn Muhammad Rūmī

Not long after we arrived in Florida posters went up around our little town announcing that there would be a tent revival out at the rodeo grounds. There was no question that we would be going. My memory of this event is mostly a series of impressions: an open field at what looked like somebody's cattle ranch, cars and pickups from the late forties and fifties parked in rows, a huge tent with thick sawdust under foot, folding chairs, handheld cardboard fans with pictures of Jesus on them, and a lot of heat and sweat. There was some singing and Bible reading, but mostly what got my attention was the preacher, who was not like anyone I had ever seen or heard before. He started off slow, but then he warmed up, pacing the stage. There was a rhythm to his words that sounded like a train leaving the station, picking up speed. There was urgency, warning, conviction, all punctuated with refrains about "JEEzuz-uh."

He said that I was mired in sin, a condition that he described as a swamp full of vipers as dangerous as those not far from where we sat. But there was hope, a lifeline, if we would but grasp it, our last chance. And then, with a shock that riveted me in my seat, the shouting began. I had never heard anything like this before. Nobody in my young life had ever made such a display of raw emotion, nor had anyone in the Friends Church my family had attended back in Indiana ever shouted back or openly cried in

1. Rumi, *Essential Rumi*, 201.

their pews. People were rocking in their seats to the cadence of the preacher's pleas, waving their arms, weeping and calling on Jesus' name. And then came the call: Come to the altar. If you are lost, alone, and scared, then come forward and receive salvation. I was all of those things, lost and alone, certainly, and especially scared, but there was nothing in me that wanted anything to do with what he was selling. There was no kindness in that preacher's voice, just fear and vivid images of hell. My brothers and I went home that night with an uneasy feeling that our young souls were just hanging out there, dangling over an abyss with no net of salvation. If we were lost, alone, and scared before that revival, we were even more so afterwards.

Years later, when I was grown and my mother was more stable, we had some wonderful conversations about faith. She acknowledged that she was disappointed in that hellfire preacher she took us to in Florida. Her Jesus was warmhearted, much like her grandfather who read Bible stories to her. She was comforted to know that I had found my own warmhearted Jesus. My brothers and I had returned to Indiana when it was clear that my mother couldn't care for us, and in the summer of my fourteenth year I attended a Quaker summer camp not far from my grandfather's farm. There was a daily worship, thoughtful counselors, and at the end of the week a preacher who said that anyone who wanted Jesus in their heart could come on up and pray. There was no fear, no threats, no talk about the depravity of our young, sweet hearts, just an invitation to come on up and get some love. I was first in line. My heart was a confused and mixed-up mess, and if Jesus wanted to move in and straighten things out, that was fine with me.

Now, I had two Jesuses, one I liked and one I didn't. As the years went by, I discovered that there are nearly countless Jesuses. Anyone with a personal or political agenda can invent a Jesus to give it religious legitimation. Biblical scholars, historians, and theologians do their best to expose flimsy reasoning and support clarity, but all of that scholarship and academic work does little to deter those bent on turning Jesus into a promoter of their own ideology.

At the end of the day, the actual, historical Jesus, who lived and taught in first-century Palestine and got himself crucified by a brutal occupying regime, resists ideological traps and rigid interpretations. I have no doubt there was an extraordinary person who inspired his followers, but the historical Jesus is hidden beneath countless layers of interpretation like so many coats of paint. We have a body of teachings, sayings, parables, and healing stories, giving us a sense of his character and vision, but these are mixed in with a variety of other elements of doubtful authenticity. Interpretations began to proliferate almost immediately after Jesus' death, so however deeply we go into the available texts, both within and outside the canon, we are almost certainly discovering just another layer of paint. What we are left with is not a Jesus of history but an image refracted through a particular writer's interests and commitments. We can be reasonably sure that each image reveals the writer, but in none of the writings do we get an unbiased picture of Jesus.

For those of us who follow him, who care about these stories and this person, Jesus is an imaginal figure in a relational field.[2] The original Light of this extraordinary person is refracted through countless lenses. Whose Jesus do we encounter: Paul's, Mark's, John's, or maybe Mary Magdalene's,[3] or the Jesus who met the woman at the well, or the Jesus of Teresa of Avila or Mother Teresa of Calcutta? In the West, our image of Jesus is likely to have been shaped more by the Roman Church than the Eastern Orthodox, and more by Augustine than the Celtic saints. In modern times, we can't help but at least notice the Jesus of Martin Luther King Jr., Dorothy Day, and Desmond Tutu, as well as the Jesus of Billy Graham, Jerry Falwell, and Jim and Tammy Faye Bakker. Whoever this singular, historical person may have been, the Jesus who now lives in the religious imagination, the Jesus we love, or hate, or are indifferent to, comes to us filtered through the lives of those who preceded us. I am inspired by some images of Jesus and appalled by others. The Jesus of my own religious imagination continually surprises me with new invitations to love, to service, to new ways of seeing and being in the world, to a deeper awakening to my own shadows, and to ongoing growth toward transformation.

I have no evangelistic impulse, no inclination to try to install my Jesus in someone else's heart. I am steeped in Quakerism and the Quaker way is to "let your life speak." This is true evangelism in any case; pushing an ideology is propaganda, not evangelism. But there are deeper reasons for my refusal to go door to door shoving tracts into the hands of unsuspecting strangers. The figure of Jesus that lives in my psyche is something like a key that can only fit the unique lock of my personality. As a therapist I have learned that

2. The term *imaginal* was introduced to depth psychology by Henri Corbin, a French scholar of Islamic mysticism. He intends the term to designate "a very precise order of reality, which corresponds to a precise mode of perception." That mode is the feature of the mind that perceives by way of images. Unfortunately, our more common term *imaginary* suggests something unreal, so Corbin uses "imaginal" to refer to an order of reality that is only perceptible by means of the imagining mind. Corbin, "Mundus Imaginalis," 1.

3. A *Gospel of Mary*, unknown for centuries, apparently written early in the second century, finally came to light in the late nineteenth century. Only a few pages exist, yet in those fragments, it is clear that this very early Christian document presents Jesus in a very different light, one that differs significantly from the Jesus enshrined in the theology of the later church. For a thorough assessment see King, *Gospel of Mary*.

I am most effective, not when I attempt to advise or persuade, but when I work at helping others find the key that unlocks their personalities and ushers them into joy and freedom. It would be ridiculous to insist that all keys and all locks must look alike.

Healthy relationships are crucibles of transformation, and that is as true in the imaginal world as it is in therapy or in a marriage. I could no more define the awakening encounter for another person than I could tell them who to love or what to dream. I have only my own story to tell. There is no conclusion to be drawn, only that who I am, and who I continually become, has been and continues to be shaped in an ongoing and evolving relationship with Jesus, whose presence has a seasoning effect on my personality. His imaginal presence was first activated in me under conditions of love and acceptance, two things I desperately needed. I have lost sight of him from time to time, but I have never had an inclination to kick him out. Why would I?

Rumi knew a greathearted Jesus and remained a Sufi. Gandhi knew a nonviolent Jesus and remained Hindu. Jesus himself lived and taught as a radical Jewish mystic, prophet, teacher, and healer. Even Paul never refers to himself as Christian, but always as a Jew and a Pharisee. Jesus will always be *before and beyond* Christianity. He is often known and followed more clearly by those outside the tradition than he is by those of us who call ourselves Christian. Within the tradition, we have a lot of sorting out to do. We have many Jesuses. Some of them are so sanitized as to be boring as wallpaper, while others have been corrupted by patriarchal, homophobic, racist, and other oppressive agendas. Of all the things that we Christians argue about, there is one question that I would pose as the most central: Whose god does your Jesus serve? I don't care whether or not you call yourself Christian, but if you're going to talk about Jesus, then I care a great deal about whether you spin your narrative toward fear or love.

Empire Christianity

In this sign, conquer.[4]

—Constantine's dream

All the best evidence suggests that Jesus placed himself in direct opposition to the driving energies of the domination system. He proclaimed love in the place of fear, nonviolence in the place of oppressive political power, and radical nonattachment in the place of greed and the unjust accumulation of wealth with its resulting oppression of the poor. It's not surprising that the domination system would be intensely invested in suppressing this Jesus, which it tried to do for the first three hundred years of the Christian era. And then the powers did what they always do; they bought out and corrupted what they could not conquer. If throwing Christians to the lions just made their love and courage more inspiring, then welcoming them into the safety and comforts of empire would finally accomplish what brutality could not. The Roman emperor Constantine did not convert to Christianity, contrary to the popular story. He converted Christianity to empire.

Some historians of Christianity are more generous toward Constantine than I am. Maybe he did have a genuine change of heart. He did, after all, build churches, establish centers of learning, redistribute some land, and feed the poor. However, he did *not* address the underlying causes of their poverty. There was nothing about Constantine's "conversion" that even remotely addressed his overwhelming political power, or undermined the sources of his wealth. But there was a lot about his conversion of Christianity into an official state religion that undermined resistance and domesticated Jesus.

Constantine had a dream, which he apparently believed, or at least told others that he believed to mean that God would give him a military victory. Whether he actually had this dream or fabricated it to serve as propaganda can't be known, but either way, what he did with its central symbol is what tyrants have been doing with the symbol of the cross ever since. He leveraged it for his own purposes, corrupting its symbolic power in the process. The cross was the very instrument that imperial Rome used to torture and execute those who posed a threat to the regime. To interpret the cross as a

4. Christian historian Diana Butler Bass writes, "In 312 the emperor Constantine (d. 337) secured his throne through military force. The night before the battle God reportedly appeared to him in a dream with a cross saying, 'In this sign, conquer.' Constantine routed the enemy and attributed the victory to the Christian God and in 313 legalized the Christian faith." Bass, *People's History of Christianity*, 132.

symbol of military victory requires a massive distortion of the image on a par with naming a nuclear submarine the *Corpus Christi*. Add to this the image of Christian bishops, all male, feasting with the emperor's delegates under armed guard in the lakeside town of Nicea, convened there at the emperor's behest for the purpose of establishing a single, orthodox, unifying ideology, and you now have a state religion complete with institutional forms, rituals, and creeds.[5] *Faith* was reduced to acceptance of a uniform ideology. The cross was sanitized of its radical confrontation of the domination system, and the poor became charity-objects bought off with just enough provision to make them dependent.

Nothing is more deadly to a movement of radical transformation than being invited into the palace and given a veneer of respectability. Constantine was shrewd enough to see clearly the dangers that Christians posed to his regime, and that continuing to throw them to the lions would just make his own brutality more evident. These early Christian martyrs, willingly, sometimes even joyfully dying for their faith, *had no more fear*, and nothing is more dangerous for a tyrant than subjects who are no longer afraid. The conversion of Christianity from a way of life and practice to an ideological cult robbed it of its radical soul. Once the conversion of Christianity to empire was complete, the brutal and bloody face of oppression could hide behind a sweet mask of piety, and Jesus disappeared behind a thick fog of distortion.

From that point on, the story of empire Christianity is a long and sordid tale of crusades, pogroms, inquisitions, and countless other examples of empire's bleak and bloody ways. Pope Alexander VI in the fifteenth century canonized the domination system even further with his toxic "doctrine of discovery," a grotesque distortion of the gospel that gave religious legitimation to conquest and genocide. Empire thoroughly absorbed Christianity into its own domination system mythology, resulting in an ideological cult that is exclusivist, dogmatic, patriarchal, and driven by missionary zeal for conquest—religious, political, and economic. Then, in a final attempt to eviscerate the Christian soul, the domination system's theology turned Jesus into a sacrificial victim of its own violent god. Empire Christianity offers ego-sustaining assurances of certainty, righteousness, and a salvation without transformation. Many of its followers are transformed anyway, which I read as a testament to the Holy Spirit's desire to flow into any heart open to it, regardless of ideology.

5. For a description of this event see Crossan, *Jesus*, 225–26. Crossan writes, "Is it time now, or is it already too late, to conduct, religiously and theologically, ethically and morally, some basic cost accounting with Constantine?"

Fortunately, there has also been another stream of Christian history, a minority report, an underground Christianity that never died out despite the oppressive ways of empire. Generative Christianity rejects the domination model and instead embraces the vision announced by Jesus as the nonviolent reign of God.[6] Were it not for this persistent, revolutionary, nonviolent remnant of radical faith, we would have to declare that the way of Jesus died in the fourth century. The faith of the early Christian community, however, persisted in this remnant that offered a way of life grounded in spiritual practice, with the goal being transformed and transforming lives. Generative Christianity never completely died out, but was forced underground and into the margins. There, it kept a candle lit while the raging beast of domination devoured the imagery, language, Scripture, culture, and symbolism of this newly emerging tradition. Sacrificial atonement was never the theology of the remnant. For them, Jesus' execution at the hands of empire, and then his resurrection, symbolized the exposure of the domination system's lies. The gods of domination and their violent mythologies were unmasked. The pillar of religious legitimation was pulled out from under empire and its bloody and oppressive ways. Jesus revealed an entirely different and revolutionary, nonviolent God in the astonishing wonder of the one he called *Abba*. Those who stood under the cross found a symbol of transformation, an awakening, and an invitation to Life. Jesus gave them a new way of seeing through the thick and distorting fog of oppression in both its inward and outward forms. The cross did not trap them in guilt; it set them free!

Given that the domination system's empire Christianity continues to be promoted in the media, by public figures, in movies, and by TV evangelists, it is small wonder that there are many sincere, good-hearted people who want nothing to do with it. They have only seen or heard of a toxic Christianity that shoves a distorted image of Jesus down the throats of anyone who has the misfortune of entering their orbit. Good people turn away from Christianity when they hear about clergy sexually abusing kids, evangelists flying around in private jets, and self-righteous preachers proof-texting Scripture to support their homophobia, sexism, racism, and self-satisfied superiority.

Do I sound angry? I hope so. My anger burns hot for those who violate the sacred, who take the very images and symbols of love and nonviolence

6. Bass describes "generative Christianity" as "a kind of faith that births new possibilities of God's love into the world. Whereas militant Christianity triumphs over all, generative Christianity transforms the world through humble service to all. It is not about victory; it is about following Christ in order to seed human community with grace." Bass, *People's History of Christianity*, 11.

and turn them into instruments of seduction, exploitation, and greed. Mine is the kind of anger reserved for those who speak of Jesus but whose lives speak hatred and fear. I am fiercely opposed to those who call themselves Christian but who have in fact stolen the tradition and poisoned it, leaving untold damage in their wake. There are many who want nothing more to do with Christianity because of them. But I'm too stubborn to abandon the field. I'm not willing to let empire Christians steal Jesus, or to let them twist and distort the words of the Bible beyond recognition. I have no issue with those who don't want to fight those battles, or with those who reject Christianity in favor of other spiritual paths, but it breaks my heart to see good people turn away from Jesus because they have never known any image of him except one so poisonous that it makes them choke on his name.

Generative Christians are leaven in the loaf, salt in the broth; they are both within and outside the traditional institutions of the church. Their nonviolent ways are evident sometimes under the very noses of the oppressors. These awakened souls, having found their way to the Divine Spring, are as fully at home sowing seeds of hope in the belly of the beast as they are outside institutional walls bearing prophetic witness. Many are well known, like Martin Luther King Jr., Dietrich Bonhoeffer, Dorothy Day, and Mother Teresa, but most are hidden in anonymity, often with a great preference for it, living lives of subversive grace. Inwardly they are sustained by a living relationship with what the Quaker Thomas Kelly called "the springs of immediacy and ever fresh divine power within the secret silences of the soul."[7] My gratitude for these Christians helps me temper my anger. The domination system murdered Jesus and then took his name, but he lives on in generative hearts.

The contrast between Jesus' teaching and domination system theology is stark and undeniable. Empire theology is *transactional*, not transformational.[8] Its patriarchal king-god sends his son who he then murders in an extreme act of ritual sacrifice deemed a necessary price of "redemption," literally a ransom, a buyout for our sins. This is very strange theology for a host of reasons: The empire god's insatiable wrath must be appeased to avoid a Divine tantrum; his son, oddly, is somehow both the incarnation of

7. Kelly, *Testament of Devotion*, 34.

8. Even *transactional* theology can be *transformational* for some believers. My argument against sacrificial atonement theology is that it is a product of empire Christianity and tends to reinforce it. However, I have worked with clients who proclaim that "Christ died for my sins" and who have found in that phrase an awakening key that has set them free from immense suffering and for profound service in the world. I take issue with the ideology but have only profound respect for the depth of those souls who have found their way by means of it.

this god and his sacrificial victim at the same time, and humanity is either frightened or seduced into distorting a healthy longing for faith into a cheap declaration of fidelity to empire ideology. This is transparent nonsense. But it serves well as religious cover for ego's attempts to ward off the costs of transformation, and it functions to legitimize oppression and to domesticate Jesus. The following are just a few of empire's distortions of Jesus' teaching:

- Ideological exclusivism replaces transformational faith.
- A patriarchal theology of the incarnation of God in a single person replaces Jesus' call to a universal, systemic incarnation.
- A theology of sacrificial atonement manipulates our small guilt over small sins so as to deflect attention from the massive systemic sins of the domination system.
- Empire Christianity makes Jesus an *object* of worship. It wants us to look *at* Jesus, not *through* him. But Jesus offers himself as a window, a lens, or perspective, inviting us to see as he sees. Empire theology wants to obscure the radically new world that comes into view when we see the world as Jesus did.
- Empire theology wants to emphasize Jesus' gender, or his piety, or portray him as a sacrificial lamb—all distractions from his prophetic voice that announces the presence of a God we never knew,[9] a God whose transformational love seeks nothing less than nonviolent revolution in both our inner and outer worlds.
- Empire Christianity anticipates a top-down domination victory that leads to world hegemony of right-wing "Christian" ideology. Generative Christianity nurtures a "bottom-up" and "inside-out" awakening to the already present Divine Spring.

As long as empire goes unchallenged in the outer world, the status quo is undisturbed, and Jesus has been safely domesticated, whitewashed, and hung on a wall. But the shadow of the idol never dies. Jesus returns in the poor, the outcast, and all those crushed by empire's relentless greed and lust for power. The teaching is clear. In the sayings, parables, healing stories, and in Jesus' own confrontations with empire, he announces that the Spring of

9. See Borg, *God We Never Knew.* In this book, Borg introduces panentheism for lay readers who may not have the inclination to read through the dense "Process philosophy" or "Philosophy of Organism" of A. N. Whitehead and others. A process theology has grown out of this movement and been richly developed by many writers. The process metaphor is deeply compatible with my focus on the critical importance of an inward/outward nonviolent revolution in soul and society.

God is immediately present, accessible within and among us. The beloved community is as close as your neighbor's hunger, accessible in the transformed heart. God's reign is at hand, already in our midst.

The world cries out for nonviolent revolution both in our hearts and in our political structures. Jesus taught this in word and deed. Then in the last hours of his life he taught in a new way, no longer with words, but by living a courageous, truthful love right in the face of a brutal Roman occupation. The story Christians return to each Easter is Jesus' most profound teaching, offered to us in his last days and what came after.

Friday

If the American empire has any similarities with that of Rome, can one really understand the theological meaning of Jesus on a Roman cross without seeing him first through the image of blacks on the lynching tree?[10]

—James Cone

The Friday that we call "good" is about a death by execution. There was nothing good about it, but we call it "Good" Friday because of the domination system's transactional theology of sacrificial atonement, a theology that obscures the reality that Jesus was executed for the single reason that the healing truths that he taught unmasked the powers, exposed the moral and spiritual bankruptcy of their gods, and cut to the root of the domination system. He was a problem for the Roman Empire so they murdered him.

Empire wears a mask of civility, but this mask is stripped off whenever its power and greed are challenged. Jesus' teaching, healing, and relentless confrontations of the domination system placed him directly in the path of empire's bloody tooth and claw. The powers didn't just kill him to get rid of him, they lynched him. It was a public torture and humiliation designed to be a warning to anyone else who might dare to challenge empire's greed and oppressive power. Cone cites a story by W. E. B. DuBois, entitled "The Son of God," that essentially retells the Jesus story in the American South: "Joshua is 'seized by a mob' that 'hanged him at sunset.' While his father, Joe, 'buried his head in the dirt and sobbed,' his mother, Mary, never loses hope and repeatedly proclaims, 'He is the Son of God.' 'Behold, the Sign of

10. Cone, *Cross and the Lynching Tree*, 63.

Salvation—a noosed rope.'"[11] Imagine the cross that hangs over countless altars. Now imagine that cross replaced by a noosed rope.

The rope and the cross are instruments of torture and execution, brutal and obscene. Yet despite knowing what it would cost him, Jesus stepped into empire's lair and poked the beast. Surely, he knew that yet another crucifixion would just add his name to a long list of domination system murders. What was the point of yet another martyr's death? None of this makes any sense unless we read the story through the lens of his teaching up until that moment, and nowhere does he speak of a transactional sacrifice. His life and teaching were all about inviting a nonviolent revolution in the core patterns that shape human perception and structure many of our institutions. Friday is the opening scene on a transformational narrative that culminated in what Walter Wink calls "an event in the history of the psyche."[12] Now, two thousand years later, empire's top-down structures of oppression are still as bloody as ever, but the Jesus story has entered the collective stream where it is seeding "bottom-up" and "inside-out" awakenings. He was not the original, nor the only teacher who taught about a revolutionary, nonviolent God, but with him there seems to have been a "tipping point." A major pillar of support has been pulled out from under the domination system's hegemony over deep structures of consciousness. Generative Christians and generative followers of other traditions are now in our collective bloodstream like a vaccine.

Fortunately, we are not all called to the literal death of a martyr, but we are all called to the journey of transformation. We cannot build a lasting nonviolent world unless we also do the inner work necessary to dismantle the false-self structures in our own minds. We are wedded to these structures, deeply attached to them. We have located our identity within them and found our security and sense of importance there. To follow Jesus through the Easter story is to see that he not only concludes his physical life on the cross; he also relinquishes the last remnants of his own ego's orbit around a god who dies with him. His death is fundamentally a psychological reality expressed in the cry, "Why have you forsaken me," and it is in this that his humanity is most fully joined with ours. We don't know what elicited this cry from Jesus, what final letting go of false hope was still necessary for him, but if we don't allow ourselves to hear his despair, and if we presume instead that his confidence never wavered, then we have made him more than human, and he is no longer one of us. Participation in this part of the story

11. Cone, *Cross and the Lynching Tree*, 106.

12. Wink, *Human Being*, 152.

calls us to see ourselves in the mirror he is holding up, and to suffer our own agonizing realization that our gods have betrayed us.

Physical death is not what truly frightens us. Ego can almost always find a way to make peace with that. Our denial of death is not about the loss of a living body, but about the loss of our gods, and the corresponding loss of an identity that is embedded in our attachments to constructs that ego uses to self-validate its life. Jesus can be the brother who helps us navigate that excruciating passage, if we let him have his humanity back, with the necessary and inevitable ego, and the necessary and inevitable letting go of ego and its attachments. We go to great lengths to avoid this picture of Jesus. We want him to be *other*, not human, not like us. Because if he is showing us what the journey to an awakened consciousness looks like, we are shocked to see how much it will cost us and how far we still have to go. Better to cling to Sunday as if Friday is merely the preamble. We want a spiritual bypass, not transformation.

Even the Gospel writers themselves are all too ready to impose their resurrection stories on the cross, as if there is something about Friday that is too unbearable to imagine unless we look backwards through a Sunday lens.[13] But this is a manic defense, a flight to the light. We can't bear the relinquishment of our gods, those egoic constructions of false hope. Jesus' vulnerability, his humanity is too close to home. We don't want to see that about him, much less about ourselves. We want to cast him as the sacrificial lamb, the designated sufferer, so as to distance ourselves as far as possible from that mirror.

This is what Mel Gibson did in his movie *The Passion of the Christ*, a film that was gruesome and shocking but ultimately trivial. It was a pornographic immersion in all of the gory details of torture and execution. The essence of pornography is a distancing of the observer, and an *objectification* of the subject being observed. Pornography separates the observer from the personal story and meaning-making experience of the person who inhabits the objectified body. Gibson's pornographic Jesus is a suffering object, to be viewed from the safety and comfort of a movie theater. Objectification is also the essence of empire theology, and the essential dynamic of oppression.

13. Only in Mark, the earliest of the Gospels, are Jesus' final words of despair, "My God, my God, why have you forsaken me?" reported with brutal finality. Yet even in Mark, commentators cannot resist adding a footnote letting us know that Jesus is merely quoting an old psalm, which ends on a note of hope. In Matthew, these words are followed by an account of dramatic supernatural events that serve as theological vindication. In Luke, this statement disappears altogether and Jesus is forgiving those who killed him, blessing those who die with him, and yielding his spirit up to God in a statement of unwavering trust. If we're reading John, then it all ends with the victorious "It is finished!"

James Cone's equation of the cross with the lynching tree is prophetic, not only because lynching exposes the raw violence of empire, but also because it exposes the domination system's fundamental dynamic: *Someone else's death* is what makes the comforts of empire possible.

Let's reject empire Christianity's objectification of Jesus and instead let the passion narratives be a *participation* story. Let Friday shatter our illusions, expose our false gods, and lay bare our persistent, secret hope that we have built our own bridge to eternity. Friday's descent into death is a stripping away. Our bridge into death is not our having believed the right things, or having done the right things, or having gained the approval of the self-appointed guardians of heaven's gate, or even having been a particularly good person. When all of our plans for self-salvation are gone, we lose all hope for heaven and all fear of hell. It never was about being good or right anyway; it was always just about being loved. We cross the bridge the only way we can, in the pure trust of the heart.

Saturday

> The dark night is a certain inflowing of God into the soul which cleanses it of its ignorances and imperfections, habitual, natural, and spiritual.[14]
>
> —St. John of the Cross

Saturday is about learning to pray in the dark. We don't yet know anything about Sunday; we are in the underworld, the land of death, learning to breathe while falling. Saturday is about learning to appreciate death's dark beauty, and the many gifts it brings that we never imagined would come to us by such excruciating means. We must learn simply to rest in the heart, and in the breath, knowing nothing, clinging to nothing, simply waiting and listening, the better to notice where we and others have built prisons for our minds and hearts. We are cast into a wilderness that requires a moment-by-moment attentiveness. Saturday is the true heart of Christian mysticism.

It is important to remember that the loss of belief does not mean that nothing is believable, only that belief is too often about a false god. The loss of hope does not mean there is no possibility of hope, only that our hopes are too often misplaced. The loss of our gods does not mean that there is no God, only that we must learn to listen with what the Buddhists

14. John of the Cross, *Dark Night of the Soul*, 75. John's mystical poems and commentary were originally composed between 1577 and 1580.

call "beginner's mind." We pray in the dark because we have left ego's well-lit house and lost all of ego's artificial lights. Having followed Jesus into the place of desolation, into the darkest of all possible nights, we must learn to inhabit the wilderness, and submit to the inflowing of Life on its own terms.

St. John of the Cross is the mystical poet and commentator who brought us the phrase "Dark Night of the Soul." He was an extraordinary explorer in the soul's wilderness, not by choice—no one chooses to experience the kind of suffering he endured—but by fate and a precociously mature spirituality. Sometime in the middle of the night, late in the sixteenth century, political forces opposed to the reformation of the Carmelite order descended upon John. He had been a protégé of Teresa of Avila, his spiritual director, who saw in him an ally in her reformation movement. By 1577, the shifting politics of the Spanish church turned against him. He was kidnapped, tortured, imprisoned, and deprived of even the simplest of life's enjoyments. But John was already a man of profound faith; an overinvestment in ego was not his condition. Because his faith was already seasoned and mature, his imprisonment plunged him ever deeper into the mysteries of Soul. He composed mystical poems, and having nothing with which to write, he committed them to memory. Then finally, in secrecy and under the cover of night, he managed to escape. Living in hiding for the next two years, John wrote down his poems. These, along with his extensive commentary, became the classic mystical texts that we now know as *The Dark Night of the Soul* and *The Living Flame of Love.*

John's descent begins, understandably, in a stripping down of all sensory attachments, for that was his actual environment, being confined in a small cell with minimal light and meager rations. His treatise, however, is not primarily about suffering, although he certainly suffers a great deal. It is rather a profound treatment of the soul's fall into a sacred darkness wherein it finds "concealment" from the devil. Now, over four hundred years later, it doesn't make sense to import into modernity John's medieval world with demons flying around attacking people. Nor can we impose the language of modern psychology onto John's writings. However, despite the differences in culture, language, and worldview, John's spiritual wisdom contains profound lessons that translate well across the generations and across cultures. Teresa of Avila, John's mentor and spiritual guide describes in her *Interior Castle* an unfolding journey that also speaks to our modern condition. John and Teresa wrote in differing styles and used different metaphors, but together, they have given us extraordinary insight into the hidden works of Love in the soul. Together, they are wise guides for Saturday's wilderness journey between Friday's death and Sunday's new life.

John is plunged into a desolation of both sense and the soul, but we must be careful here not to confuse what he calls the soul's dark night with what modern psychology calls depression.[15] If John experienced anything that a modern therapist would see as depression, he did not write about it. Rather, his journey was into a profound darkness of the soul where, as in Dante's opening lines to *The Divine Comedy*, "the true way was wholly lost." He is not spared Friday's excruciating loss of all his gods. He loses all of his ideological bearings and is forced to fall into the pure trust of the heart. He falls into uncharted territory where he must wait for the Breath of Life to animate him moment by moment. He suffers terribly, and his journey can be instructive for ours. On Friday, our gods get killed off and we lose our bearings; we get lost in a dark wood. However, with John and Teresa as our guides, we can learn to walk with suffering in a way that does not activate all our abandonment fears. When ego is forced to relinquish its certainties, we have a choice. We can cling ever more desperately to the false hope of a familiar but limited world, or we can follow the trailhead into the wilderness where we must learn a moment-by-moment trust of the heart. This is where many of us are on the journey. We know Friday's terrible suffering, and we have had some glimpses of Sunday, but we mostly inhabit Saturday's wilderness. We are in the desert, somewhere between Friday's suffering and Sunday's promised land.

John teaches that the soul enters its dark night when it descends into a secrecy so profound as to fall out of reach of ego altogether. If I may translate John into my nonviolent model of the self, I would say that John's two dark nights, the first of sense, the second of the soul, parallel ego's descent.[16] The first part of the journey comes with ego's fall into the transitional self where it must fully face the shadow, and learn humility. The second comes with the transitional self's fall into Soul where every notion, name, image, belief, and sense of God is stripped away and we fall into a depth so profound that no light can search it. In John's *Dark Night of the Soul* every self/god constellation has finally been emptied out, a condition that the mystical theologians call the *kenosis* of God.

15. *Depression* is an imprecise term since there are many different kinds of depression with many different etiologies, some purely genetic, organic, or chemical in origin, some psychodynamic, and some spiritual, and all of these commonly overlap one another. The best treatments look through multiple lenses, body, mind, and Soul.

16. John speaks of *the* soul in a sense that suggests he means the whole person. I am proposing a different model of the personality in which *Soul* (capitalized and without the article *the*) is more of a dynamic opening onto the Divine Spring. Despite these differences in terminology, I believe we are speaking of the same spiritual dynamic. John comes to a place of ongoing encounter where he finds an inflowing of God animating his being.

The paradox of kenosis is that emptying is not negation but opening. There is a final breaking of the idols, images, and names that freeze lived experience into concretized form. When the idols finally break, we awaken to No-Thing-Ness. Buddhist scholar Masao Abe says that "[Christianity can share] with Buddhism the realization of absolute nothingness as the essential basis for the ultimate. This can be accomplished through the notion of the kenotic God—not through losing Christianity's self-identity, but rather through deepening its spirituality."[17] However, many of us are confused by this notion of Nothingness; to us it always sounds like a prescription for despair. But this is ego's worry. Soul finds its true home there and can only speak of it paradoxically—death becomes life, emptiness becomes fullness, and darkness becomes light.

Teresa's imagery also takes us along this path, although by means of different metaphors. She takes us through a description of trials and temptations that we might understand as ego's gradually yielding to the inward work of Love. We pass through various chambers or anterooms on the way to the innermost center where God dwells. In the fifth chamber, or "Dwelling," she compares the soul to a silkworm, which in its maturity, "begins to build the house where it will die."[18] Her language becomes paradoxical, as mystical language always does. There is a complete dissolution and then a reformation in the silkworm's transformation into a butterfly through union with the Beloved.

For Teresa, there is ultimately a "Divine marriage," a union with the Beloved, "But in total union no separation is possible."[19] Eventually, even the butterfly dies "with the greatest joy because Christ is now her life."[20] This condition is one of "darkness" but only because in union with the Beloved, both the soul and God are obscure. There can be no sensible perception when all separation has been overcome. Teresa says, "We are conditioned to perceive only external light. We forget that there is such a thing as inner light, illuminating our soul, and we mistake that radiance for darkness."[21] Thus, for both John and Teresa, the descent into the dark night is an unbroken fall into mystery, into depths beyond ideologies, beyond ancient patternings of thought, beyond even ideas about the soul itself. For John and Teresa, God is dark. Their God is obscure, like Rilke's. But theirs is not a *dark god*, like Jung's. Both John and Teresa reach beyond the psyche's *imago Dei*, and

17. Abe, "Kenotic God," 17.
18. Teresa of Avila, *Interior Castle,*128.
19. Teresa of Avila, *Interior Castle,* 269.
20. Teresa of Avila, *Interior Castle,* 270.
21. Teresa of Avila, *Interior Castle,* 261.

relinquish attachment even to inner states, to feelings, consolations, spiritual experiences, to images and visitations. All these disappear in the Beloved Union. We indwell God, who indwells us.

Both John and Teresa fall into the No-Thing-Ness of God, the very *kenosis* that saves them from attachment to an image or idea. Perhaps No-Thing-Ness is the ultimate groundless ground where all spiritual paths meet. Out of that No-Thing-Ness comes an inflowing of Love. Darkness becomes Light. Not a visible light, but rather a "Living Flame of Love." It is in this darkness that love emerges as a "sweet burn" and "delicious wound."[22] John falls through the bottom of his spiritual darkness into an inexpressible peace. His spiritual intuitions defy speech and can only be spoken of with difficulty because, as he says, "they relate to matters so interior and spiritual as to baffle the powers of language."[23] They both touch the place of the soul's full opening into the Divine Spring. In this awakened state, Teresa has a vision of the Christ child who asks her, "Who are you?" and she replies, "I am Teresa of Jesus, who are you?" And he replies, "I am Jesus of Teresa."[24] John finds that he is "undiscovered by the evil one," for evil can find no entry into the non-dual mind. It finds nothing there to support it. There are no more devils to pray for. Finally, in Teresa, we find her amused: "These metaphors make me laugh at myself. I'm not satisfied with them, but I can't come up with any others. Think whatever you want. What I have said is true."[25] Friday's entry into the wilderness becomes a free fall into the soul's dark night on Saturday. And then, out of bottomless depths, there comes for John a "Living Flame," and for Teresa, laughter and inexpressible joy.

Sunday

> Until we pour ourselves in the story, until we become the story in ourselves, in our blood, flesh, and bones, it doesn't fully come alive.[26]
>
> —Adyashanti

John's living flame of love and Teresa's irrepressible joy arise out of unfathomable depths. They lived the story in their blood, flesh, and bones. Their writings

22. John of the Cross, *Dark Night,* 162.
23. John of the Cross, *Dark Night,* 161.
24. Starr, "Introduction," in Teresa of Avila, *Interior Castle,* 10.
25. Teresa of Avila, *Interior Castle,* 275.
26. Adyashanti, *Resurrecting Jesus,* 225–26.

are important because they show us that, like them, we too can reach to the bottom of our disorder and find new life, new passion for living, and new joy. Sunday's awakening is a surprise, a pure gift that arrives from somewhere far outside our horizons of perception. Mary comes to the empty tomb and believes that she has not only lost Jesus but that even the opportunity to dress his body for burial has been taken from her. She pleads with a man she takes to be a gardener to tell her where they have taken his body. She does not recognize Jesus until he calls her name: "Mary." And she responds, "Rabboni!"[27] It is a moment of awakening, of love recognized and restored, a homecoming to the Beloved. Like Mary at the empty tomb, we are in desolation, in grief, all hope is lost. And then, astonishingly, Love once again calls our name.

I cannot emphasize strongly enough that the story that begins with Friday's agony and comes to its surprising joy on Sunday is a participation story. It offers a narrative structure and mythic depth that precisely describes the soul's journey to awakening. It is a harrowing journey. The Apostles' Creed states that between the crucifixion and resurrection, Jesus descends into the land of the dead. Adyashanti writes, "When self is annihilated, there is often a temporary sense of living in ashes, living among the dead."[28] There is no more hope for a recentering of ego. That which rises is carried into being solely on the currents of Love. But this is intensely disorienting because we don't know how to live without drives, goals, agendas, and ego's meaning-making programs. Adyashanti goes on: "It's not immediately clear what life is going to look like. One's whole sense of passion and of drive belongs to the self, to the ego, even when it's very positive or for the benefit of all beings. It's very hard to convey what moves you when all of that is gone."[29] There is still a life to be lived, even after all the drama of our personal story falls away. But it is a life that cannot be grasped within our usual frames of reference. We surrender to mystery and to wonder.

Ego hates surrender, so it is no surprise that it has many devices for warding off the call to transformation. Spiritual bypass, a quick leap to Sunday, is an immense temptation for many. Another is the objectification of Jesus. Not only do we make him the designated sufferer on Friday, we also make him the designated awakened one on Sunday. We want to keep the focus on Jesus' journey and not our own. Objectification, literalism, and the trivialization of myth as merely a quaint story are all defenses, as is a preoccupation with the physical resurrection of Jesus' body. As will become clear in the next chapter, I am perfectly comfortable with the idea that Jesus

27. John 20:14–16.

28. Adyashanti, *Resurrecting Jesus*, 192.

29. Adyashanti, *Resurrecting Jesus*, 193.

reanimated his physical body, but I do not anchor my faith in it. If we can relax these defenses and read the passion narratives as Jesus' most profound teaching, then we will understand why he insisted that the Teacher must go so that the Spirit may come.[30] He sees our temptation to make it all about him. He wants to make it all about us.

At the heart of the matter is our surrender to Love's refining fire, and awakening to its irrepressible joy. Transformed lives become transforming presences in the world. This is not to suggest that the good works that rise from a literal, moral, or political reading of the gospel are without value. I only want to insist that our world is at a critical point of emergence and we can no longer afford to be guided by frames that fail to reach the bottom of the disorder. Our world calls for a profound awakening, a leap forward in our collective evolution of consciousness that will be characterized by a critical mass of people living sacramental lives.

Sunday's awakening is in invitation to such a life. Prayer is made visible in how we live and act. Suffering persists. The question is not whether we suffer, but how. Obviously, we want to relieve the personal and political conditions of suffering, but the outward condition never tells the whole story. We can no longer afford to split the inward/outward journey, even less to pit them against one another. The mythic journey from Friday to Sunday allows us to carry our suffering in a new way, and to live in the midst of a suffering world with a new simplicity and creativity.

The world did not change while we were in the midst of Friday's death or Saturday's descent into the dark night. But now we can meet the world with an open heart rather than a fearful one. Sunday, of course, is followed by Monday, or as the Zen proverb puts it, "after enlightenment, the laundry." Nothing has changed, and yet everything has changed. We begin to see creation and the human family with new eyes and we begin to see people living sacramental lives all around us. They are far more common than we realize. None of them are saints, nor are they spared the struggles that go with every human journey, but they are in our midst. We recognize them because they always seem to stir something awake in others. There is always some invitation to connection. Something in them always leans in the direction of kindness, toward compassion rather than judgment, more toward love than fear.

When not animated by the Fountain of Life, our programs for psychological and political change are often little more than sophisticated cover for the soul sickness that lies hidden under the fierce defenses we deploy against the dying and rising that is the true ground of healing. I raise this challenge

30. John 16:7.

to my brothers and sisters on the political right and the political left, to my brothers and sisters of color as well as to those who share my Euro-American ancestry, to my Christian family across the full spectrum, and to all those within the psychotherapy community who want to serve healing more than cure. We are addicted to our political, psychological, and religious ideologies and our addictions are killing us. Our backs are against the wall, and neither the New Being,[31] nor the emerging world can come to birth unless we take the first step of admitting our powerlessness and embracing a new willingness to surrender to the journey of transformation. Awakened lives are free, no longer trapped in ideological prisons. They enjoy a new creativity, love, and joy that can break free of institutional walls and tribal constraints.

Paradoxically, it was a group of cloistered Trappist monks who taught me this. They certainly believed things; they lived moral lives and followed the Benedictine Rule, but they didn't preach or moralize, and they understood that the Rule is there to serve Life and not the other way around. I find it both instructive and amusing that some of my most profound learning about Jesus was gained in the presence of nine men who didn't talk about him! In fact, they didn't talk at all! But their love and joy were unmistakable. They laughed their scapulars off when I backed their dump truck with a full load of dirt into a ditch. Fr. Joseph, who was prior at the time, gathered the whole community together to dig me out. Brother Bernie made some sandwiches and Brother George coordinated the work. Even Brother Raphael came down from his hermitage to grab a shovel. The rule of silence was broken for the essentials like organizing the tasks and teasing their Quaker guest. Forgiveness was abundant without being spoken. Jesus was present without being named. The Trappists taught me that the Jesus of so much talk is not the Jesus who has risen in our hearts and is a trickster and a shape-shifter, a fox in the henhouse of our certainties. From Vigils to Compline, we kept our hearts open to the one whose own heart was so radically open to the Divine Spring. My brother monks were happy to be lost in the wilderness with Jesus. The cloister actually intensifies the wilderness; it was never meant to keep it out.

The resurrection does not deny death, but rather dances with it, and it calls us to dance with our own death, to embrace it, and to find in this mysterious partner, new ways to dance with life. The Jesus journey falls through death into the dark night, all the way into No-Thing-Ness. Everything empties out, including the tomb. No thing is there. Then, in the days following, our hearts begin to burn.[32] There is new Life, Fire, and Joy.

31. 2 Cor 5:17.

32. Luke 24:32.

CHAPTER 11

Walking on Water

I will open my mouth in parables,
I will utter things hidden since the creation of the world.[1]

Peter could have stayed in his boat and just admired Jesus from afar. He was amazed to see him walking toward him across the water. The disciples were at first terrified, and then astonished, and even more convinced of this man's extraordinary teaching. But as understandable as those states are, fear and then amazement, these can be experienced without much risk. Clinging to his boat, Peter could have marveled at Jesus, seeing him as someone with special powers, and he would not have had to give up anything about his own identity, or his sense of how the world works for him and the rest of us mere mortals. But the story takes a surprising turn. Peter calls out to Jesus and wants to meet him on the water. Jesus invites him out of the boat, and then Peter himself walks on the water until fear overcomes him and he starts to sink.[2] It's all on the line for Peter—certainly his familiar world and the identity he had formed within it—but also all of his background assumptions about the way things are. He bets it all—the grand wager—identity, purpose, meaning, life itself. The surprise in the story isn't that Peter started to sink into the waves but that he stepped out of the boat at all, and even walked a few steps. For me, the story holds the full drama, some would say foolishness, of leaving ego's familiar world, and casting one's life onto the waters of the Spirit.

1. Matt 13:35.
2. Matt 14:25–31.

Perhaps because I'm fascinated by dreamwork and have seen how dreams can initiate processes that lead to profound healing, I have a preference for reading such stories as if they were dreams. I don't want to discount other approaches; I only want to add this one to our tool kit. Dreams often present in a matter-of-fact way events that the waking ego would never accept. Walking on water? Sure. Being chased by lions? Why not? Final exams are today and you didn't know? Ok. Dreams suspend everyday reality so as to place us within narratives that challenge fundamental assumptions. Dreams, like parables, show us that we are never located in just one story. We do not have to be trapped by a single, rigid narrative about who we are or what is possible for our lives. If we listen and are willing to suspend our taken-for-granted certainties, dreams and parables can confront our illusions about ourselves, alert us to shadows, and awaken us to surprising new ways of seeing the world and our place in it.

Usually, our prayers for healing are little more than pleas for Jesus to hurry up and get in the boat so we can be healed where we sit. We want faith without risk, on our terms. We're happy to be astonished at Jesus, but we don't want to give up what is familiar, safe, and comfortable. But the call to faith is radical. Step out onto the water. That's what I hear in the story. Whether or not such stories are actual historical events is secondary. After all, what's the point of a story about raising Lazarus from the dead?[3] Surely, he eventually grew old and died again. These accounts are teaching tales. Stories about raising the dead, or restoring sight to the blind or healing a case of paralysis, when read like a newspaper report, might be occasions for astonishment but they do not awaken the soul. When read as parables, however, they can fundamentally shift our perceptions of the conditions within which we navigate the soul's journey.

I find, for example, in the healing of the ten lepers,[4] a cautionary tale about getting the cure but missing the healing. All ten were freed of their affliction, but only one came back with gratitude and curiosity. Ten were cured but only one was healed. What about the nine? They received the gift but left it unopened.

I find in the story of the paralytic healed by the pool at Bethesda a tale of awakening.[5] He was firmly fixed in his victim identity, and firmly fixed in his beliefs about the source of healing being in the troubled waters. But Jesus cracked open all of that and the man walked away from the pool without ever getting wet. If Jesus had picked him up and carried him to the

3. John 11:44.

4. Luke 17:11–19.

5. John 5:1–8.

water, he might have been cured, but then he also would have been even more firmly fixed in his delusions. Jesus asks him if he wants to be healed. This seems like an odd question to ask. The man has been waiting there for thirty-eight years! But Jesus isn't asking if he wants to be cured; his question is about whether he is ready to be transformed. He offers him a way of *no longer being paralyzed by an idea*.

I take from this that for all of our efforts to fix, cure, repair, reform, serve, and otherwise try to make the world a better place, if we are not even more deeply committed to awakening, our good works will not ultimately address the underlying limitations of consciousness. *How* we see shapes *what* we see and even what we can imagine for our future. An outward cure will not make much of a lasting difference if the underlying consciousness is not also transformed. Freud discovered early in his career that an unresolved complex will inevitably re-create the world it envisions in an endless repetition compulsion. Unfortunately, this is a dynamic that is true collectively as well as for individuals. It is the unconscious narrative that shapes what we see, and keeps us trapped in stories that are too small for the soul. It is testament to the power of the unconscious that even with a dramatic cure, nine former lepers are still not healed, or that a man sitting by a pool for thirty-eight years still must be asked if he really wants healing. We want a cure for our physical, psychological, and political ills, but we don't want to get out of our physical, psychological, or political boats. We want to define the terms of our healing. We think it's great that Jesus can walk on water, but what does that have to do with me? We want to get Jesus off the water and into the boat so he can help us out. But none of the healing stories are just about cure; there is always an invitation to walk on the water, always the invitation to transformation. Awakening is the real healing, and sometimes we get a cure as well.

In another story, Jesus makes mud out of dirt and spit and rubs it on a blind man's eyes.[6] There is clearly an action, though not one that any modern ophthalmologist would endorse, and our habit is to read this story as a tale about cause and effect, a healer and the healed. But let's not get too literal. What if Jesus' actions are not causative, but ritual enactments intended to draw attention into depths beyond the surface of the action itself? This is really the nature of ritual, after all. Rituals are not simple transactions but symbolic enactments intended to awaken consciousness. If Jesus had rubbed some medicinal plant in the man's eyes, the story would make more sense as an account of cause and effect. But why mud and spit? As symbolic elements they associate to things most of us would prefer to avoid. Jesus is

6. John 9:6.

always lifting up the exile, the poor, the outcast in the political world, and he is always exposing the shadow in the inner world. What does he want to "rub in our eyes," what does he want us to see?

Our habits of interpretation tempt us to see healing events as involving a specially gifted healer, someone who knows secret techniques or has special knowledge and powers. But Jesus seems to assume that anyone can do it, and even scolds us when we fail to take him at his word. There is even one story in which Jesus himself is entirely passive. He is not actively engaged at all; he is simply an awakened being whose mere presence becomes an occasion for healing. The story is about a woman who was healed merely by touching his garment as he passes by.[7] Jesus is on his way elsewhere, doing nothing other than walking by. He notices that someone touched him and was healed. He doesn't even know who it was but has to ask, "Who touched me?" Then when he sees who it was, he credits her for her own healing. Most of our translations have him saying "Your faith has made you whole," but this too can easily be read as transactional, as if just believing or trusting in the right way is a causative agent. But I suspect that Jesus was not talking about causality at all, but rather commenting that someone whose consciousness has awakened naturally participates in the ever-flowing stream of God.

Although my interpretive preference is to read these stories as parables and dreams, I also want to affirm that I suspect that they are also historical accounts. Most biblical scholars agree on the authenticity of the healing stories. But it isn't only the scholarly consensus that persuades me; it is also because I know that such accounts are present in all religious traditions, and in many anecdotal accounts past and present. Most people, given assurances that they will be taken seriously, will report personal experiences of healing or other extraordinary events. Grace-filled occasions of protection, provision, healing, and guidance are hidden in plain sight, one of our best-kept secrets that most people don't talk about unless they're sure you won't think they're crazy. Jesus didn't seem to care about that. He taught and healed, and proclaimed good news for the poor. He knew that the domination system would eventually kill him, but he did it anyway. He was deeply attuned to interior and collective dynamics that many shamans, sages, teachers, and healers across the centuries have known about, but that are hidden to those of us who cling to our boats. Having eyes, we do not see. We are paralyzed by our ideas.

7. Matt 9:20; Mark 5:27; Luke 8:44.

The Inside-Out World

To indigenous people, matter is the skin of Spirit,
a permeable boundary between the dimensions.[8]

—Malidoma Patrice Somé

A Brazilian doctor performs "psychic surgery," without anesthesia. A Native American healer has a dream that leads him to the medicinal plant that he needs to heal his patient. Dagara healers from West Africa see their ancestors, sometimes physically present and embodied, sometimes in spirit form. Some southern Appalachian Pentecostal Christians handle poisonous snakes, speak in tongues, and claim dramatic healings.

Anyone can dismiss such stories as the naïve fantasies of the gullible, tales told by a "primitive" imagination. I prefer an approach that combines healthy skepticism with an open-minded willingness to be shocked into a new way of seeing. Some claims about extraordinary phenomena are certainly embellished if not invented outright. But I am not convinced they all are. Events that are unexplainable by conventional understandings of the natural world are ancient, enduring, and appear across cultures and in all religious traditions. Knowing that we "see" according to socially constructed patterns of perception that are enshrined in culture and language, patterns that may obscure more than they reveal about reality, I am willing to accept that there's more going on than meets the eye.

Modernity, that is, the worldview that emerged in Western European consciousness following Descartes and the unfolding of the age of science and technology, has erected an apparently impenetrable barrier between the inward and outward worlds of human experience. This view has dominated Western thought but it has never been without its challengers. Baruch Spinoza, a brilliant Sephardic Jewish philosopher and contemporary of Descartes, was already unwilling to separate mind and matter to the extreme degree that Descartes did, even at the beginning of modernity, and later philosophers continued to revise Descartes's radical dualism. Contemporary philosophers, as well as advances in modern science, have shown that Cartesian dualism obscures more than it reveals. Of course, indigenous people don't need advances in Western philosophy and science to tell them that there can be no separation between body, mind, heart, and soul. They have known this for centuries. But those of us with Western European ancestry are just beginning to learn that we can no longer separate the inward

8. Somé, *Healing Wisdom of Africa*, 63.

and outward. Important distinctions can be made without separation; we can acknowledge that sometimes one is in the foreground and the other in the background. But extreme dualism is no longer tenable.

We have much to learn from people whose Spirit-based worldviews have not been colonized to extinction by Western European insistence on privileging the perspective of the detached observer. Throughout history, across religious traditions, and among contemporary indigenous cultures, there have been and continue to be shamans, healers, and adventurers in multidimensional worlds for whom what we call extraordinary phenomena are actually the ordinary and expectable outcomes of certain ancient and refined spiritual practices. The Dagara people of West Africa, for example, according to Malidoma Somé, a healer and teacher from that tradition, understand the visible world as the outward "skin" of the invisible. He says, "Ritual is the principal tool used to approach that unseen world in a way that will rearrange the structure of the physical world and bring about material transformation."[9] The boundary between the inward and outward is permeable and that which is out of order in the spirit world will be disordered in the more visible worlds of personal and communal life.

Many of Jesus' followers claim that, like Dagara ancestors, he walked physically among them after his death. He also healed the sick and raised the dead, and then said that we should go and do likewise. Really!? I am one of those readers of the Gospels who wants to take these things seriously, but I've never had much luck raising the dead or walking on water. I get annoyed at Jesus' tone of exasperation in his "Oh you of little faith!" And then I remember that he is the Teacher, and I'm the student, so I try to listen again with less annoyance and more willingness to hear what is being asked of me. The clear implication is that Jesus sees, knows, and experiences a reality that I am blind to, and that he obviously expects, even demands, that I get out of my boat of assumed certainties and walk on the waters of the Spirit. It isn't the magic trick that interests me. Literally walking on water seems like bending spoons. There's not much point to it and it's hard on the spoon. But I am endlessly fascinated by the invitation. Jesus' teaching is an unmistakable indictment of my world. What am I not seeing? What is the direction of inquiry and spiritual growth that would bring me a little bit closer to his way of seeing?

Perhaps our learning to see everything around us and within us as an inclusive, multidimensional, relational universe will be the next evolutionary advance in consciousness. Perhaps when we can see that everything is woven into an interconnected ecology of being, and that what we take to be

9. Somé, *Healing Wisdom of Africa*, 23.

our individual life is actually a precipitate of the interweaving of our collective life in Soul, perhaps then we will finally be able to answer Jesus' call to "go and do likewise." This kind of transformation of consciousness goes to the root of everything we take for granted. We understandably cling to the cultural world we've learned to inhabit because of its familiar orientation in time and space, and especially because it comes with a secure sense of identity. But if we are willing to risk awakening to an interconnected, relational, ecological world, then the call to a loving partnership world would just make sense. Perhaps then we would not see extraordinary events as something requiring special healing powers, or as an intervention from above, but simply as the natural outward expression of profound work in the unseen world.

Those of us who have been socialized within the collective background of thought that has dominated Western European worldviews since the Enlightenment have a lot of work to do. The first step is to consider loosening our grip on certain fundamental assumptions that are the "common sense" of our culture. As these begin to fall away, and we begin to see with new eyes, we might hear the question, "Having eyes do you not see?" as another way of saying that extraordinary phenomena are extraordinary only to eyes that have not yet learned to see from the perspective of the nonviolent soul.

Scientific Materialism

The whites always want something; they are always uneasy and restless.
We do not know what they want. We do not understand them.
We think that they are mad.[10]

—Ochwiay Biano
Elder of the Taos Pueblo

The dominant ideology of Western, technological culture, the view that emerged during the Enlightenment, is characterized by "scientific materialism." Alfred North Whitehead, originator of the philosophy of organism, or "process" philosophy, defines it as a "fixed scientific cosmology that presupposes the ultimate fact of an irreducible brute matter, or material, spread throughout space in a flux of configurations."[11] Science brings wonderful blessings of curiosity and discovery, and the benefits of inquiry into the

10. Biano in Jung, *Memories, Dreams, Reflections*, 248.

11. Whitehead, *Science and the Modern World*, 17.

properties of the material world. But scientific *materialism* is a worldview that makes ideological assumptions about the world's essential nature. Whitehead rejects the assertion that matter is "brute," "ultimate fact," and "irreducible." "In itself such a material is senseless, valueless, purposeless. It just does what it does do, following a fixed routine imposed by external relations which do not spring from the nature of its being."[12] Scientific materialism reduces the world to inanimate matter.

Anything spiritual has no place in such a world, so must be denied, explained away as "primitive" fantasy, or exiled to another world, a supernatural realm, split off from the everyday world we inhabit. When the living soul of the world is excluded from our perceptual field, we see only the surface of things, objectified as brute, irreducible, senseless, valueless, and without intrinsic purpose. Devoid of subjectivity, the material world is simply an insentient object passively subject to manipulation, responsive only to externally imposed forces, and available for exploitation. It is no wonder that this attitude, imported onto the American continent by European colonizers, would appear to the native people as sheer insanity. Ochwiay Biano's words, which were spoken in a conversation with C. G. Jung when he visited the American West in 1925, were further explained when Jung asked him why he thinks the whites are mad:

> They say that they think with their heads, he replied.
> Why of course. What do you think with? I asked him in surprise.
> We think here, he said, indicating his heart.[13]

Many indigenous people around the world do not merely have a different picture of the world, they also have a different relational stance within it, and a spiritual "technology" for engaging forces that are invisible and inaccessible to those of us who can only think with our heads. Beings move in and out of visibility and meaningful coincidences occur among apparently unrelated events, a phenomenon for which Jung coined the term *synchronicity*. Malidoma Somé says that "countless illnesses that could not be healed at the local infirmary . . . were perfectly curable at the hands of Dagara healers."[14] A dismissive attitude toward such things begins to appear not only ignorant but arrogant. We have eyes but we cannot see. We are blinded by our cultural assumptions. We are not trapped by matter but by materialism.

12. Whitehead, *Science and the Modern World*, 17.
13. Jung, *Memories, Dreams, Reflections*, 248.
14. Somé, *Healing Wisdom of Africa*, 7.

When extraordinary events do occur, they present Western consciousness with a massive problem. Typically, we pretend we don't see them, or we try to explain them in ways that don't challenge our worldview. But when they intrude into awareness in ways that are so vivid as to be undeniable, and unexplainable, our last resort for avoiding a transformation of worldview is to invent a special category to account for them. Thus, we call extraordinary events "miracles." Our materialism presupposes the existence of laws that only miracles can set aside. But the implicit theology behind miracles requires an empire god who intervenes from somewhere outside and above creation. As we have already seen, the domination system's gods come with a Pandora's box full of excruciating questions like, why are some healed and not others, and is there something wrong with me or my faith, given that I have not been healed? We are thrown back into wondering why God "allows" suffering to persist for some and not others. Spirituality loses all vitality. Some abandon all hope. Others cling to hope in an empire god that they secretly doubt could possibly exist. Some, however, will learn to see with new eyes.

Fortunately, we are getting help from emerging discoveries in science, and from new perspectives in both the philosophy of science and religion. New discoveries that cannot be explained within the Cartesian paradigm are being paired with emerging postmodern theologies, and together they are overcoming the science/religion split that has plagued modernity for almost four hundred years. In addition, new approaches to cultural anthropology, as well as insights arising from studies in the sociology of knowledge and from depth psychology, are all contributing to a growing willingness to question some of our most fundamental assumptions about the nature of reality. Those of us steeped in a Western, Eurocentric, Cartesian, domination system mentality are beginning to see that the detached, analytic mind, the mind that objectifies what it sees, commits what Whitehead called "the fallacy of misplaced concreteness,"[15] that is, it takes what is essentially an abstraction, or an interpretation, for concrete reality.

What seems to be happening, concurrently in the worlds of science, philosophy, religion, and depth psychology, is a revolution in epistemology, that is, in how we think about the processes by which we come to know something. Most of us adopt what is called "naïve realism," classically expressed by Samuel Johnson. The eighteenth-century British literary scholar didn't like the idealist philosophy of Bishop George Berkeley, who favored the idea that reality is more mind than matter. With what I imagine must have been a tone of superiority if not contempt, Johnson declared that he

15. Whitehead, *Science and the Modern World*, 51.

could prove Berkeley wrong simply by kicking a stone. We've come a long way since then. Ian Barbour, a leading scholar in the dialogue between science and religion, trained in both physics and theology, writes, "There is, in short, *no uninterpreted experience* of the sort which the positivist posits. We don't simply see; we 'see as.' In the act of perception, the irreducible 'data' are not isolated patches of colour or fragmentary sensations, but total patterns in which interpretation has already entered."[16] Scientific materialism is an interpretive habit. It conditions us to treat the whole world like Johnson's stone. Only certain kinds of experience are possible within the horizons of its perceptual field. Extraordinary experience requires a wider perceptual field and a different consciousness. By now, you will not be surprised to hear that I believe that emerging styles of consciousness fit within my four-quadrant model.

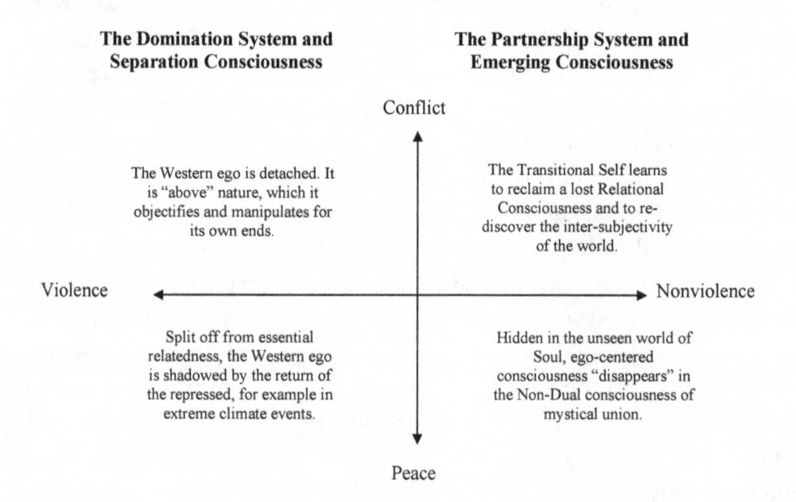

16. Barbour, *Myths, Models, and Paradigms*, 120.

Separation Consciousness

> The idols are tough and hard to crack, but through the first real fissure we make in them we find ourselves looking, how deeply, into a new world![17]
>
> —Owen Barfield

The everyday science that impacts our lives is essential, incredibly helpful, and we can't do without it. It is like the ego in that regard, also essential, helpful, and we can't do without it. The parallels don't stop there. Also like the ego, modern technology casts a shadow. The ego/shadow constellations in the inner world are writ large in the world of technology. All is well, as long as ego finds its proper relationship to Soul, for then the shadow can come into view. But everything goes off the rails when ego is cut off, inflated, when it denies the shadow and ignores Soul. Likewise, science without Soul casts a shadow that is immense, dangerous, and potentially catastrophic. We have a long list of reasons, from climate collapse to nuclear proliferation, to insist that the work of reconnecting science and Soul is more urgent than ever.

"Science" has an interesting etymology. The Latin *scientia*, or knowledge, derives from the root *scire*, which is the common root for precision, incision, excision, decision, and, of course, scissors. In each case, something is being cut, divided, separated out from the general field so as to be examined in its presumed individuality. The Western ego itself has also been carved out from nature. Phenomenologist and depth psychologist Robert Romanyshyn finds the separate self emerging in the invention of linear perspective painting in the early fifteenth century. Prior to this invention, paintings depicted a world in which both the painter and the viewer are embedded in the scene. But, according to Romanyshyn, "with the advent of linear perspective vision we have managed to spatialize time, to distance ourselves from the body, and to remove ourselves from the midst of things."[18] David Abram finds the first hints of this emergence of an ego carved out from nature in the transition from pictographic to alphabetic writing, as far back as 1500 BCE: "The senses that engaged or participated with this new writing found themselves locked within a discourse that had become exclusively human. Only thus, with the advent and spread of phonetic writing, did the rest of nature begin

17. Barfield, *Saving the Appearances*, 72.

18. Romanyshyn, *Technology as Symptom and Dream*, 36.

to lose its voice."[19] I suspect an even more ancient origin in the advent of the domination system.

Fast-forward to modernity and we find a modern Western ego, and a scientific-technological world, both of which are formed in an artificial separation from our native embeddedness in the world. Separation consciousness has emerged as a worldview that requires the observing subject to split off and stand apart from the observed world. The world becomes object, from *ob* ("in front of," or "against") and *iacere* ("to throw"), a root shared with e-ject, re-ject, and of course, pro-jectile. Separation consciousness is always dissecting things, like bodies, and splitting things, like atoms, and then throwing them apart and sometimes against one another. The stance of the Western ego is to stand apart from and unrelated to that which is objectified. There are obvious benefits to this stance because what separation consciousness can dissect and analyze, it can also sometimes manipulate until all the parts work better. Our modern medical and technological world is the direct result.

The blessings of science are obvious. When I consult with my cardiologist, I'm very happy for her to see my heart as a pump and my arteries as plumbing. I count on her to let me know if the plumbing is clogged or the pump needs some new parts. If I ever need surgery, I want a focused and competent mechanic. But I am on a quest to push the horizons out beyond the technical fix. I want to know what the shamans and faith healers know that I don't. This is dicey territory, in part because there's so much snake oil in it that it can be a challenge to sort out the nonsense from the profound, the merely weird from the truly wise. But I believe there is treasure in that field. I also know that the shadow of the Western ego and the scientific-technological world is extremely costly. The ego formed in separation consciousness is cut off, alienated, isolated, and alone in a cosmos imagined as impersonal and devoid of subjectivity. We long for a reanimation of the world, a restoration of our place in the family of things.

Sometimes in order to see a new world we have to get out of the boat and walk on the water of the Spirit. Listening, reaching out for the Guide, suspending all our certainties, and allowing our familiar narratives of place, identity, meaning, and vocation to drop away so as to look deeply into a new world—these are the disciplines of a wilderness spirituality. But "the idols are tough and hard to crack." Separation consciousness serves the surgeon but not the lover; it serves science but not Soul. I am grateful for my cardiologist and her training. But if she decides she needs to use her scientific scissors on me I will also want a wise and spiritually grounded chaplain

19. Abram, *Spell of the Sensuous*, 138.

nearby. I'll need someone whose job it is to see my heart through a different lens, someone who knows that I'm more than a machine. My cardiologist and my chaplain do not see the same heart.

Relational Consciousness

Listening in wild places, we are audience
to conversations in a language not our own.[20]

—Robin Wall Kimmerer

Learning to see with a relational eye, or the eye of the heart, opens a new mode of perception. When we learn to have an "I-Thou" relationship with the cosmos as a whole and with everything in it, we finally overcome the insanity of standing apart from it all. We are freed from the cosmic loneliness of feeling exiled from the family of things. The relational world has always been there, but it is only when we allow the separate observer mind finally to become quiet that we begin to hear the world's many voices. The spirits of the world come out of hiding, revealing their faces, showing us how they participate in the dance of reality. The whole world begins to offer itself for relationship.

A university professor in environmental sciences with a PhD in botany, Robin Wall Kimmerer is also an enrolled member of the Citizen Potawatomi Nation. She writes that she once heard a Navajo woman lecture for hours on the plant communities in her valley. This woman had no training in botany, and she didn't speak in the detached language of the scientist. Instead, she spoke of communities, and plants as subjects, not objects. Her lecture was about who likes to live where and with whom. She spoke of to whom each plant prefers to give itself as food or nest material, and how it wants to share its medicine. She spoke of plants as carriers of stories and teachings. To someone of Western European heritage, this description would be heard as an anthropomorphic projection. But one gets the feeling in reading Kimmerer and the writing of other Native people that these are descriptions of an obvious and original reality. For those steeped in relational consciousness, separation consciousness looks like a self-inflicted wound.

One must already be outside of nature in order to pro-ject something into it. But we are not separate from nature except in our own Cartesian fantasy. We are fully immersed in it and inseparable from it. Those who

20. Kimmerer, *Braiding Sweetgrass,* 48.

have not yet learned that they can shift their epistemological stance from observer to participant are still trapped in a world that divides the cosmos into subjects and objects, and that denies subjectivity to most of it except the human.[21] This creates a unique dilemma for the Western ego, for it cannot see outside the limits of its own perceptual habits and cannot imagine "conversations in a language not our own." No one is suggesting that the natural world has human vocal cords, or that French trees speak French, and British trees speak English! Rather, learning to hear nature's speech is a matter of recognizing that long before there were human words, there were already meanings, requests, instructions, warnings, playfulness, celebrations, and mourning, all expressed in a language of communion for and among all the elements of the natural world. Relational consciousness requires a relational ego, located within an intersubjective matrix of being.

The natural world is speaking to us; it's just that we usually dismiss such things, if we admit to them to at all. A dear friend once asked me if I would take an old writing desk to the Habitat donation center for her. It had belonged to her mother, was out of style, and she needed the space. I loaded it into my truck and was on my way when I felt a distinct unease; something was out of sorts, misaligned. I decided to take her desk to my home and to listen until I could feel the plumb line come to center. I placed it where I could touch it as I passed it by, say hello, listen for its story, feel its history, and then one day I could feel something shift. We came together into an understanding, an "aha" moment of recognition that if translated into words would have been "I want to be a chair!" I felt an immediate rush of excitement, the joy of feeling something *true*, and went to work freeing the ancient oak from a form it no longer wanted and refashioned it into an Adirondack chair. It gave me a special pleasure to see my friend's eyes glisten when I took it back to her and said, "Here is your mother's desk. It didn't want to go to Habitat. It wanted to be a chair. May you feel your mother's arms around you when you sit in it."

I don't offer this story as proof of anything, nor do I believe that any such experiences will ever satisfy the rigors of scientific proof. But for those who inhabit a relational worldview, these things don't need proof. It makes perfect sense that all beings want to be in meaningful relationship with the

21. *Objectification* justifies exploitation. I suspect that the splitting of the phenomenal world into a binary subject/object frame is closely linked to the rise of the domination system. Once that original split took hold, it then widened from humans objectifying nature, to men objectifying women, to lighter-skinned races objectifying people of color. Its inherent ranking of value ultimately yields a virulent narcissism that reserves all subjectivity to a "self" encased in an isolated, increasingly delusional, but nevertheless fiercely defended world. "Freedom" becomes entitlement to exploit, and exclude the neighbor from consideration in the name of individual "rights."

whole. This piece had long service as a desk, but when its service was no longer needed, I could feel its sorrow at being hauled away. Perhaps I was honoring the wood's own longing, or perhaps I was honoring my friend's mother as an ancestor in returning her desk to her daughter in a more useful form, or if you insist, I was projecting my own feelings onto it. Whatever the analytic mind wants to say about it, when I honored relational consciousness, something opened my awareness to a new way of perceiving and engaging the task before me. If I frame this story drawing on the language of Quakerism, I would say that when I was on my way to the Habitat donation center "I felt a *stop* in my mind." I sensed that I was "running ahead of the Guide," and when I turned my truck around, I was "responding to a leading." I needed to wait, listen, and pray until "way opened" for me to take a different path. The only proof I need was in my friend's delight and gratitude and my own deep joy in reuniting her with her mother's desk.

In a small way, this experience was "shamanic," in that it arose out of a sense of intersubjective relatedness, and sought a new way of continuing a relationship. The shamanic traditions around the world affirm that we must attend to disruptions in the ecological and spirit communities. Doing so is key to restoring not only ecological balance but also to healing human illness and disorder. The shaman's primary objective is to repair broken relationships, especially in the invisible world, the relief of symptoms is the natural result. According to David Abram, the shaman "functions primarily as an intermediary between human and nonhuman worlds, and only secondarily as a healer."[22] He adds, "The medicine person's primary allegiance, then, is not to the human community but to the earthly web of relations in which that community is embedded—it is from this that her or his power to alleviate human illness derives."[23]

This is also the case in Native American healing practices where the creatures of nature are allies, companions, and bearers of healing powers. Vine Deloria in a fascinating study in which he brings Jungian psychology into conversation with Native American spirituality, writes, "The Sioux felt that the animals actually *chose* the people they wanted as human companions."[24] He goes on to quote Luther Standing Bear:

> While in the spirit condition the dreamer was in contact with the spirits of all things of the world, though in the case of the Bear Dreamer only the bears spoke to him and gave him bear powers. The bears told him to recognize all things of nature and

22. Abram, "Ecology of Magic," 305.
23. Abram, "Ecology of Magic," 305.
24. Deloria, *Jung and the Sioux Traditions*, 127.

> to observe and learn from them. *The animals would thereafter observe and learn from the dreamer, and he should do likewise.*[25]

Animals appearing in dreams were frequent guides for healers, often bringing specific remedies to the attention of the dreamer. In other accounts, the people were guided to certain medicinal herbs or methods for warding off pests or disease. In every case, it was the attitude of respect and willingness to listen that opened the door to the help and wisdom the dream figure was offering.

In the deep embodied silences of wilderness, we can begin to feel nature's original, interrelational speech. Listening in wild places brings us into conversation with a world where meaning is sensual, and language communicates by way of an embodied, felt sense of knowing. Language, in this sense, is foremost an intersubjective dance, a series of gestures within a relational field. Only secondarily, and only in its highly abstracted forms, is human speech *about* something. If we Western Euro-Americans can learn to fall deep into the silences that live in the relational body, to drop below the detached, separation consciousness of our heritage, we can once again "become animal," as David Abram puts it. He is not saying that we become something we've never been, but that we can remember something we've always been but have forgotten.[26] We can reawaken our native capacity to entertain all of nature's fellow travelers who appear on the horizons of consciousness, bearing gifts, strange customs, knowledge of different worlds and new ways of seeing and experiencing reality. If, as most Native peoples affirm, we participate in a vast ecology of being, we can learn from them how to find our way back to right relatedness within a partnership world.

25. Deloria, *Jung and the Sioux Traditions*, 127. Deloria added the emphasis to the Standing Bear quotation.

26. "The things of the world continue to beckon to us from behind the cloud of words, speaking instead with gestures and subtle rhythms, calling out to our animal bodies, tempting our skin with their varied textures and coaxing our muscles with their grace, inviting our thoughts to remember and rejoin the wider community of intelligence." Abram, *Becoming Animal*, 40.

Non-Dual Consciousness

> Love neither rules, nor is it unmoved;
> also it is a little oblivious as to morals.
> It does not look to the future, for it finds
> its own reward in the immediate present.[27]
>
> —Alfred North Whitehead

Each perspective, each location of "self," and each style of consciousness, has its approach to healing. Each approach is a unique fit within its universe, effective within its horizons of perception, and each style of healing is in profound service to its mission of alleviating suffering. Science and the separated, observer ego have brought us modern medicine and the wonders it brings to our illnesses and injuries. Shamanic practices and certain psychological approaches that work within relational consciousness heal at the level of the relational mind and the narrative structure of the psyche. But healing that proceeds from non-dual consciousness is of an entirely different order. I suspect that the healings reported in the Jesus story are neither scientific nor shamanic but are of a type that arise naturally in the presence of profoundly awakened beings. We step into a powerful current of Love when in the presence of someone who is so radically open to the Divine Spring. Healings result not so much from one agency acting upon another; they arise more because we are drawn into that current. Our unconscious resistances are overcome and we yield to a naturally ordering Love.

But a strong caution is in order here! How easy it is to look for fault when prayers for healing seem to go unanswered. We want to blame somebody's sin, or wrong thinking, disobedience, or lack of faith. Let's not add "unconscious resistance" to the list! Blaming thoughts arise because of our bias toward individualism, whereas resistance to a naturally ordering Love is collective. I propose that there is *never* a condition in which seemingly unanswered prayer is the fault of the one who suffers; *never* is it because of the unsteady faith of the intercessor, and *never* is it the act of a withholding or abandoning God. I find it essential to trust that every prayer matters and that every prayer helps the whole in our collective struggle to yield to the hidden works of Love. Healings are breakthrough moments when "top-down" collective resistances weaken enough for the "bottom-up" and "inside-out" forces of the Hidden Spring of Love to reorder the structures

27. Whitehead, *Process and Reality*, 343.

that keep disorder in place. They are the natural outcome of persistent nonviolent pressures that originate in the nonviolence of God. It is far beyond anyone's reckoning to know how, when, or where that will happen, but I trust that my praying is never in vain. If we can lay down our individualistic bias and our Cartesian blinders, we might begin to see through an ecological lens that brings a collective, intersubjective world into view. The simplest desire to open the heart to Love participates in a collective work of wearing away resistance. We belong to one another. We are broken together and we heal together.

Healings that arise out non-dual consciousness originate in a Divine Presence that Whitehead described as dwelling "on the tender elements of the world, which slowly and in quietness operate by love."[28] One gets the impression of a God who prefers anonymity. Perhaps the ultimate mystery is shy of any names and wants to work from hiddenness in the way that water flows into underground crevices. There is a radical humility in this God who will work through any means or person that is open and willing. The Divine Fire is as present in a child's prayer as a surgeon's knife, and will work through a dream, a shamanic ritual, or a country preacher. Healing is not our work but God's. There is no secret technique, or proper ritual or belief, there is only the openhearted desire to make oneself a willing instrument, like the wooden flute that gives itself to the Musician's breath. Anyone can pray and anyone can confidently open the heart to the Divine mystery of healing. It doesn't take much. Jesus compared healing faith to a mustard seed. Just do it. Show up. Tell the truth. Listen. It's not about getting the beliefs or the technique right. It's about praying from the heart, joining our small love to that large Love that is already at work in the secret places of the soul.

Sometimes the veil drops away. We see Love in action, and confidence soars. But mostly our lives are lived with the veil firmly in place, and we must pray in the dark. Another Quaker aphorism that speaks to this is "Don't doubt in the darkness what you learned in the Light." Praying in the dark requires the discipline of everyday practices, gestures of the heart and soul that help us lean into the sacred. There are many such practices but in one way or another, they all unclothe the heart, bringing us to a condition of undefended vulnerability. Inevitably, I engage the world and those I encounter with my interpretive habits and defenses in place. But in prayer I must cultivate a deep awareness of the limitations of my own vision and for the many subtle ways that ego has of clinging to the protective covering of fixed ideas. Praying in the dark works at noticing and then shedding the

28. Whitehead, *Process and Reality*, 343.

many barriers we erect to protect us from the immediacy of the present moment. We are participants in a sacred work that is greater than anything we can imagine.

When we do get glimpses, and our eyes are briefly opened, we see the earth and everything in it as the incarnation of the holy. There is no more duality between the observing ego and nature, between self and other; there is no more supernatural, domination system god either making things happen, or refusing to; there is only *this* present moment, *this* Divine Fire animating our love and awakening prayer. Our holy longing, which we assumed would only be met in some other world, is suddenly met in this one. We spend most of our lives in duality, behind the veil, seeing through a glass darkly. But there are occasional glimpses of non-duality. I suspect that most of us are favored with brief moments of awakening; they are not really that rare. Perhaps in a moment of reverie, or waking from a dream, or resting in a deep stillness, something drops away and suddenly the Divine Fire blazes through every stone, every creature, and every blade of grass. In those moments, there is nothing more to heal. "All is well, and all shall be well," as Julian of Norwich wrote in the fourteenth century. Even in the midst of overwhelming oppression, "life is beautiful," as Etty Hillesum wrote. Sometimes we are allowed to go up to the mountain and look over, as Martin Luther King Jr. said so powerfully on the eve of his death, and then we can say, even in the face of all that threatens to break our hearts and steal our hope, "I have seen the promised land."

CHAPTER 12

The Truth Is in the Music

Earth's crammed with heaven,
And every common bush afire with God;
But only he who sees takes off his shoes.[1]

—Elizabeth Barrett Browning

The cathedral at Santiago de Compostela is constantly teeming with exhausted hikers who have completed a five-hundred-plus-mile pilgrimage known as the Camino de Santiago. The Mass that is celebrated for them feels medieval, with its bustling, unwashed crowds, merchants hawking souvenirs outside, and Romani beggars roaming the streets. The crowd settles down when the priests enter the chancel and the Mass begins. It is a high-church service with elaborate robes, bells, organ, and eight robed men, or *tiraboleiros* who pull on the ropes that swing the giant incensor. The *Botafumeiro,* as it is called, at its full arc reaches nearly to the cathedral ceiling on both sides of the transept and gives sacramental expression to the prayers of all those who bring their sweat and blisters to that moment. For some, it's just a spectacle, a tourist attraction. But for others, it is a soaring image of longing and hope. Some are brought to their knees.

Hiking the Camino was a way of giving myself over to five weeks in which my only task was to walk. Walk and pray. A Soul friend joined me on the journey. Our shared reflections, seasoned by long silences, fell into greater depths because of the unhurried and uncomplicated pace of the

1. Browning, "Aurora Leigh."

Camino. In my everyday life back home, apart from my occasional vigils in the dark, and the twenty minutes or so that I set aside before heading off to see clients, I am swept away by life's incessant demands, forcing me to pray on the fly. It took the first two weeks, beginning at St. Jean Pied de Port in southern France, hiking across the Pyrenees, and well into northern Spain before I could feel my body begin to slow down. I felt like one of those giant 747s that shuts down its engines and you come back later and can still hear the turbines turning. I was halfway through the pilgrimage before I felt like I had finally become quiet. Just walking, listening, noticing, lying down in the sun, eating an apple. I finally remembered something long forgotten, something I hadn't experienced for many months—just being. Somewhere along the way I had the thought that I was beginning to remember how to be a human being. Coming back to the States was the most difficult part of the journey. Having finally become sane, I knew I was returning to the insanity of a sped-up life, complex technology, and what feels like *never* enough time. This is the everyday "normal" for lives that are considered "sane."

It was no wonder that I was on my knees before the *Botafumeiro,* captivated as it threw its incense toward the heavens. That incensor threw my prayers aloft with every pull on the rope and I could feel it in my bones. Embodied, sacramental gestures have always parted the veil for me, a gift for which I thank the Trappists. Another pilgrim, next to me in the pew, was happily chatting with a friend. Did she not see the Holy Fire burning right in front of us? Can mystical perception be true, or does "truth" now belong only to those facts that can be demonstrated by science? Was I the delusional one for seeing *more* than was there, or was she for seeing *less*?

Dancing on the Edge of Language

> The best that can be done, it seems to the religious person,
> is to fluctuate between silence and the indistinct borders of language.[2]
>
> —Paul Van Buren

Throughout this writing I have been trying to revive, rescue, and perhaps rehabilitate some seriously endangered words. "God," and "prayer" are certainly in the ICU if not in hospice. "Truth" is on life support. "Jesus" has become an ideological icon for the right and an exclamation point for the left. For many people, religious words have become so laden with toxic

2. Van Buren, *Edges of Language*, 117.

associations that they have been rendered virtually useless. Truth has suffered relentless assault in recent years, not only from postmodern relativism, but even more directly by a president who behaved as if he could invent it on the fly.[3] To rehabilitate "truth" as a word that can be used meaningfully in religious discourse, we must first distinguish religious words that live at the edge of language, from the important but more strictly defined truths that are subject to scientific or legal proofs. Religious words are "liminal" or threshold words that inhabit the borderlands between the known and unknown. Each one is a trailhead that leads into the wilderness. They are more like wild animals than those tame creatures that sleep at the foot of the bed.

In order for religious truth to spring free of meanings that have been ex-plained, literally flattened out (from *ex-planare*), the words themselves must be pressed beyond the limits of what language can say. For many of us, this feels like an impossible task because such words have been trapped and domesticated by the small gods of our concretized images. They have had all the life drained out of them. In order to reanimate them, it is important to understand how we arrived at such a condition. Like the stranger in the pew next to me in Santiago, we do not realize that our perceptions have been shaped by forces of modernity set in motion centuries ago and far outside of our awareness. In fairness to her, I must admit that she may have been fully awake to the Divine Fire and had simply returned to chopping wood and carrying water. But more likely she was influenced less by Elizabeth Barrett Browning and more by scientific materialism. Even to suggest that her perception of reality has been shaped by influences outside of her awareness would strike her as absurd. Like most of us, she would hear my talk of a Holy Fire as merely poetic, naïve, pious, or worse, suspiciously mystical, but not grounded in the hard facts of reality.

Our differences in perception are rooted in soil many centuries deep, perhaps as old as the domination system itself. But it was in the seventeenth century when one of the more visible fractures occurred. The opening scene has Galileo in the Pisa Cathedral where he also observed a swinging object suspended by a rope, in his case a chancel lamp. Having already developed the observer's eye of separation consciousness, he devoted his mind to measuring the duration of the arc, using his pulse as a timekeeper. He discovered

3. Relativism is a useful concept when used to show the diverse views that arise from diverse social locations. It is a scourge when applied to "truth," whether scientific, legal, or religious. Scientific and legal truths strive for the precision of fact: The 2020 election was not stolen. The COVID-19 virus is effectively contained by vaccination. These are facts, firmly established within the rules of our legal system, and those of the scientific method. Religious truth is not about facts but mysteries. Relativism does not apply here either. Mystery is mysterious for everyone.

that the duration of the swing was always the same regardless of the length of the arc. Galileo is considered the father of the scientific method.

He got in trouble with the church, as we all know, but perhaps not for the reasons we've been taught. Many of us assume that *heliocentrism*, or the theory of the earth's rotation around the sun, was the sticking point. But Copernicus had already promoted that view, and centuries before him, it had been promoted by Aristarchus of Samos in the third century BCE. This was not a new idea. In fact, the church had supported the sciences, and some within its academies had already supported heliocentrism. Why would the church force Galileo to "abjure, curse, and detest" his "errors," when even the pope had previously been an admirer of his work, and Galileo had been and remained a faithful Catholic? It was not the theory that got Galileo in trouble. The deeper issue was that he presented his theories in writings that insisted on a distinction between matters of faith and matters of science, where the latter could arrive at conclusions about the nature of reality by methods outside the church's control. There were powerful forces in the church that were outraged by Galileo's encroaching on territory that the church had staked out for itself, namely the authority to determine what can be accepted as "true." Conflict was inevitable.

What is missing in many interpretations of this turning point in history is a broader contextualization. The political power and authority of empire Christianity embodied in the Roman Catholic Church had fractured under the Protestant Reformation. The ashes from that fire were still hot when Galileo was writing his treatises. In fact, the Thirty Years' War did not finally end until after Galileo's death. Empire can't survive without the perception of legitimacy, and the church believed that absolute authority was essential. As long as church authority wasn't questioned, it supported the sciences. But Galileo was advocating a method of inquiry that left truth open to discovery. He was embracing what religious scholar James Carse calls "a higher ignorance," a deep appreciation for uncertainty. The church, on the other hand, was deeply entangled with wealth and political power, and was subject to the inevitable pull toward what Carse calls "willful ignorance," that is, an intentional choice to ignore or even dispute claims that are threatening to one's self-interest.[4] A tragic polarization ensued between an emerging scientific method that favored an open, curious, experimental stance toward a possibly inexhaustible truth, and an empire Christianity embodied in a politically dominant church that demanded final ideological authority. The conflict was political. The controversy over ideas was secondary. Galileo recanted and avoided torture, imprisonment, and possibly

4. Carse, *Religious Case against Belief*, 13–14.

death, although he suffered house arrest for his remaining years. Empire won that round, but the revolution had begun. In 1642, the year Galileo died, Isaac Newton was born.

Without the corrupting influence of empire, the emerging scientific method and those sensitive to generative Christianity might have been able to preserve the common ground of science and religion in a more nuanced epistemology and an appreciation for the metaphoric basis of mind. But the political context forced a polarization that initially suppressed the emerging science. Within a generation, that suppression gave way to what is aptly called the scientific revolution. It was not an overt political upheaval, but rather a cultural revolution with political consequences. Four centuries later those consequences are obvious and immense. Like the tragedy of a bad divorce, the siblings got split between the parents. The church got custody of "God" and science got "truth." As the scientific method evolved and took hold, "truth" would gradually be drawn into the objectified world of separation consciousness, eventually yielding the new ideology of scientific materialism.

The grandchildren of this divorce include the rise of fundamentalism in the late nineteenth century, which tries to compete with science in its emphasis on biblical inerrancy, literalism, and more recently creationism. Others surrendered the *natural* world to science and retreated further into *super*naturalism, and others, like Christian Science, simply rejected modern science altogether. Ultimately, these essentially conservative efforts to preserve some claim to truth are countered with an emerging liberalism that tries to make accommodation with science.

Freud and Jung were developing their ideas during the early part of the twentieth century. Their falling out was the result of many factors, but placing it within the context of the seventeenth-century divorce of science and religion sheds some important light. At the heart of the matter was their disagreement over the nature of the unconscious. For Freud it is essentially an old trunk in the basement that holds all the family secrets and all our repressed thoughts, disowned feelings, and forbidden wishes. Jung does not deny this aspect of the personal unconscious, but he also sees a collective unconscious. For him this is the underwater part of the iceberg, so much bigger than the visible part and ultimately barely distinguishable from the ocean that holds it. Inevitably, this difference significantly influences their approaches to religion. In Jung's view, Freud was too reductionistic. Science had become the senior partner in the conversation with religion, much like Freud, nineteen years older than Jung, considered himself the senior partner in their collaboration. In a kind of parallel process with religion being asked to submit to science, Freud insisted on Jung's loyalty to his ideas. But

Jung was unwilling to accept this arrangement. Motivated by a profound religious sensibility, Jung took the stance of the explorer. He believed that religion must be approached phenomenologically.

Now, in the twenty-first century, we are still caught in tensions set in motion in the seventeenth century. The great-grandchildren of this divorce appear in a soulless technology and the "New Atheism" of writers who don't seem to be aware that there are some very intriguing alternatives to the ideological religion of empire Christianity. Those of us who cannot find a home in any of the current forms of conservatism or liberalism, and who are not willing to give up on either God or truth, struggle to find a way to get these estranged siblings back under the same roof. Fortunately, some reconciliation is beginning to occur in emerging conversations across disciplines. New advances in science, depth psychology, and theology are promising, although they are still a generation away from acceptance in the wider culture.

Like so many of us, my modern friend in the pew next to me in Santiago can no longer see the Holy Fire that our ancestors saw. It does not enter her field of perception, even if she considered it a possibility, which she surely does not. Now, she can only see a pendulum, faithfully obeying Galileo's law. The argument we are having in my imagination over whether the *Botafumeiro* actually blazes with a Holy Fire or is merely a dead object swinging on a rope, is unnecessary and unfortunate. The argument simply vanishes when we begin to talk about the emergence of new ways of seeing, about the links between language, culture, and perception, and about the mythic mind. When separation consciousness is in the foreground, it objectifies the world, and language strives to be definitive and precise. When relational or non-dual consciousness is in the foreground, a different world comes into view and we dance on the edges of language, always striving to say more than language can say. Must I assume that only the well-lit, "common sense" world of separation consciousness is true? If I dream of a Divine Fire, must I dismiss that image as soon as I am awake? Or, have I merely awakened to a different kind of sleep, and might there be another, more profound awakening yet to come? If so, then perhaps I can one day learn to see a Divine Fire burning in every common bush and illuminating the faces of strangers.

We are working with mysteries more than certainties, and both religion and science deal in matters that live far beyond the edges of language. They must learn to dance together. They both touch the sacred, and they both ultimately fall into a holy silence where the only reasonable thing to do is to take off one's shoes.

The Bottom of the Disorder (III)

God is dynamically interior to creation.[5]

—Ilia Delio

I suspect that when our habits of seeing only an objectified world finally drop away and the sacred is revealed, we will see what those near death sometimes see. A pastor friend once told me of being at the bedside of a parishioner. Just moments before he died, he exclaimed, "Oh!" His eyes widened and joy spread across his face. When the veil drops, the shoes come off, and we fall to our knees. Perhaps when we arrive at the threshold of mystery, we come to a confluence of streams where the Real meets the perceptible. I don't know what this man saw, or whom, but according to my friend, his joy was unmistakable.

I wasn't there, but now I have a story. My friend told me, and now I'm telling you. We will each make of it what we will. I have heard that some brain researchers have come up with the idea that those near death may experience hallucinations due to changes in the brain, perhaps as an adaptation to help ease the passage. Maybe these are the same researchers who have studied the brain chemistry of love. Ok. Not my thing, but I can appreciate the curiosity and creativity that goes into that kind of research. Now, ask yourself, what is your mind doing right now with these two stories? Each one invites a certain conclusion. Did this man see something profound, or was his brain playing tricks on him? Neither version actually proves anything. We are not rescued from our interpretive responsibilities. If you lean toward the religious interpretation, what do you do with your doubt? If you lean toward the scientific interpretation, what do you do with your doubt? Do you have a way of holding these two perspectives together, or perhaps moving back and forth between them? We are mapmakers, interpreters of experience, and we must not forget that we cover the phenomenal world with images and ideas, like we cover our feet with shoes.

Ilia Delio is a Franciscan nun who holds doctorates in both theology and pharmacology. I am inspired by her vision of God. It isn't the scholarship that convinces me, however, impressive as that is, but the inspiration. I believe these things, not because I can prove them, but because they bring me joy, and they ground me in a creative life that helps me show up for service each day without getting overwhelmed by the tragedies and suffering of the world. I choose to embrace a picture of the world that has God

5. Delio, *Unbearable Wholeness of Being*, 125.

working from the inside out and the bottom up. The top-down structures are ours, and they must constantly be refreshed by the Life that sustains them. Otherwise, they are a cut flower, enduring in form perhaps but without the animating forces that keep them creative and able to support nonviolent peace and the ecology of justice. I see this picture of God as the Lover of the universe, who refuses to be named, or boxed in by our fears, or trapped in our cults of religious, psychological, or political ideas. The Lover of the universe patiently endures our cautious approaches to prayer, and will always seek out the places of least resistance to love. The Lover of the universe wants intimacy and will work through, or in some cases in spite of, our very human and inevitably limited words and ideas, our halting attempts to figure out what to believe, and what to do with our doubt.

We reach the bottom of our disorder, not when we finally discover, name, or grasp truth, but when we *become true* in these moments of falling into the dynamic heart of creation, which is therefore also the dynamic heart within each of us. Becoming true sets us free *from* possession by our internal complexes, and *for* service in the world in ways that are unique to our personalities and gifts. We use words to make reference to that which cannot be named, because these gestures of speech can call us home. But words can also misdirect, so it is essential that we engage religious speech very differently than how we engage the language of science or law. Religious words are more like living beings. We must engage them aesthetically, sensually, relationally, noticing how some divide us from ourselves and others seem to awaken us into a wholeness of being. Then when we come to the limits of what words can say, we let them go. When we pray in the dark, the thousand names all fall away.

We reach the bottom of our disorder when we live on "the edge of the raft," as Sallie McFague puts it, "our models are *only* models, and while we advance evidence energetically to support them over against other models, we should do so in the spirit of passionate nonchalance, that is, in the spirit of prayer."[6] It is with this in mind that I insist that we find and engage those practices that bring us into contact with the Hidden Spring of Love, and to offer ourselves and our gifts in the service of nonviolent peace and the ecology of justice. I insist on this passionately, because I believe in this journey, and because I'm excited by the possibilities it offers. But I also offer it with the nonchalance of one who knows that I am advocating a wager and not a certainty. But isn't that how we *must* live—with passionate nonchalance—throwing ourselves with wholehearted abandon into the breach between belief and doubt, laughing our scapulars off when the dump truck goes in the

6. McFague, *Metaphorical Theology*, 144.

ditch? We live our lives on this side of the veil, so the best any of us can do in this world with all of its problems is simply to gather the community, make some sandwiches, and start digging ourselves out. Choose love. Choose it because there's plenty of evidence to support the belief that it's an excellent idea. But, even when it seems like all the evidence is to the contrary, we can, like Etty Hillesum, choose love anyway.

We reach the bottom of our disorder when we inhabit the transitional self, with one eye on the world, and the other on Soul, because we know that every construction of identity has its god and every god has its devil. Every "self" dies and takes its god with it, and every god dies and takes its devil. We are embedded in our personalities, each one with a subjectivity that projects a world, and every location of "self" is subject to crises of emergence that will require its death. There is always a more deeply interior mystery that animates every finite and circumscribed world. We hit bottom not when we find bedrock that supports our limited structures, but when we learn to breathe while falling, moment by moment, each one an invitation for dying into new life and into a new configuration of the world.

We reach the bottom of our disorder when we realize that creation, as Catherine Keller asserts, is not *ex nihilo,* but rather *ex profundis.*[7] There is no watchmaker god who stands outside of the mystery, tinkering with Nothingness, fashioning a world, but rather a God of depth who is Self-revealing in a vast diversity of incarnational moments. The psyche is a polytheistic image maker, endlessly fertile and creative, always pouring forth new images, narratives, and bids for engagement. But its images are always penultimate. There is no final *imago Dei.* We must bring discernment to our images and narratives, but we must also go beyond the image and surrender to the ever-deepening journey into depth. There we find the One in the Many and the Many in the One. We search in vain for primal origins. The world rests on the back of a turtle, according to one Native American story of creation. That turtle rests on another. How many are there? "It's turtles all the way down" goes the tale, expressing the futility of searching for the bottom turtle, the final revelation. Turtles are simply one more means of God's Self-revelation.

We reach the bottom of our disorder when we *become true,* not when we lay hold of some new god and but when we fall into that mystery that "animates the sphere of being from within."[8] Then we become more like jazz musicians who find immense joy in *truth's emerging conversation with itself.* Great jazz is full of authentic encounters. Jazz artist, teacher, and

7. Keller, *Face of the Deep,* 155.

8. Delio, *Unbearable Wholeness of Being,* 125.

theorist Mark Levine says, "There are almost as many 'jazz theories' as there are jazz musicians."[9] He goes on to note that artists like Louis Armstrong, Duke Ellington, Art Tatum, Charlie Parker, Thelonious Monk, John Coltrane, and others all "could have played with each other and understood one another,"[10] despite their differences. Truth comes to life in moments of musical conversation. We don't *know* truth so much as find it happening in the heat of engagement. Levine says that "'theory' is the little intellectual dance we do around the music, attempting to come up with rules so we can understand why Charlie Parker and John Coltrane sounded the way they did."[11] Jazz theories dance around the music like the best of our theological and psychological ideas dance around the mystery of God and Soul.

We reach the bottom of our disorder when we can participate in a multitude of creative encounters that invite our own creative voices to respond. Truth wants a relationship more than agreement. Like great jazz, it wants conversation, tension, amplification, creativity, and new experiments in authentic expression that invite answering voices from other instruments in the ensemble. Even the Bible is a jazz ensemble, a conversation, even an argument, but never a conclusion.[12] Our religious, psychological, and political ideas, like music theory, are important, but nevertheless provisional structures. Truth persuades through inspiration and invitation. It is always playing with new forms, and it lives not by dominance, but by the awakening persuasions of love.

Awakening in the Dark

God hates visionary dreaming.[13]

—Dietrich Bonhoeffer

For five weeks we had walked across northern Spain. We kept count of the countries represented among the pilgrims we met along the way, twenty-seven in all, so many different languages, cultures, and beliefs. And then

9. Levine, *Jazz Theory Book*, vii.

10. Levine, *Jazz Theory Book*, vii.

11. Levine, *Jazz Theory Book*, vii.

12. Some conservative Christian readers will take issue with this statement, but it is no surprise to Jewish readers who are steeped in midrash, an ancient practice of vigorous sparring over interpretations. For an inspiring argument in favor of a conversational approach to the Bible see Moore, *Practicing Midrash*.

13. Bonhoeffer, *Life Together*, 27.

all these pilgrims finally came to the city, and the plaza, and the cathedral, and then to the altar at its center, at the completion of the journey, the end point that we had been walking toward for so long. There was a beggar by the steps of the cathedral door, and I caught myself walking past her, barely noticing. Something stopped me and I could almost hear the voice of Jesus as I passed by, saying, "Do you really want to come all this way, thinking you're going to find me at that altar, and never realize that you passed right by me on your way into the church?"

I chided myself for needing to learn that lesson, yet again. I shifted focus and considered the possibility that the whole point of the journey was to be brought to this very tangible moment of compassion, with its invitation to share what I had and to find new ways to confront the domination system powers that create the conditions of her poverty. But then, just as quickly, I saw that my dream of justice for the poor could be equally blinding. The part of me that is a Social Gospel Christian can forget my own need for mercy and healing, for facing my shadows and my poverty of soul. On the other hand, the part of me that wants to weep and shout, and that falls to my knees before the *Botafumeiro*, can forget that God's amazing grace does not save me *from* this world, but *for* it. I did not have to choose between the altar and this beggar; I couldn't possibly choose in any case. We're the kindling, not the Fire. Without the Holy Fire I found burning at the altar I had nothing to bring to the work of peacemaking, and without yielding to Love's call to pour itself out, I had nowhere to go with the gift. What good is a Fire that doesn't warm anyone, and what kindling can ignite itself?

The Camino became the journey in which the monk and the activist finally found a way to live together within me. Their reconciliation became possible when I realized that the monk had become wedded to a spiritual vision, and the activist had become wedded to a political vision, and it was their devotion to their ideals that blinded them and kept them divided. I finally understood Dietrich Bonhoeffer's statement, a line that shocked and disturbed me when I first read it. The Camino was a physical journey whose rigors taught me the folly of living in devotion to an idealistic goal. It was incredibly easy to spend most of the journey walking like we were trying to get somewhere, blinded by even a small goal like finding a place to sleep for the night. We had to discover over and over that the true discipline was simply to walk. Just walk, notice, listen, share a thought, observe silence, have a meal, drink water, sleep, and then do it all over again the next day. How difficult that was when the path was strewn with rocks, or we were baking in the sun of the high central plateau called the *meseta*. It was difficult to just let go. Just be. But in those moments when we did, our eyes and hearts opened, and we experienced amazing synchronicities. There were always helpers, some visible, others not. We always had a meal and a place to sleep and we eventually learned simply to trust. The Camino taught us simplicity. It was a requirement for the journey. Just be awake, in this moment, without our visionary dreaming getting in the way. That was always the best way to navigate each day's challenges. Attached to my vision of finding a bed for the night, I got lost in my anxiety. Letting go into the present moment, the bed found me.

But wait! Wasn't Martin Luther King Jr. a visionary dreamer? Didn't John Lennon sing about being a dreamer, and didn't he call us to imagine a time when "the world will be as one"? Visionary dreamers have always inspired me, and Bonhoeffer's statement feels like sand in the gears. But the more I read, the more I saw in him a profound integration of the mystic and the activist. Bonhoeffer helped me see that we misunderstand our heroes when we fail to see that their journeys were also punctuated with agonizing spiritual trials, sleepless nights spent in prayer, harrowing experiences of being tempered in the fires of spiritual struggles in which they were forced to confront their demons. Nobody comes to spiritual maturity without first being dragged into an underworld of shadows, as Jesus was immediately following his baptism, when the Spirit drove him into the wilderness. It is in the "swamplands of the soul" where we do some of our most raw and painful inner work.[14] No wonder we are so tempted to take King, Gandhi, or Bonhoeffer purely as moral leaders, to be followed in form, but not into the wilderness of agonizing struggles like those that shaped them. And how common it is to be disillusioned when we discover their flaws. We faithfully follow these very human and inevitably flawed teachers, not by simply doing what they did, or by idealizing them, but by submitting to the fires of transformation in our own lives.

Bonhoeffer also helped me to see how my own tradition keeps falling into divisions and splits. Too many of us are visionary dreamers. Whether theological, moral, or political, and whether right, left, or center, too many of us have become ideological. I've had to face the uncomfortable truth that my own interior divisions have mirrored the larger splits within my denomination. The activist finds a home in a Social Justice Quakerism that is interpreted primarily through a political lens. The monk finds a home in an evangelical Quakerism that is interpreted primarily through a theological lens. There are many Quakers, of course, across the spectrum, who pour their lives into service precisely because they hear a message of overwhelming and transforming Love. But some of us, and I have been one of them,

14. For a wise and helpful exploration of this theme from a Jungian perspective, see Hollis, *Swamplands.*

have allowed ourselves to become so deeply attached to our political or theological ideals that we would rather split than find a way to make music together. Bonhoeffer teaches that when we love our ideologies more than each other, we fail the God we seek to serve.

We need egos and their stories to navigate everyday life. We need agency, analytic ability, and strategic thinking in order to be effective peacemakers. We need the theological mind to help us name false gods and to point us toward the mystery beyond the gods. We need the psychological mind with its ability to open awareness to the unconscious, to expose our complexes and learn from those many symptoms and tricksters who throw obstacles across our paths. We need science and the rule of law, and the institutional structures of society that keep our lives working. Most of all we need awakened people to serve within these outward forms. We need undercover mystics inhabiting all these roles, people who have learned to hold our inevitable egos, as well as their gods and devils, with the sensitivities of Soul. We need calculating contemplatives, mystic activists, fierce strategists brave enough to face the domination system with passionate nonchalance. We need Holy Fire and wild hearts. We need people who have not abandoned prayer, but who have doubled down and fought their way to an authentic spirituality that brings them fully alive and reacquaints them with joy.

One night in the middle of the Camino, I had gone to sleep in one of the many pilgrim hostels, exhausted from a long day, and then far into the night something awakened me. I was completely disoriented. I had no idea where I was or why I was in a room full of snoring people. Gradually, I began to regather my named-world around me like a familiar cloak, but there were several long moments when I simply experienced a world without words, before naming, in its pure living immediacy. There was neither fear nor hope, just Presence. Like a newborn, without identity or memory, I knew nothing, nor felt any need to. I was simply awake in the dark. It was just a few moments, and then identity, memory, place, ideas, and all my neuroses came back online. But the shell of my world had briefly cracked open. That moment gave me a glimpse of eternity, beyond all the horizons of knowing. Momentarily relieved of the mind's incessant grasping after some narrative frame, it was painful to be returned to my habitual story. But I now know that the stories I inhabit, and all the ways I locate my sense of self within them, are fragile shells that can crack open. Now I am much more willing to feel my way past the edges of language, into the wilderness, where the world presents itself on its own terms.

Awake in the dark, in a world set free of my need to colonize it with interpretations, I fell into wonder. Now when I pray in the dark, I remember this moment and its gift of a brief glimpse of the unbroken web of being.

Now I can see why "pray for your enemy" is perhaps Jesus' most profound teaching, for "enemy" is a construction of the narrative mind, and prayer throws a long line of love across chasms we believe are impossible to cross. The Love that sustains us is fierce and unrelenting. It wants to be born into our lives and through us into the world. Seek first the Divine Spring. From that will flow what we need. And then, refreshed by its Living Water, we can give our lives and our gifts in service to the emerging world.

Epilogue

Nonviolence: America's Better Angel

We are not enemies, but friends. We must not be enemies. Though passion may have strained it must not break our bonds of affection.[1]

—Abraham Lincoln

Everybody knows where they were on September 11, 2001. Everything stopped. Most of us instinctively reached out for family and friends, seeking support in our shock and grief. I was at Pendle Hill, the Quaker center near Philadelphia. An impromptu meeting for worship was called and the community gathered to center in prayer. The residential student term was about to begin and I was planning my fall term class on nonviolence. We all knew that everything we hoped for that year had suddenly been framed by this event. My three course offerings, "Nonviolence in Personal and Political Life," "Prayer and Peacemaking," and "Forgiveness and Reconciliation," would have to answer the challenge of 9/11 with both head and heart. Nothing less than fierce realism, clarity, and persuasive strategy woven into whole cloth with depth of meaning, and healing power would be sufficient. Grief, fear, and rage would be in the classroom, animating our conversations, and they would be relentless interrogators of nonviolence, prayer, and especially of forgiveness. How can any of these be possible in the face of such brutality?

1. Lincoln, *First Inaugural Address*, para. 35.

As I complete the journey of this writing, aware of so much more that could be said, I also know that the journey now is to trust all you who read this to take away what feeds your soul and to leave the rest. I know that we are all looking out of our windows onto a world that is terribly broken but that is also, and even more deeply, exquisitely beautiful. My grief for this world has been too heavy at times, and I am learning that there is too much pride in my grieving, as if the world is mine to carry. It is not. We are created by Love, for love, and that Love carries us through all of our days, and all of our nights, breath by breath, heartbeat by heartbeat. Love breaks our hearts over suffering, our own and that of our neighbor; it cracks open our worlds and causes our painted roofs to collapse. Our iconoclastic God, hidden in mystery, weans us off our addiction to light, knowing, and certainty. I write, teach, and practice my vocation because I believe that we discover the heart's true home when we learn to pray in the dark, and because I want to invite, nurture, and support a shift in our collective inner landscape. I believe that our way forward will never be the way of agreement in religion or politics; we will always be immersed in a vast diversity. Rather our way will be guided by Love's transforming Fire.

The Pendle Hill classes that year went deep into our shared broken-heartedness over our national tragedy. Many of us participated in anti-war protests, shocked by how quickly plans for war started coming out of Washington. We worked, studied, prayed, played, and acted, all core pillars of Pendle Hill's mission. We explored nonviolent alternatives to war.[2] But we saw our protests drowned out in a drive toward war that was awash in a flood of fear and rage. We grieved that year, over lives lost and over boneheaded decisions made in Washington. We feared for our country and raged against our felt sense of powerlessness. But we also lifted each other up, found opportunities for care, for worship, and, always, for laughter. Joy found its way with us, even in the midst of our sorrow. We saw the wild beasts for what they were, unleashed into the world, but we also found them in ourselves and we did our best to lean toward our better angels.

There are at least two narratives that compete for how we tell our national story. The one most of us were taught in school, the popular, patriotic one, is that the US is a beacon of democracy, a model for the world, a land of freedom and opportunity. The democracy narrative is beautiful and largely

2. A year later, Peter Ackerman and Jack DuVall, founders of the International Center on Nonviolent Conflict, wrote that "a leading nonviolent Iraqi oppositionist expressed exasperation that the Bush administration appeared to be considering every possible military strategy for regime change without realizing 'that 22 million Iraqis detest Saddam Hussein' and that they represent an enormous potential resource in ungluing critical levers of his control." Ackerman and DuVall, "Weapons of the Will," 3.

true, at least in the broad strokes, but demonstrably false in the details, especially for marginalized people. The second narrative, often ignored by many who benefit from the democracy story, is that the US was founded on genocide, economically built on slavery, and has become dependent upon a caste system of oppression where wealth inequality has been steadily growing.[3] This narrative is about the drive for power and wealth, often on the backs of others, surely not one of our better angels. The democracy narrative obscures this reality by insisting that wealth is directly and exclusively tied to merit and hard work. The second narrative clearly exposes that lie.

Democracy has never been easy. It requires vigilance and persistent determination to hold the critical tensions of difference, resisting their flying apart into polarizations. Our angels and their shadows live side by side. Lincoln's first inaugural address, in which he calls on the better angels of our nature, was his attempt to preserve the deeper unity of a democracy on the brink of dissolution. His words are worth remembering at every moment in our history when we are tempted to deepen our hatreds rather than find our common ground. Lincoln called us with eloquent words that we must hear again and again. We must not fall into enmity, sacrificing our democracy on the altar of our differences. We can be discerning without being condemning. We can hold the tensions of our disagreements and work together to build and preserve a more perfect union.

Nonviolence is a way of doing democracy. Perhaps it is even democracy's deepest and most complete expression. The Southern Christian Leadership Conference, a critical organization advocating nonviolence during the civil rights movement, had as its motto, "To redeem the soul of America."[4] Let's continue to be faithful to that journey. Let's not break the bonds of our affection, but rather find new ways to make music out of our dissonance. Let's lead by partnership rather than domination. Let's lay down our pride and judgments, the better to welcome the stranger. Let's study the history and strategies of nonviolence, so that we can bring to birth an emerging world where children no longer have to fear the planes flying overhead. Let's be fierce in our commitment to inner work, embracing our individual and collective shadows. Let's learn to pray in the dark, allowing consciousness to grow beyond the limiting horizons of our ideologies. Let's redeem the soul of America, and tend the soul of the world, so that the whole of creation can fall into the surprise of awakening.

3. Wealth distribution statistics vary, but the Pew Research Center reports that the US now has the highest income inequality of all the G7 nations. See Schaeffer, *6 facts*.

4. Cone, *Cross and the Lynching Tree*, 82.

APPENDIX

Strategic Nonviolence

THE LITERATURE ON NONVIOLENCE has grown substantially in the last fifty years. There are many wonderful resources and it is easy to be overwhelmed. In selecting resources to list in this appendix, I limited myself to ten volumes and chose them for their accessibility, inspiration, depth of history, and careful strategic thinking.

Ackerman, Peter, and Jack Duvall. *A Force More Powerful: A Century of Nonviolent Conflict*. New York: St. Martin's, 2000.

Chenoweth, Erica, and Maria J. Stephan. *Why Civil Resistance Works: The Strategic Logic of Nonviolent Conflict*. New York: Columbia University Press, 2011.

Engler, Mark, and Paul Engler. *This Is an Uprising: How Nonviolent Revolt Is Shaping the Twenty-First Century*. New York: Nation, 2016.

Gandhi, Mohandas. *The Essential Gandhi: An Anthology of His Writings on His Life, Work, and Ideas*. Edited by Louis Fischer. New York: Vintage, 1962.

Lakey, George. *How We Win: A Guide to Nonviolent Direct Action Campaigning*. Brooklyn, NY: Melville House, 2018.

Lynd, Staughton, and Alice Lynd, eds. *Nonviolence in America: A Documentary History*. Rev. ed. Maryknoll, NY: Orbis, 1995.

Schell, Jonathan. *The Unconquerable World: Power, Nonviolence, and the Will of the People*. New York: Henry Holt, 2003.

Sharp, Gene. *From Dictatorship to Democracy: A Conceptual Framework for Liberation*. Boston: The Albert Einstein Institution. No copyright. The author has intentionally placed this material in the public domain.

———. *How Nonviolent Struggle Works*. Boston: The Albert Einstein Institution, 2013.

Wink, Walter, ed. *Peace Is the Way: Writings on Nonviolence from the Fellowship of Reconciliation*. Maryknoll, NY: Orbis, 2000.

Online Resources:

The Albert Einstein Institution, www.aeinstein.org.

A variety of monographs and pamphlets are available in PDF as free downloads.

International Center on Nonviolent Conflict: https://www.nonviolent-conflict.org.

> "ICNC focuses on how nonviolent movements struggle effectively and win. Our mission is educational. We develop and share knowledge and educational resources related to civil resistance with interested recipients throughout the world. This includes citizens and activists, scholars, educators, nongovernmental organizations, media professionals, and members of the policy community."

Global Nonviolent Action Database: http://nvdatabase.swarthmore.edu.

TED Talks

(www.ted.com)

Jamila Raqib: The Secret to Effective Nonviolent Resistance
https://www.ted.com/talks/jamila_raqib_the_secret_to_effective_nonviolent_resistance.

Scilla Elworthy: Fighting with Nonviolence
https://www.ted.com/talks/scilla_elworthy_fighting_with_non_violence.

Srdja Popovic: How to Topple a Dictator
https://www.ted.com/talks/srdja_popovic_how_to_topple_a_dictator.

Julia Bacha: Pay Attention to Nonviolence
https://www.ted.com/talks/julia_bacha.

Erica Chenoweth: The Success of Nonviolent Civil Resistance
https://www.youtube.com/watch?v=YJSehRlU34w.

Bibliography

Abe, Masao. "Kenotic God and Dynamic Sunyata." In *The Emptying God: A Buddhist-Jewish-Christian Conversation,* edited by John B. Cobb Jr. and Christopher Ives, 3–65. Maryknoll, NY: Orbis, 1990.

Abram, David. *Becoming Animal: An Earthly Cosmology.* New York: Vintage, 2010.

———. "The Ecology of Magic." In *Ecopsychology: Restoring the Earth; Healing the Mind,* edited by Theodore Rozak, Mary E. Gomes, and Allen D. Kanner, 301–15. San Francisco: Sierra Club, 1995.

———. *The Spell of the Sensuous: Perception and Language in a More-Than-Human World.* New York: Vintage, 1996.

Ackerman, Peter, and Jack DuVall. "With Weapons of the Will: How to Topple Saddam Hussein—Nonviolently." *Sojourners,* September-October 2002. https://sojo.net/magazine/september-october-2002/weapons-will.

Adyashanti. *Resurrecting Jesus: Embodying the Spirit of a Revolutionary Mystic.* Boulder, CO: Sounds True, 2014.

Bailie, Gil. *Violence Unveiled: Humanity at the Crossroads.* New York: Crossroad, 1995.

Baldwin, James. *The Fire Next Time.* New York: Random House, 1962.

Barbour, Ian. *Myths, Models, and Paradigms: A Comparative Study in Science and Religion.* New York: Harper and Row, 1974.

Barfield, Owen. *Saving the Appearances: A Study in Idolatry.* 2nd ed. Hanover, NH: Wesleyan University Press, 1988.

Bass, Diana Butler. *A People's History of Christianity: The Other Side of the Story.* New York: HarperCollins, 2009.

Berger, Peter L., and Thomas Luckmann. *The Social Construction of Reality: A Treatise in the Sociology of Knowledge.* New York: Doubleday, 1966.

Bernstein, Jerome. *Living in the Borderland: The Evolution of Consciousness and the Challenge of Healing Trauma.* New York: Routledge, 2005.

Berrigan, Daniel. "Connecting the Altar to the Pentagon." In *Peace is the Way: Writings on Nonviolence from the Fellowship of Reconciliation,* edited by Walter Wink, 93–97. Maryknoll, NY: Orbis, 2000.

Bleiker, Roland. *Nonviolent Struggle and the Revolution in East Germany.* Monograph Series Number 6. Cambridge, MA: Albert Einstein Institution, 1993.

Bonhoeffer, Dietrich. *Life Together.* Translated by John W Doberstein. New York: Harper and Row, 1954.

Borg, Marcus J. *The God We Never Knew: Beyond Dogmatic Religion to a More Authentic Contemporary Faith.* San Francisco: HarperSanFrancisco, 1997.

Brinton, Howard. *The Quaker Doctrine of Inward Peace*. Pendle Hill pamphlet number 44. Wallingford, PA: Pendle Hill, 1948.

Browning, Elizabeth Barrett. "Aurora Leigh." https://www.bartleby.com/236/86.html.

Carse, James. *The Religious Case against Belief*. New York: Penguin, 2008.

———. *The Silence of God: Meditations on Prayer*. San Francisco: HarperSanFrancisco, 1985.

Chergé, Dom Christian de. *The Last Testament of Dom Christian de Chergé*. https://ocso.org/history/saints-blesseds-martyrs/testament-of-christian-de-cherge/.

Coffin, William S. *The Courage to Love*. New York: Harper and Row, 1982.

Cone, James. *The Cross and the Lynching Tree*. Maryknoll, NY: Orbis, 2011.

Corbin, Henri. "Mundus Imaginalis or the Imaginary and the Imaginal." *Spring: A Journal of Archetype and Culture* (1972) 1–19.

Crossan, John Dominic. *Jesus: A Revolutionary Biography*. New York: HarperCollins, 1994.

Delio, Ilia. *The Unbearable Wholeness of Being: God, Evolution, and the Power of Love*. Maryknoll, NY: Orbis, 2013.

Deloria, Vine, Jr. *C.G. Jung and the Sioux Traditions: Dreams, Visions, Nature, and the Primitive*. New Orleans: Spring Journal, 2009.

Dempsey, Judy. "A Counterbalance to Communists." *International Herald Tribune*, April 2–3, 2005.

Diangelo, Robin. *White Fragility: Why It's So Hard for White People to Talk about Racism*. Boston: Beacon, 2018.

Dillard, Annie. *Holy the Firm*. New York: Bantam, 1977.

Eckhart, Meister. *Meister Eckhart: A Modern Translation*. Translated by Raymond Blakney. New York: Harper and Row, 1941.

Eisler, Riane. *The Chalice and the Blade: Our History, Our Future*. New York: HarperCollins, 1987.

Fell, Margaret. *An Epistle to Convinced Friends in 1656*. Glenside, PA: Quaker Heritage, http://www.qhpress.org/texts/oldqwhp/mf-e-3.htm.

Finley, James. *Merton's Palace of Nowhere*. Notre Dame, IN: Ave Maria, 1978.

Fox, George. *The Journal of George Fox*. Rev. ed. Edited by John L. Nickalls. Philadelphia: Philadelphia Yearly Meeting of the Religious Society of Friends, 1997.

Fox, George, et al. *A Declaration from the Harmless and Innocent People of God called Quakers against all Plotters and Fighters in the World*. Twenty-first day, eleventh month, 1660. http://quaker.org/legacy/minnfm/peace/A%20Declaration%20to%20Charles%20II%201660.htm

Freud, Sigmund. *The Future of an Illusion*. Translated and edited by James Strachey. New York: W. W. Norton and Company, 1989.

Gandhi, Mohandas. *An Autobiography: The Story of My Experiments with Truth*. Translated by Mahadev Desai. Boston: Beacon, 1957.

———. *Essential Writings*. Selected by John Dear. Maryknoll, NY: Orbis, 2002.

Gilligan, James. *Preventing Violence*. New York: Thames and Hudson, 2001.

Grossman, Dave. *On Killing: The Psychological Cost of Learning to Kill in War and Society*. New York: Little, Brown, 1995.

Haidt, Jonathan. *The Righteous Mind: Why Good People Are Divided by Politics and Religion*. New York: Vintage, 2012.

Hannah, Barbara. *Jung: His Life and Work: A Biographical Memoir*. New York: G. P. Putnam's Sons, 1976.

Hartshorne, Charles. *Omnipotence and Other Theological Mistakes*. Albany: State University of New York Press, 1984.

Havel, Vaclav. *Open Letters: Selected Writings 1965–1990*. Selected and edited by Paul Wilson. New York: Vintage, 1991.

Hedges, Chris. *War Is a Force that Gives Us Meaning*. New York: Anchor, 2002.

Heschel, Abraham J. *Essential Writings*. Selected by Susannah Heschel. Maryknoll, NY: Orbis, 2011.

Hillesum, Etty. *An Interrupted Life: The Diaries, 1941–1943, and Letters from Westerbork*. Translated by Arnold J. Pomerans. New York: Henry Holt, 1983.

Hillman, James. *A Terrible Love of War*. New York: Penguin, 2004.

———. *The Thought of the Heart and the Soul of the World*. Woodstock, CT: Spring, 1982.

Hollis, James. *Swamplands of the Soul: New Life in Dismal Places*. Toronto: Inner City, 1996.

Holmes, Barbara. *Joy Unspeakable: Contemplative Practices of the Black Church*. 2nd ed. Minneapolis: Fortress, 2017.

Hopkins, Gerard Manley. *The Poems of Gerard Manley Hopkins*. 4th ed. Edited by W. H. Gardner and N. H. MacKenzie. Oxford: Oxford University Press, 1967.

John of the Cross. *The Dark Night of the Soul* and *The Living Flame of Love*. Compiled by Robert Van de Weyer. *The Dark Night* translated by Benedict Zimmerman and *The Living Flame* translated by David Lewis. London: HarperCollins, 1995.

Johnston, William, ed. *The Cloud of Unknowing and the Book of Privy Counseling*. Garden City, NY: Image, 1973.

Jones, Rufus. *The Double Search*. Reprint of 1906 ed. Richmond, IN: Friends United, 1975.

Jung, C. G. *Answer to Job*. 2nd ed. Translated by R. F. C. Hull. Princeton: Princeton University Press, 1969.

———. *Memories, Dreams, Reflections*. Rev. ed. Edited by Aniela Jaffe. Translated by Richard and Clara Winston. New York: Random House, 1961.

———. *Modern Man in Search of a Soul*. Translated by W. S. Bell and Cary F. Baynes. New York: Harcourt Brace Jovanovich, 1933.

Kalsched, Donald. *The Inner World of Trauma: Archetypal Defenses of the Personal Spirit*. London: Routledge, 1996.

Kazantzakis, Nikos. *Report to Greco*. Translated by P. A. Bien. New York: Simon and Schuster, 1965.

Keats, John. *Letter to George and Thomas Keats*. December, 1817. http://keats-poems.com/to-george-and-thomas-keats-hampstead-december-22-1817/.

Kegan, Robert. *The Evolving Self: Problem and Process in Human Development*. Cambridge, MA: Harvard University Press, 1982.

Keillor, Garrison. "Garrison Keillor Signs Off." Interview with Jane Pauley, June 26, 2016. https://www.cbsnews.com/news/garrison-keillor-signs-off/.

Keller, Catherine. *Face of the Deep: A Theology of Becoming*. London: Routledge, 2003.

Kelly, Thomas. *A Testament of Devotion*. New York: Harper and Row, 1941.

Kierkegaard, Søren. *Works of Love*. Edited and translated by Howard V. Hong and Edna H. Hong. Princeton: Princeton University Press, 1995.

Kimmerer, Robin Wall. *Braiding Sweetgrass: Indigenous Wisdom, Scientific Knowledge, and the Teachings of Plants*. Minneapolis: Milkweed, 2013.

King, Karen L. *The Gospel of Mary of Magdala: Jesus and the First Woman Apostle*. Santa Rosa, CA: Polebridge, 2003.

King, Martin Luther, Jr. "Letter from Birmingham City Jail." In *A Testament of Hope: The Essential Writings and Speeches of Martin Luther King Jr.*, edited by James M. Washington, 289–302. New York: HarperCollins, 1986.

———. "The Power of Nonviolence." In *A Testament of Hope: The Essential Writings and Speeches of Martin Luther King Jr.*, edited by James M. Washington, 12–15. New York: HarperCollins, 1986.

King, Ruth. *Mindful of Race: Transforming Racism from the Inside Out*. Boulder, CO: Sounds True, 2018.

Korten, David. *The Great Turning: From Empire to Earth Community*. San Francisco: Barrett-Koehler, 2006.

Levi-Strauss, Claude. *Myth and Meaning: Cracking the Code of Culture*. New York. Schocken, 1978.

Levine, Mark. *The Jazz Theory Book*. Petaluma, CA: Sher Music Company, 1995.

Lincoln, Abraham. *First Inaugural Address*. 1861. https://www.bartleby.com/124/pres31.html.

Lorenz, Helene Shulman, and Mary Watkins. "Silenced Knowings, Forgotten Springs: Paths to Healing in the Wake of Colonialism." *Radical Psychology* (Fall 2001). http://www.radpsynet.org/journal/vol2-2/lorenz-watkins.html.

Maass, Peter. *Love Thy Neighbor: A Story of War*. New York. Random House, 1996.

Macy, Joanna. Preface to *Rilke's Book of Hours: Love Poems to God*, 1–6. Translated by Anita Barrows and Joanna Macy. New York: Riverhead, 1996.

Marx, Irmgard. *Hier konnte jeder reden—unzensiert und frei*. In *Die Kirche (Wochenzeitung für Anhalt und die Kirchenprovinz Sachsen)* Nr. 41 vom 11. Oktober 2009. 18. Sonntag nach Trinitatis. Evangelische Verlagsanstalt GmbH. Personal translation.

Mathai, M. P. *Mahatma Gandhi's Worldview*. New Delhi: Gandhi Peace Foundation, 2000.

McFague, Sallie. *Metaphorical Theology: Models of God in Religious Language*. Philadelphia: Fortress, 1982.

———. *Super, Natural Christians: How We Should Love Nature*. Minneapolis: Fortress, 1997.

Mindell, Arnold. *Sitting in the Fire: Large Group Transformation Using Conflict and Diversity*. Portland: Lao Tse,1995.

Moore, F. Timothy. *Practicing Midrash: Reading the Bible's Arguments as an Invitation to Conversation*. Eugene, OR: Wipf and Stock, 2018.

Moore, Thomas. *Care of the Soul: A Guide for Cultivating Depth and Sacredness in Everyday Life*. New York: HarperCollins, 1992.

———. "Developing a Mythic Sensibility." *Sphinx 4: A Journal for Archetypal Psychology and the Arts* (1992) 53–61.

Nagler, Michael. *Is There No Other Way? The Search for a Nonviolent Future*. Berkeley: Berkeley Hills, 2001.

Newell, Roger. "Reflection on Pastor Christian Führer of the Nikolai Church in Leipzig." *Contemporary Church History Quarterly*, September 2014. https://contemporarychurchhistory.org/2014/09/reflection-on-pastor-christian-fuhrer-of-the-nikolai-church-in-leipzig/.

O'Grady, Joan. *The Prince of Darkness: The Devil in History, Religion, and the Human Psyche*. Shaftsbury, Dorset, England: Element, 1989.

Oliver, Mary. "Praying." In *Thirst*, 37. Boston: Beacon, 2006.

Otto, Rudolf. *The Idea of the Holy: An Inquiry into the Non-rational Factor in the Idea of the Divine and its Relation to the Rational*. Translated by John W. Harvey. New York: Oxford University Press, 1958.

Owens, Lama Rod. *Love and Rage: The Path of Liberation through Anger*. Berkeley: North Atlantic, 2020.

Pagels, Elaine. *The Origin of Satan*. New York: Random House, 1995.

Palmer, Parker. *Let Your Life Speak: Listening for the Voice of Vocation*. San Francisco: Jossey-Bass, 2000.

Penington, Isaac. *The Inward Journey of Isaac Penington: An Abbreviation of Penington's Works*. Edited by Robert Leach. Pendle Hill pamphlet number 29. Wallingford, PA: Pendle Hill, 1944.

———. *Knowing the Mystery of Life Within: Selected Writings of Isaac Penington in Their Historical and Theological Context*. Selected by R. Melvin Keiser and Rosemary Moore. London: Quaker, 2005.

Penn, William. "Extracts from William Penn's Preface to the Original Edition of George Fox's Journal, 1694." In *The Journal of George Fox*, rev. ed, edited by John L. Nickalls, xxxix–xlviii. Philadelphia: Philadelphia Yearly Meeting of the Religious Society of Friends, 1997.

Reagon, Bernice Johnson. "Bernice Johnson Reagon: Interview Excerpts." Veterans of Hope Project interview with Vincent Harding. http://www.veteransofhope.org/veterans/bernice-johnson-reagon/.

Rilke, Rainer Maria. *Letters to a Young Poet: A New Translation and Commentary*. Translated by Anita Barrows and Joanna Macy. Boulder, CO: Shambala, 2021.

———. *Rilke's Book of Hours: Love Poems to God*. Translated by Anita Barrows and Joanna Macy. New York: Riverhead, 1996.

Rogers, Annie. *A Shining Affliction: A Story of Harm and Healing in Psychotherapy*. New York: Viking Penguin, 1995.

Rohr, Richard. *Art: Week 2: Joy Unspeakable, Wednesday, May 23, 2018*. https://cac.org/joy-unspeakable-2018-05-23/.

Romanyshyn, Robert. *Technology as Symptom and Dream*. New York: Routledge, 1989.

Roszak, Theodore, et al., eds. *Ecopsychology: Restoring the Earth; Healing the Mind*. San Francisco: Sierra Club, 1995.

Rumi, Jelaluddin. *The Essential Rumi*. Translated by Coleman Barks, John Moyne, A. J. Arberry, and Reynold Nicholson. Edison: Castle, 1997.

Rushdie, Salman. "One Thousand Days in a Balloon." In *The Rushdie Letters: Freedom to Speak, Freedom to Write*, 13–24. Edited by Steve MacDonogh. Lincoln: University of Nebraska Press, 1993.

Schaeffer, Katherine. *6 facts about economic inequality in the U.S.* Pew Research Center, February 7, 2020. https://www.pewresearch.org/fact-tank/2020/02/6-facts-about-economic-inequality-in-the-u-s/.

Schell, Jonathan. *The Unconquerable World: Power, Nonviolence, and the Will of the People*. New York: Henry Holt, 2003.

Schwartz, Richard. *Internal Family Systems Therapy*. New York: Guilford, 1995.

Sells, Michael. *Mystical Languages of Unsaying*. Chicago: University of Chicago Press, 1994.

Sharp, Gene. *From Dictatorship to Democracy: A Conceptual Framework for Liberation*. Boston: The Albert Einstein Institution, 2002. No copyright. The author has intentionally placed this material in the public domain.

———. "Gene Sharp 101." Interview with Metta Spencer, *Peace Magazine*, July/September 2003, 16–27.

———. "Gene Sharp: A Dictator's Worst Nightmare." Interview with Mairi Mackay, CNN Profile. http://www.cnn.com/2012/06/23/world/gene-sharp-revolutionary/index.html.

———. *The Politics of Nonviolent Action: Part One: Power and Struggle*. Boston: Porter Sargent, 1973.

———. *The Politics of Nonviolent Action: Part Two: The Methods of Nonviolent Action*. Boston: Porter Sargent, 1973.

———. *The Politics of Nonviolent Action: Part Three: The Dynamics of Nonviolent Action*. Boston: Porter Sargent, 1973.

Smith, Steve. *Living in Virtue, Declaring Against War: The Spiritual Roots of the Peace Testimony*. Pendle Hill pamphlet number 378. Wallingford, PA: Pendle Hill, 2005.

Snyder, Daniel O. *Quaker Witness as Sacrament*. Pendle Hill pamphlet number 397. Wallingford, PA: Pendle Hill, 2008.

———. *The Spirituality of Restlessness*. Philadelphia: Friends World Committee for Consultation, Section of the Americas, 2009. https://www.fwccamericas.org/pub/Snyder2010.pdf.

———. "Violence and Nonviolence: Quaker Spirituality and the Treatment of Domestic Violence Offenders." In *Out of the Silence: Quaker Perspectives on Pastoral Care and Counseling*, 155–75. Edited by J. Bill Ratliff. Wallingford, PA: Pendle Hill, 2001.

Somé, Malidoma Patrice. *The Healing Wisdom of Africa: Finding Life Purpose through Nature, Ritual, and Community*. New York: Jeremy P. Tarcher/Putnam, 1998.

Stafford, William. "A Ritual to Read to Each Other." In *Ask Me: 100 Essential Poems*, 16. Minneapolis: Graywolf, 1960.

Starr, Mirabai. "Introduction." In *The Interior Castle* by Teresa of Avila, translated by Mirabai Starr, 2–27. New York: Riverhead, 2003.

Steere, Douglas V., ed. *Quaker Spirituality: Selected Writings*. New York: Paulist, 1984.

Stephen, Caroline. "Letter to Miss E. Wedgwood, December 9, 1872." In *The Quaker Reader*, selected by Jessamyn West, 449–50. Wallingford, PA: Pendle Hill, 1962.

———. *Quaker Strongholds. Third Edition.* [*London—1891.*] South Yarra, Victoria, Australia: Leopold Classic Library, 2016.

Stoltzfus, Nathan. *Resistance of the Heart: Intermarriage and the Rosenstrasse Protest in Nazi Germany*. New Brunswick, NJ: Rutgers University Press, 1996.

Teresa of Avila: *The Interior Castle*. Translated by Mirabai Starr. New York: Riverhead, 2003.

Thandeka. *Learning to Be White: Money, Race, and God in America*. New York: Continuum, 2001.

Thurman, Howard. *With Head and Heart: The Autobiography of Howard Thurman*. New York: Harcourt Brace Jovanovich, 1979.

Tillich, Paul. *The Dynamics of Faith*. New York: Harper and Row, 1957.

Ulanov, Ann and Barry. *The Healing Imagination: The Meeting of Psyche and Soul*. New York: Paulist, 1991.

Ury, William. *The Third Side: Why We Fight and How We Can Stop*. New York: Penguin, 2000.

Van Buren, Paul. *The Edges of Language: An Essay in the Logic of a Religion*. New York: Macmillan, 1972.

Van der Kolk, Bessel A. *The Body Keeps the Score: Brain, Mind, and Body in the Healing of Trauma*. New York: Penguin, 2014.

Wehr, Demaris S. *Making it Through: Bosnian Survivors Share Stories of Trauma, Transcendence, and Truth*. Asheville, NC: Chiron, 2020.

West, Cornel. *Democracy Matters: Winning the Fight against Imperialism*. New York: Penguin, 2004.

Whitehead, Alfred North. *Process and Reality: An Essay in Cosmology*. Corrected ed. Edited by David Ray Griffin and Donald W. Sherburne. New York: Macmillan, 1978.

———. *Science and the Modern World*. New York: Macmillan, 1925.

Wink, Walter. *Engaging the Powers: Discernment and Resistance in a World of Domination*. Minneapolis: Fortress, 1992.

———. *The Human Being: Jesus and the Enigma of the Son of the Man*. Minneapolis: Fortress, 2002.

———. *Jesus and Nonviolence: A Third Way*. Minneapolis: Fortress, 2003.

Winnicott, D. W. *The Maturational Processes and the Facilitating Environment: Studies in the Theory of Emotional Development*. Madison, CT: International Universities, 1958.

Woolman, John. *The Journal and Major Essays of John Woolman*. Edited by Phillips P. Moulton. Richmond, IN: Friends United, 1971.

Printed in the USA
CPSIA information can be obtained
at www.ICGtesting.com
LVHW051311140823
755191LV00009B/225

9 781666 731910